BOHEMIAN NEW ORLEANS

BOHEMIAN NEW ORLEANS

THE STORY OF THE *OUTSIDER* AND LOUJON PRESS

JEFF WEDDLE

UNIVERSITY PRESS OF MISSISSIPPI

JACKSON

www.upress.state.ms.us

The University Press of Mississippi is a member of the Association of American University Presses.

First edition 2007

Library of Congress Cataloging-in-Publication Data

Weddle, Jeff.
Bohemian New Orleans : the story of The Outsider and Loujon Press / Jeff Weddle. — 1st ed.
    p. cm.
Includes bibliographical references and index.

ISBN 978-1-4968-3082-1
                                1. Loujon Press—History. 2. Small
presses—Louisiana—New Orleans—History—20th century. 3. Book industries
and trade—Louisiana—New Orleans—History—20th century. 4. Publishers and
publishing—Louisiana—New Orleans—History—20th century. 5. Webb, Jon
Edgar. 6. Outsider (New Orleans, La.) I. Title.
    Z473.L84W44 2007
    686.209763'350904—dc22

                                                                2006102205

British Library Cataloging-in-Publication Data available

❖ ALWAYS FOR JILL ❖

CONTENTS

PREFACE AND ACKNOWLEDGMENTS

EDWIN BLAIR, TALL, FIT, AND BALDING, a dedicated book collector and long-time New Orleans resident, leaned forward in his chair and considered his words: "This was a romantic couple. This was *La Bohème*, people giving everything up for art." Blair was describing his friends, the late Jon Edgar Webb and Webb's widow, Louise, who sat opposite Blair in the cramped office, a room filled to overflow with books and memorabilia of the Beat Generation, New Orleans culture, and the Webbs' remarkable press, Loujon, which originated in the Crescent City in 1960 and died along with Jon in 1971 in Nashville, Tennessee. It was a warm February day in 2005, and for the past hour Louise, almost ninety years old, had been telling stories of her life with Jon. She was dressed in black, a beret on her head and a black cane clutched in her hands. Silver and turquoise jewelry dangled from her neck and wrists. She radiated energy and good humor.

Louise told stories of Charles Bukowski, about how she once matched him drink for drink in a tiny French Quarter apartment and about how Loujon launched his career. She spoke of hard times, of how she and Jon barely got by as they worked their press and sold their magazine, the *Outsider*, as well as fine press books by Bukowski and Henry Miller. She told of a baby lost in a childbirth that almost killed her, too. Mostly, she told a love story of hard-eyed dreamers who worked like the possessed to create their art, along the way crossing paths with Ernest Hemingway, David Goodis, Sherwood Anderson, Kenneth Patchen, and many other bright lights of American literature.

After the stories, Blair and Louise led a walking tour through the French Quarter. Louise's gait was slow and sometimes halting, but her voice was strong as she pointed out landmarks such as the apartments where she and Jon lived on Ursulines and Royal streets. The tour ended in Pirate's Alley, where she spent sixteen years painting street scenes and clowns to sell to tourists. She pointed out a corner in the courtyard of St. Louis Cathedral where she surreptitiously buried her baby's ashes. Three young women lounged in chairs along the sidewalk as Louise spoke. One of them asked her name and what she was doing. It was a friendly question, and Louise fell briefly into conversation with the women. One of them, a pretty twenty-something with both arms covered in tattoos, asked if Louise was an artist.

"Used to be," Louise replied.

"Once an artist, you're always an artist," said the woman.

Another of the women remarked that Faulkner had once lived in the building behind where they sat. Louise corrected her: "No, he used to live in a building down the street where my husband and I lived." A few moments later, the tour moved along. It was clear that the French Quarter was home for Louise Webb, but it was equally clear that this Quarter was much different from the one where she had lived. There was a time when everyone knew her. Now, she was anonymous, just an old woman telling stories of days long gone to keep them from disappearing like the morning fog off the Mississippi.

The first issue of the *Outsider* appeared in 1960 in an edition of three thousand copies and required a year of production work. It was typeset, collated, and bound in the Webbs' tiny Royal Street apartment in New Orleans's French Quarter and sold globally with the help of the B. DeBoer distribution company and a network of friends in the United States and abroad. The second issue appeared a year later, this one from a place on Ursulines Street, where the Webbs also labored over issue three. It was in this apartment that Bukowski's first major poetry collection, *It Catches My Heart in Its Hands* (1963), came to be. The remaining Loujon catalog consists of Bukowski's *Crucifix in a Deathhand* (1964) and Henry Miller's *Order and Chaos chez Hans Reichel* (1967) and *Insomnia, or the Devil at Large* (1970). *Crucifix in a Deathhand* was the last Loujon publication done in New Orleans. The Miller books and a final, double-issue *Outsider* (1968–69) were published in Tucson, Las Vegas, and Albuquerque, respectively.

The Webbs did their work with style, and people in the know understood that, while there were other good publishers, there really was no better small press operation in the country than Loujon. One reviewer called the *Outsider* the Rolls-Royce of little magazines. Charles Bukowski said the magazine was "the cave of the gods and the cave of the devils . . . it was the place, it was in . . . it was literature jumping and screaming." It is past time that the Webbs and their contribution to our literature are given a close look. That is the purpose, and the journey, of this book.

Many people are responsible for this journey. The first is John Patterson, a friend from my college days. John was my downstairs neighbor at the

Minor-Dixon, an old apartment building at the corner of Limestone Street and Leader Avenue in Lexington, Kentucky. John put many things in motion one afternoon in the early 1980s when he pounded on my door and thrust two books into my hands, demanding that I read them. The books were Kenneth Patchen's *Memoirs of a Shy Pornographer* and Charles Bukowski's *Mockingbird Wish Me Luck*. I read these books and my life changed. It seems like everyone I knew in the Minor-Dixon ended up reading and talking about Bukowski: John Spears, Tom Chapuk, Jeff Hinton, Roger DeRossett, Debbie Martin, Stephanie Brown. These conversations put me further down the path that led eventually to the Loujon Press.

Curtis Robinson and George Cline are my brothers-in-arms. I watched them start a half-dozen weekly newspapers and learned the pirate spirit of publishers on the knife edge of ruin and glory. Curtis and Wayne Ewing began filming *The Outsiders of New Orleans: Loujon Press* in early 2005. Our conversations with Louise Webb, Ed Blair and the young women in Pirate's Alley described above were shot for that documentary. The film premieres in late 2007.

My dear friends at Morehead State University, Eric Cash, Paula Fountain, Jerry Williams, and George Eklund, helped me understand where poetry came from and why the small press is important. Eric and I embarked on a crash course in little magazine publishing when he suggested we start our own. *Misnomer* lasted four issues, and I now know that there is no way to understand the small press unless you live the small press. Later, at Ole Miss, Dr. Ann Fisher-Wirth helped me piece together the threads of modern poetry.

The earliest formal rumblings of this book began as a paper for Dr. Ed Caudill's seminar in communication historiography at the University of Tennessee. I am indebted to Ed and to Dr. Elizabeth Aversa, Dr. Allen Dunn, and Dr. Doug Raber, who read and commented on early drafts of this manuscript. My first tenure-track faculty position was at Mississippi University for Women, better known as "the W," in Columbus, Mississippi. I wrote much of this book there in the evenings and between classes and during one memorable week in the aftermath of a tornado that leveled much of the campus. I extend sincere thanks to my old boss, Dr. Anne Balazs, for having the faith to hire me, to my dear colleagues Dr. Marty Hatton, Dr. Van Roberts, and Eric Harlan for their forbearance and support, and to all of the W students who touched my life. This goes double for the staff of the *Spectator*.

My current colleagues at the University of Alabama's School of Library and Information Studies have given me support and encouragement at every opportunity during the past year and a half when I have mostly hidden away in my office, stealing every free moment to write and revise. Dr. Culpepper Clark, former dean of the College of Communication and Information Sciences, our parent unit, has been supportive from the moment we met. Dean Loy Singleton, who replaced Cully in 2006, has likewise supported my efforts with this book. Elizabeth Aversa moved here from Tennessee to assume the directorship of the School of Library and Information Studies and recruited me to this faculty. I also acknowledge with gratitude Dr. Gordon Coleman, Dr. Margaret Dalton, Professor Anna Embry, Dr. Stephen MacCall, Professor Michael Malinconico, Professor Steve Miller, Dr. Charles Osborne, Dr. Annabel Stephens, and Dr. Tonyia Tidline. SLIS staff members Clay Davis, Linda Hord, Cherry Quinn, and Beth Riggs have solved more crises and fixed more emergencies for me than I can count. Students in my American literary small press seminar have given me insights into all aspects of little magazine history that I might never have come to on my own, and these insights have enriched this book. My graduate assistants, Katie Guerin, Beth Downey, and Phillip Anglin, worked above and beyond the call of duty. A special thanks to Phillip for indexing this book.

Alan May, formerly of the University of Alabama Libraries and now with the University of Montevallo Libraries, read this manuscript in an earlier form. His wise comments helped shape that crude document into this book. I am indebted to a number of other librarians who went far out of their way to aid my research. Special Collections at the University of Tennessee, Knoxville, provided easy access to their Loujon Press materials, as did Special Collections at Mississippi State University and the University of North Carolina at Chapel Hill. At Northwestern University's Charles Deering McCormick Library of Special Collections, R. Russell Maylone, Scott Krafft, Sigrid P. Perry, and Susan R. Lewis graciously gave me full access and support during two intense, whirlwind research trips there. Without this archive, there would be no book. Christopher Harter and his colleagues at the Lilly Library at Indiana University were equally generous and helpful. Kelly Reiss at the Newberry Library came to my aid in a time of desperation and saved me.

For bearing witness to what they saw or for giving me permission to quote, I thank Marvin Bell, Ed Blair, Neeli Cherkovski, Cordley Coit, Joyce Corrington, Darlene Fife, Michael C. Ford, Dennis Formento, Jack Grapes,

Robert Head, John Martin, Simon Perchik, James Sallis, Carol Tinker, Ben C. Toledano, Miller Williams, Anne Rice, Jory Sherman, and Diane Wakoski. I am forever indebted to Linda Lee Bukowski.

For their seemingly endless patience with me as I completed this book, I am grateful to Seetha Srinivasan and her staff at the University Press of Mississippi. Seetha believed in this book from the start, and her thoughtful suggestions and guidance were invaluable. Without her, this book would not have been possible.

For reasons known to them: Donna Dowling Robinson, Cathy Dowling, Philip Bruce Bishop, David Banner Leslie, Gary Randall Burruss, Thomas James Blackburn, Steve Farmer, Roger DeRossett, Grandmaster Hyun Ok Shin, and Gary, Ann, and Amy Grogg.

My parents, Leo and Laura Weddle, and my sister, Lynn Weddle, have supported and encouraged me my entire life. My wife, Jill, and son, Gus, believe in me. Without them, nothing matters.

Dr. Jon Edgar Webb, Jr., has been generous, enthusiastic and supportive. He has supplied thousands of pages of correspondence and other materials from his personal archive. Our telephone and e-mail conversations have given this book a life to which it could not otherwise have aspired. Jon and Louise Webb lived the lives that this book celebrates. I reserve my greatest thanks for Louise, who shared her grand adventure with me.

BOHEMIAN NEW ORLEANS

INTRODUCTION

THE FIRST GOLDEN AGE OF little magazine publishing came in the 1920s. Among the important magazines of the era was the *Little Review*, which, with its flamboyant editor, Margaret Anderson, emerged from Chicago to engage the world in a dynamic conversation on beauty, art, and social change. In the South, New Orleans's the *Double Dealer* set up shop in part to spite H. L. Mencken for unkind remarks about the region made in his essay "The Sahara of the Bozart." Along with the satisfaction of spiting Mencken, the *Double Dealer*'s editors also had the pleasure of introducing to the world such talented unknowns as William Faulkner and Ernest Hemingway. The *Anvil*, *Contact*, and *transition* were other fascinating small press operations, each with a vision and a manifesto to ensure that readers understood what that vision was. The era of modernism was upon the world, and the little magazines were helping to lead the way.

There had been a good run-up to this explosive era, with magazines like Alfred Stieglitz's Dadaist *291*, which ran twelve issues in 1915–1916 and, in England, *Blast*, Wyndham Lewis's Vorticist journal that appeared a total of two times and disappeared. Having a brief life as these magazines did, unfortunately, has long been the rule, not the exception. What kills most little magazines is the deadly combination of poverty and exhaustion. The people responsible for getting them out slave over their work and, only if they are smart and lucky, do not go deeply in debt in the process. Though most little magazines come and go with astonishing speed, some do last. The most resilient of them all, Harriet Monroe's *Poetry*, took root in 1912 and never stopped publishing.

By the 1940s, the little magazine world had entered a gray period. As veteran Malcolm Cowley observed, writers and editors showed high levels of skill in those days, but the cutting edge, the excitement, had dulled. The problem, as Cowley saw it, was "critical inbreeding carried almost to the point of incest." He longed for the old, vital spirit and half-predicted its return: "Some day the fire may be rekindled. When printing and paper are a little cheaper, or when it once more becomes possible to print little magazines abroad at a ridiculously low price (with a dozen typographical errors on every page) and when the veterans now in college are graduated and begin to make their way in literature, then we may once again see informal and impertinent and wildly venturesome reviews, like those which flourished after the other war."

As it happened, Cowley was a prophet. Not much more than a decade passed between his essay and the start of a new golden age. This "mimeograph revolution" can be traced to the 1960 publication of *New American Poetry 1945–1960*, an anthology which showcased the work of people like Gregory Corso, Allen Ginsberg, and Robert Creeley. Editor Donald Allen was reacting against the safe verse celebrated in Donald Hall's 1957 collection, *New Poets of England and America*. Allen sought to highlight poets in the emerging traditions of Ezra Pound and William Carlos Williams: "They are our avant-garde," he wrote, "the true continuers of the modern movement in American poetry."

By the early 1960s, little magazine operations were springing up in garages, apartments, and living rooms across America. There was a genuine excitement about new writers and new kinds of literature. The Beats and other counterculture poets caught the public's attention, and, with things moving so quickly, it was a good time for people involved in the movement to step back and take account of what they were doing—to determine what importance, if any, it had. It made sense for such accounting to take place within the pages of a little magazine. In 1962, Walter Lowenfels invited about a dozen of his friends in the small press world to do just that. Lowenfels asked these people to submit brief essays on the state of little magazine publishing in America to *Mainstream*, where he served as contributing editor. Though there was no physical meeting of the participants, Lowenfels dubbed the collected essays "Little Magazines in America: A Symposium."

Mainstream was an important little magazine with roots dating back to 1911, when it first appeared as the *Masses*. It was a good venue for a serious discussion of little magazine publishing. Lowenfels, too, was well suited to initiate this discussion. He had a long history with little magazines and the small press. As an expatriate in Paris during the 1920s and 1930s, he published regularly in *transition*, an important magazine of the day. For a time he was a partner in the Carrefour Press, a leader in the short-lived "anonymous movement," which sought to remove competition from the arts by not crediting authors with their work. Remembering Lowenfels's contributions to *transition*, Kenneth Rexroth later wrote, "In his young days he was certainly one of America's best poets."

Some in the symposium had pedigrees stretching back to the 1930s; others were relative newcomers. In many cases, they worked in both the small press/little magazine world and in the world of commercial publishing. The biggest name was probably Millen Brand. His credits included several novels on the theme of madness and recovery and an adaptation of Mary Jane Ward's *The Snake Pit* for the screen. The film received multiple Oscar nominations, including best picture, in 1948. Curtis Zahn, associate editor of *Trace*, was another commercial success. Zahn was a Southern California playwright, short story writer, and poet known in the 1950s for, among other things, hosting writers' workshops in his Malibu home. These gatherings included famous names such as Henry Miller, Anaïs Nin, and Christopher Isherwood, but unknowns were welcome and frequently attended. Zahn was also a member in good standing of the Hollywood community, often socializing with people like Sam Peckinpah and Tuesday Weld, who was Zahn's next door neighbor. In 1959, Zahn founded the Pacificus Foundation, a literary arts group whose loosely defined mission was to help struggling writers. Zahn once said that if a destitute writer knocked at his door and told him he needed a typewriter, Zahn would give the writer as much as two hundred dollars to buy one.

Other symposium contributors were less well connected but still important players in the little magazine world. In 1957, Leslie Woolf Hedley's Inferno Press was the first publisher to include Richard Brautigan's work in a stand-alone book, *Four Poets*. Hedley described Brautigan and the others in this book as representing "the silent generation." While introducing Brautigan to the world was probably not fully appreciated in 1962, Hedley also had the distinction of editing and publishing eleven issues of the San Francisco-based little magazine *Inferno* in the years 1950 to 1956.

John William "Bill" Corrington, an English instructor at Louisiana State University, was a regular contributor to a number of literary magazines. Corrington was born in Ohio in 1932, but moved with his family to Shreveport, Louisiana, during his boyhood, and the city remained his spiritual home for the rest of his life. Corrington argued that little magazines "remain the breeding ground of much significant contemporary talent—and almost the only ground upon which the poet (as distinguished from the novelist, essayist, or short story writer) can set his feet with any degree of assurance." Corrington also saw dangers which demanded a constant vigilance from editors and publishers. He suggested that these publications were "eternally trapped in the slim ground between two destructive forces," which he identified, respectively, as "becoming a kind of esthetic curiosity," and becoming "for better or worse, 'totally committed.'" The "esthetic curiosities" championed obscure, exclusive literary movements, and were unwilling to engage the broader world outside their "charmed circle" of followers. Among this group, Corrington included the *Chicago Review, Big Table*, the *Partisan Review*, and the *Sewanee Review*. These magazines, Corrington wrote, "smack of clique." The "totally committed" picked a political or literary cause and chose their content based upon its usefulness to that cause. As an example, Corrington offered *Mutiny*, which had recently organized a petition drive to declare that the Beats were not actually poets.

Like Corrington, Jack Lindeman was a teacher by profession and, between 1955 and 1961, the editor of the little magazine *Whetstone*. When the symposium was published, he was a year away from his first poetry collection, *Twenty-One Poems*. Not all symposium participants were writers or editors. Philip Kaplan was a Russian-born artist and book collector who immigrated with his family to the United States in 1911, when he was seven years old. The family eventually settled in Cleveland, Ohio, where Kaplan remained until adulthood. During the 1920s he joined and later became president of Cleveland's Kokoon Arts club, an organization more or less at the center of the city's artistic community.

Charles Bukowski was a Los Angeles postal worker and poet who had briefly helped his wife at the time, Barbara Fry, edit her magazine, *Harlequin*. He worried that little magazines tended to fold under the pressure to conform. Bukowski was a small press regular, his work having already appeared in dozens of magazines, and offered that "the little magazines, on the whole, are a xxxxx mess." He didn't like the term "little magazine," which he called a "mind state that builds smallness," and despised editors who compromised their artistic vision. In Bukowski's mind, most editors eventually succumbed to such pressure. As if wishing to illustrate Bukowski's point, *Mainstream* editors replaced a four-letter word with "xxxxx."

If Bukowski's view was bleak, others' were more so. Carl Larson, editor of *Rongroad, Brand X,* and 7 Poets Press, for example, wrote that, while "little magazines fill a need," that need had more to do with amateur writers finding a place to publish their work than it did with providing serious literature to readers. Zahn agreed that little magazines provided a necessary means to publication for amateur writers, especially those with something to protest: "Generally, the littles are 'protesting' the status quo, and it is sorely needed. But 'Protest' requires more than words like 'fuck' or sadistic violence, or erotic sex." Readers searching for important new writing in the little magazines might instead be faced with work that was "nothing more than the other side of the coin—no more truthful, accurate, artistic, realistic" than material found in commercial publications.

Hedley compared the current crop of littles with their 1920s counterparts and found the current magazines wanting. He disagreed with Kaplan's enthusiasm for the perceived taboo-free content of many postwar magazines and argued that the little magazines of the 1960s were less vital than were those of the twenties and thirties, "when most writers and editors were deeply concerned with their time and the task of honestly rendering that changing reality into vibrantly authentic language, a communication not just limited to provincial life in New York City or some university faculty, but made of and from the mainstream speech and conditions of the American continent." Hedley believed that to understand little magazines one had to understand both their context and their intent. He asked: "If there is a literary and philosophical Resistance and Underground in this country, what are their intentions? Resistance to what? Underground for what purpose? In what direction are they going?" These are excellent questions, but Hedley provided no answers. The closest he came to any resolution was the observation that: "Such movements, like a good poem, must mean as well as be, and we should thoroughly comprehend its meaning."

The most consistent venue for discussing little magazines of this era was James Boyer May's *Trace.* The struggle to make sense of little magazines and their place in the broader culture—literary and otherwise—made up a large portion of *Trace*'s content. *Beatitude* editor William Margolis called *Trace* the "binding force, the common ground" for the little magazine subculture. Margolis believed that, along with the emergence of Beat Generation poetry, *Trace* was a primary reason for the boom in little magazine production in the mid-twentieth century: "For *Trace,* guided by James Boyer

May, has been the one place where usually accurate information about the little magazines can be found; and where the various editors and publishers and contributors could express themselves to each other about the trends and problems and controversies of the little magazines and of poetry in the English speaking world. By making such internal communication possible *Trace* made, is making, possible the growth of little magazines and of interest in poetry."

Lowenfels was probably the strongest connecting force among the symposium participants. After all, he chose the group. Another participant with strong ties among the panel was Lowenfels's good friend and protégé, Jon Edgar Webb. For Webb, editing was a family affair. He worked with his wife, Louise, editing and publishing the *Outsider* from a small apartment in New Orleans's French Quarter. Several in the symposium were Webb's friends and also contributors to the *Outsider*. These included Brand, Zahn, Corrington, and Bukowski. These men had radically different ideas about the nature of art, but they all agreed on Webb's skills as an editor.

Brand chose to discuss Webb and the *Outsider* to make a point about the nature of little magazine culture and publishing. For Brand, the notion of being an "outsider" had much to do with being outside of the social injustice of segregated America. Brand wrote that "a dark and radiant thought breaks in my mind, that perhaps the only good thing to be is an outsider until white can eat with black, until black can travel with white, and until we don't have to go to prison to be insiders." Admitting that such a definition might be limiting, Brand offered that "Outsiders are against all forms of alienation and distortion and to put it simply, they have to stick with it until things can be turned inside out."

Like Brand, Jon Edgar Webb appeared in the symposium's first installment. Webb was more concerned with the health of the little magazine subculture than with social change. In Webb's view, the economic poverty of most little magazines was matched by an impoverished view of their own potential. Webb believed the conservative editorial policies of many little magazines often discouraged talented new writers. The dynamic attitude Webb looked for in little magazine editors hearkened back to the publications of the 1920s and 1930s. His fellow Clevelander, Kaplan, remembered that little magazines of the golden age "were started in prison cells, speakeasy joints, colleges, universities, any place where there were a few rebels. The most popular subjects were Sacco-Vanzetti, Eugene O'Neill, Picasso, Russia, Freud, Birth Control and hundreds of injustices. However, poetry was the mainstay of the Little Mags. The poets took the lead; they were the most vociferous and articulate. If a poet had any hopes of having a book published, a credo of his work in Little Mags was important."

Kaplan noted that a new type of little magazine arose in response to "a desperate need" of new, young poets in the post–World War II period. "Now the language was more daring; no subject was taboo, and this new freedom attracted new converts everywhere." Webb was blunt in his dislike of editors who did not embrace the new freedom. "Little mag editors afraid to 'let go' in any creative direction they wish to, afraid to denounce anything they believe needs denouncing, who go on publishing the same old cliché rot of the academy they sprang from (playing safe and decent) ought to be lined up and shot—into immediate obscurity." To his credit, Jon Edgar Webb practiced what he preached. With the *Outsider* and a handful of fine press books, he, for a time, became a force in American literary publishing. While there is probably no such thing as a typical little magazine or small press publisher, a close look at what Jon Webb and his wife, Louise, accomplished, and the challenges they faced, offers a window onto that world.

Like so many before and since, the Webbs went without luxuries for their art. Sometimes they were hungry, and they often worked themselves past exhaustion. But they knew everyone there was to know in the little magazine world and beyond, even to such figures as Sherwood Anderson, Tennessee Williams, and Henry Miller. They also came to know America, skipping again and again between the West and South, always looking for a home that eluded them. And they published works of art that have stood the test of time to become classics of their kind. This is their story. It is a story about publishing, but at its core it is a love story. It begins in Cleveland and, like *Poetry*, it endures.

FROM CLEVELAND TO NEW ORLEANS

JON EDGAR WEBB WAS BORN on February 1, 1905, in Cleveland, Ohio, the first child of carpenter and building contractor T. W. Louis Webb and the former Ella Neely. Louis was born in Canada in 1878, the son of English emigrants. Ella was a year younger than her husband and, like her father, hailed from Philadelphia. Her mother was born in Ireland. The Webbs eventually had five children, with the addition of sons Harry, Thomas Louis, and William, and a daughter, Mary. Though blue collar, the Webbs were reasonably well-off. They were land owners, possessing a number of houses and a total of perhaps seventeen pieces of real estate. In 1930, their family home was valued at ten thousand dollars, a substantial sum. Louis and Ella sold their property some time before Louis's death in the late 1950s. After the death of her husband, Ella moved to Florida, where she remained until her death in 1968.

Turn-of-the-century Cleveland was a boom town, growing in population from just over seventeen thousand in 1850 to almost four hundred thousand in 1900, making it the seventh-largest city in America. It was a progressive city and a regional transportation hub with the excitement of electric streetcars, a professional baseball team, and the country's first indoor shopping center. In 1905 the *Cleveland News* published its first issue, and the popular attraction Luna Park opened on thirty-five acres situated between Woodland Avenue, Woodhill, Mt. Carmel, and East 110th Street. Luna Park lured families in droves for thrill rides, swimming, roller skating, and culture. The great tenor Enrico Caruso once sang in the park's concert garden. The grand Hollenden Hotel, which proved a favorite stopover for several United States presidents and other celebrities over the next six decades, was brand-new. John D. Rockefeller built his summer home, Forrest Hill, in Cleveland in 1890 and used it regularly until it was taken by fire in 1917. The massive Cuyahoga County Soldiers' and Sailors' Monument, dedicated in 1894 to Cleveland-area residents who fought for the Union in the Civil War, towered over downtown's Public Square.

Jon Webb grew to manhood in this city. He was short and lean, but well-proportioned, with the thin, sharply defined features of an aristocrat. In 1924, he married a local girl named Opal Marie Bennett. Jon was nineteen, Opal a year younger. The couple sneaked away to Flint, Michigan, for the ceremony, perhaps a bad omen. Their union was stormy at best. Opal was sexually promiscuous and a drinker who spiraled into alcoholism. The couple eventually had three children. Barbara was born in 1926, Joyce arrived the following year, and a son, Jon, Jr., came in 1928. Jon supported his family by working as a reporter at one time or another for both the *Cleveland News* and the *Toronto Star*, but there was never enough money in the house. This was before the Cleveland Newspaper Guild formed in 1934, and reporters with three or more years' experience could expect to earn only twenty to twenty-five dollars a week. Jon, Jr., recalled that it was not uncommon for Opal to take the children to a breadline in order to keep them fed. Sometimes meals consisted of no more than hardtack bread and oranges.

In 1932, Jon worked the police beat for the *News*. As part of the routine, he spent time at a precinct each day with competing reporters, digging for stories or waiting for a newsworthy event. When something big happened, the reporters raced to the scene and angled to get the best story. The life of a reporter could be stressful, combining long hours with low pay. The job mixed stretches of intense boredom with flurries of excitement when a good story broke. In Jon's case, the pressures of work, family, and finances eventually acted upon him in a way probably no one would have expected. He decided to commit armed robbery.

As he told it to his son years later, Jon picked out a jewelry store in upscale Cleveland Heights and carefully planned his crime. He went to the police station as usual on the day of the robbery. After a time, he went to the men's room, climbed out a window and made his way to the jewelry store, where the robbery went off without incident. The next part of the plan was ingenious. Rather than flee Cleveland, he returned to the police station, climbed back through the bathroom window, and rejoined the other reporters. Very soon, word came that a jewelry store in the vicinity had been robbed. Like everyone else, Jon scrambled to get to the scene of the crime and write the story.

Jon hid the jewels in a flophouse room he had rented just for that purpose. He pulled a board loose from the floor, placed the jewels beneath it, replaced the board, and covered it with a rug. Unfortunately, a housecleaner noticed the loose board and found the jewels. She called the police, who were waiting for Jon when he returned. He did not go quietly. According to Jon, Jr., his father "was shot in the calf muscle when he was eluding the cops and treated himself by soaking a handkerchief in peroxide and running it in and out of the wound." Years later, Jon showed his son the scar from his gunshot wound. It was about the size of a nickel.

Jon was convicted of armed robbery and sent to the state reformatory in Mansfield, where he spent the next three years. The prison was designed in 1896 after the style of a medieval castle by Captain Levi T. Scofield, a Civil War veteran and, like Webb, a Cleveland native. Scofield intended the aesthetics of his architecture to have an uplifting effect on inmates, perhaps even help rehabilitate them. Naïve though Scofield may have been, he was also prolific. During the second half of the nineteenth century, he designed a number of well-known Ohio buildings, including the Raleigh Penitentiary and insane asylums in both Athens and Columbus. For many years, his best-known work was probably the Cuyahoga County Soldiers' and Sailors' Monument, still a Cleveland landmark.

Being a prisoner was doubtless an awful experience, especially for a man with Webb's independent streak. Mansfield was a dangerous place. The guards could be brutal, and many inmates kept homemade knives or other deadly weapons for protection or to exact vengeance on an enemy. Even so, Jon was determined that he would not cower in his cell; he made sure his time in prison would not be wasted. Probably because he was a highly articulate, professional writer, Jon taught English to the other inmates, eventually going so far as to join the National Council of Teachers of English. He also edited the institution's newspaper, the *New Day*, printing work from convicts and writers on the outside. One of these nonincarcerated writers was Millen Brand, who was impressed enough with Webb and the *New Day* to write affectionately of both decades later: "Years ago, so long ago I shiver to think of it, Jon Edgar Webb edited a prison paper published in some Ohio State Penitentiary and called *The New Day*. Some of the young writers of the Thirties would send poetry to this paper and the paper circulated exclusively in the prison and among this group of writers. In that way, with an audience of nonconformists, thieves, murderers, and each other we got things out that we might not have got out otherwise and had a sense of print audience and communication."

Jon found he enjoyed literary publishing and decided he could write fiction as well as the authors he published in the *New Day*. He determined he would make his career as a short story writer and novelist. Mansfield provided a deep well of source material from which he would draw for years. With his reporter's eye, he noted the details of prison life, from the feel of the cells to the natures of the men who inhabited them. He began writing short stories while still in prison and submitted them, without immediate success, to literary magazines. It was only after his release that his efforts began to bear fruit. "All Prickles, No Petals," about lonely misfits serving time in a penitentiary, appeared in the May–June 1935 issue of *Manuscript*, out of Athens, Ohio.

A picture of the dapper young man appeared on the journal's "Discovered by *Manuscript*" page. Webb is nattily attired in a dark coat and tie and posed for dramatic effect in the striking head-and-shoulders photograph. His body angled roughly one hundred eighty degrees from the camera, Webb stares over his shoulder, directly at the viewer. The picture, showing a man with dark, wavy hair parted in the middle and combed straight back, neatly trimmed moustache, and hint of a grin, could as easily be a publicity photograph for a 1930s film actor. This polished image hardly matched the "outsider" subject matter of his story. Already, the dichotomy which would characterize much of Jon Webb's professional life was developing: the merger of outré literature—his story deals with such themes as sexual obsession, fetishism, voyeurism, misogyny, poverty, and death—with high-style presentation. The accompanying biographical sketch also hinted at Webb's literary ambitions: "Mr. Webb's story in this issue is his first work published in a magazine with national distribution, however, he has seven stories placed with various magazines for early publication."

Though some of Webb's companions in that issue never achieved literary success or are long forgotten, others were notable. There was Irving Shulman, who later wrote the screenplay for *Rebel without a Cause*, the novelization of *West Side Story*, and a biography of 1930s screen siren Jean Harlow. Richard Johns, editor of the important and long-lived (1925–1970) little magazine *Pagany*, contributed a poem, as did August W. Derleth, later to achieve fame as an author of supernatural fiction and, in 1939, as founder of Arkham House publishers. Novelist, poet, and Iowa Writers' Workshop faculty member Hubert Creekmore contributed a short story. The lyrically named Dorothea Spieth and Fleet Munson also had work in that issue, but they have otherwise faded from memory.

Jon continued to publish short fiction, sometimes in prestigious publications such as *Esquire* or Martha Foley and Whit Burnett's excellent *Story*. Like *Manuscript*, *Story* claimed to be the first nationally distributed magazine to publish Webb's fiction; his "Night after Night" appeared in their August 1935 issue. Publication dates being somewhat capricious, it may be that *Story*'s August issue was on sale before the May–June issue of *Manuscript*, but obviously each magazine published very early work of Webb's. More important is the claim itself. Though generally innocuous, it may suggest a faith that Webb's fiction was considered noteworthy. Indeed, Edward O'Brien, editor of the respected *Best Stories of the Year* anthology, recommended several of Jon's stories to readers throughout the 1930s. *Story*'s February 1936 issue contained the magazine's second Jon Edgar Webb short story, "The Key in the Lock," and two pages of letters from Webb to the magazine's editors.

In these letters, Webb wrote of his time as a prisoner at Mansfield, a topic he later avoided. The letters explain this later reluctance: "Before leaving the reformatory I decided to drop all the old friends and make new ones," he wrote. "I would keep my past a secret and start all over again in a different community. Well, it hasn't worked out. I made new friends and for a while got along fine. Then whispers began and presently the new friends were avoiding me. I had been discovered. I was an ex-convict. It would be very unwise to associate with me. I found that it is impossible to run away from the past."

Jon moved his family every few months, going from bad neighborhood to worse, and worse still, trying to make a new life. At each new address, his neighbors stopped being friendly when they learned of his jail time. Though clearly bitter about this treatment, he admitted that there was some justification. "They are both right and wrong in their persecution of an ex-felon," Jon wrote. "They are not shocked so much—they're afraid." Jon believed his neighbors feared him because he "let go and got away with it." Here he was, a felon, walking the streets. "Served a few measly years and out—free—a menace. Avoid him!" Like *Manuscript*, *Story* published Webb's photograph. The difference between the two pictures is striking, and together they offer a glimpse into the contradiction that was Jon Webb. The *Manuscript* photograph, showing the well-groomed and ambitious young author, is in stark contrast to the *Story* photo, in which Webb is lying on a bunk in his Mansfield cell. Webb claimed this was the "first snap of an individual cell ever taken in this dump, and it was hard taking."

Small literary magazines typically do not pay their contributors, so Jon had to find other ways to make money. He landed a job with the Annals of Cleveland, a WPA project whose goal was to index and archive the city's early newspapers. It was a large project, employing dozens of former white-collar workers displaced by the Depression, and a fortunate position for a man with a prison record to acquire. He was also able to generate income from his writing. The 1930s were a heyday for lurid pulp magazines hawking stories of kidnapping, murder, torture, and rape. These magazines had titles like *Official Detective, Actual Detective, Startling Detective,* and *Front Page Detective.* The writers usually highlighted unsavory sexual details of the perpetrator's past or of the crimes themselves, much to the public's delight. The magazines sold extremely well. Jon's past made him a natural reporter for the true crime pulps, and he supplemented his income with regular submissions to their pages. Writing about crime and criminals was his forte, be it in fiction or nonfiction. And there may have been more in Jon's background than his jewelry store robbery and years at Mansfield which made him at home in this genre. According to his son, Jon was also a self-styled abortionist. Jon, Jr., claims his father performed several coat hanger abortions on Opal, burying the aborted fetuses in the backyard of their home. Though Opal was sometimes unfaithful, Jon, Jr., maintains that his father was also the father in the aborted pregnancies.

Jon's first real commercial literary success came in the March 1937 issue of *Esquire* with the prison-themed story "The Idiot in Cell 33," in which a series of misadventures begins with a prisoner looking for a match to light a cigarette and ends with another prisoner coughing himself to death. The *Mansfield News-Journal* noted Webb's success in a front-page column. After identifying him as a former inmate at the state prison, the column described his story as "a simply written episode which conveys the drab emptiness of life behind bars, where little things take on monumental importance." While it is not certain how much *Esquire* paid for this story, a then-unknown Harriette Simpson Arnow published her short story "Two Hunters" there in 1938 and received one hundred twenty-five dollars. It is likely that Webb received similar compensation.

Esquire chose George Grosz, a German national with hard-left political leanings, as illustrator. Grosz was known as a satirist, but thought of himself as a social propagandist and critic of capitalism. During a 1928 visit to Germany, Henry Miller thought of Grosz after seeing a group of ragged, debased German workers, heads shaved and begging cigarettes from tourists they clearly despised. Grosz had drawn such men, and these drawings had been labeled caricatures, but Miller knew better. "The man is the most painstaking photographic realist," Miller wrote. Grosz also illustrated stories in the issue by Allen McGinnis and screenwriter Robert Meltzer. Other short story writers appearing in this issue of *Esquire* included celebrated Canadian journalist and Hemingway friend Morley Callaghan, Kentucky local colorist Jesse Stuart, and Italian-American socialist Pietro di Donato.

Jon relocated Opal and the children as a family a final time in 1938. The Webbs moved to a two-story house on Silvia Street in Cleveland's northeast corner. Between the WPA and the pulp magazines, Jon was at last doing fairly well financially, and the new house reflected this. It had a large country kitchen with a gas stove and oven, two bedrooms, a family room, and a large basement with a furnace. There was an expansive backyard with grapevines covering an overhead framework. This house was near "Euclid Beach," as the popular Euclid Beach Amusement Park on the shore of Lake Erie was commonly called. The park opened in 1895 and spent its first few years as a seedy, lowlife destination patterned after Coney Island, with gambling, freak shows, and a beer garden, but by 1906 new ownership had transformed it into a family-friendly spot with no beer sold inside and no one admitted who had been drinking at any of the nearby bars. There was even a dress code, with adults forbidden to wear short pants. According to a 1907 ad in the Cleveland *Plain Dealer*, the park boasted the first theater in America designed specifically to show moving pictures.

The Webb children loved going to Euclid Beach, a place Jon, Jr., called "the joy of our lives." Neither Jon nor Opal took them there often, but Opal's brother-in-law, Gill Sindeldecker, sometimes piled them into his old Chevrolet for the forty-five-minute drive and an afternoon of fun. The park held many rides, including several roller coasters. Its most distinctive feature was the breathtaking view to be had from the end of a pier stretching into Lake Erie. Trees lined the shore, thick and deep, in both directions, blocking much of the Cleveland skyline. It was like entering a different world. Drawing youngsters from all over the city, Euclid Beach was also a good place to make friends or even find romance. On one excursion, Jon, Jr., met and fell in love with a lovely young girl named Connie Pleshinger. Though their relationship did not work out, they kept in touch for many years. Meanwhile,

Jon and Opal's marriage had become almost unbearable. Jon buried himself in his work, and Opal escaped as she could into a bottle.

The Webbs lived next door to Lucido Madaio and his wife, Rosina, who had lived on Silvia Street for about a year when the Webbs arrived. Rosina's father made money by buying dilapidated houses and refurbishing them for resale. The Madaio family lived in these houses while they were being repaired. Lucido emigrated from Italy in 1905, Rosina in 1912, though, as of the 1930 census, neither was able to read or write in English. Lucido Madaio, said to have been possessed of a strong temper, was a cement finisher by trade, making cement flower pots and owls for the garden from pebbles he gathered at Lake Erie. Rosina was a homemaker who gave birth to seven children, four of whom died in infancy. She spent much of her time looking after the three who survived, Lena, Louise, and Antony. Louise still lived with her parents in 1938, and it was not long before she caught Jon's eye. The first time Jon saw the striking, raven-haired, twenty-one-year-old, she was washing windows in her parents' house. He thought she was beautiful.

A few days later, Jon was trying to concentrate on his writing but a barking dog kept distracting him. He stormed out of the house, intending to complain to the dog's owner. It turned out that the dog belonged to Louise. This was his chance to meet the young woman who had captivated him, and his anger quickly vanished. They became friends on the spot. Louise was a book lover, savoring modern novelists such as William Faulkner and Sherwood Anderson. She was also a fledgling songwriter and a skilled typist. She sometimes heard Jon typing and was equally curious about the writer who lived next door, but her parents would not let her meet him because he was married. When they finally did meet, "It was easy for us to get along, since I was a writer and she had read the great writers of the day," Webb later told a reporter. "She amazed me."

Jon, Jr., was curious about the Madaio family, too. The boy sometimes peeked over the fence to watch the quick-tempered Mr. Madaio at work on his pots and owls. It was during one of these times that Jon, Jr., first met Louise, who "would come out there and prance around and we'd talk over the fence every now and then." It seemed almost natural to the boy when Louise moved across the lawn and took up residence with the Webbs. "I was really too young to comprehend what was going on. My mother was drinking quite a bit and she moved in with us and it seemed like a normal thing. You know, a kid doesn't think about those ramifications and what this means." Living conditions in the Webb household could not have been easy, and they were undoubtedly made worse by the hardships of the Great Depression. On one occasion, Opal made a spaghetti dinner but, in her drunkenness, fell and splattered the food on the floor. Louise heard the crash and came to help clean up. Food was scarce and the women were hungry, so after they got the spaghetti back into a bowl, they ate it anyway.

It was an odd situation, but somehow it worked for a while. To find privacy, Jon and Louise sometimes went walking in nearby Wade Park. There were benches there and, since they had little money, sitting on a park bench and talking was like having a night on the town. But it could also be dangerous. One night in the park, Jon had to excuse himself to urinate in the bushes. While he was away, two young men approached Louise. She was frightened and became more afraid when Jon reappeared and said, forcefully, "Don't you touch that girl. I've got a shiv on you." The young men ran away, and Louise realized that her mild-mannered lover could be dangerous if the situation demanded.

Louise loved Jon and liked Opal, and when there was a little extra money in the house the three of them sometimes went out together for beers at a local bar. One day Opal asked Louise if she loved Jon. Louise said that she did love Jon and wanted to marry him. Opal understood that this was how things were going to be. "Well, I guess so," she told her rival. Through all of this, Jon remained dedicated to his writing. He had switched from short stories to the novel by the mid-1930s, and devoted much of his energies to a book he later described to Sherwood Anderson as "a gigantic piece of work." He wanted to make a splash with his novel and sent it to Anderson, a man he did not know. Anderson had a richly deserved reputation for helping young writers, though, and Jon thought it was worth taking a chance. He had helped launch Hemingway and Faulkner, so why not Jon Edgar Webb? Anderson liked the manuscript well enough to solicit Houghton Mifflin on Jon's behalf, recommending him for the publisher's prestigious annual fellowship, an award which came with a thousand-dollar prize.

Jon did not win the fellowship and lost faith in what he had written. When Houghton Mifflin returned his manuscript, he destroyed most of it and began again in earnest. After three weeks of intense effort, the manuscript was back to about forty thousand words, enough for Jon to send it to his agent, Ann Watkins. This time, he was successful. Watkins arranged for a reading at Harcourt, Brace and Company. A week after Watkins submitted the work in progress, Harcourt drew up a contract and forwarded Jon a five-hundred-dollar advance. He wrote Anderson to update him on the situation: "Anyway, I'm sure that when you read the novel, part of which appeared in *Story*, you will not be sorry you recommended me when I sorely needed your help. I want to thank you again for your confidence."

Somewhere in all of this, Jon divorced Opal, and the household split apart. Jon and Louise moved out of the Silvia Street house and relocated to the nearby community of Euclid. The children were parceled out to relatives, some of whom probably also cared for Opal. Jon was free of the marriage, but still tied down financially. The court awarded Opal alimony in the amount of twenty-five dollars per week, a substantial amount in the mid-1930s. Jon's prospects were thus anything but certain when he asked Louise to marry him. Jon loved Louise and had an animal need for her that went beyond romance. As he later told Anderson, "I can't work without a woman around near, and I never went for whores."

Jon and Louise were married in Cleveland in a civil ceremony on June 15, 1939. About a month after their wedding, Jon approached Louise with an idea he had for keeping their marriage healthy. He asked her to sit in the kitchen with him and drink a beer. When they were settled he told her his idea: "Every Thursday night we'll go in the kitchen. We'll sit across from each other, we'll drink beer and we'll tell what we don't like about the other person."

"Like what?" Louise asked.

"Like if you snore . . . something about you I don't like."

Louise agreed, and they made the Thursday night sessions a ritual for years thereafter. The only rules were to be honest and not get angry. If either broke the rules, the other would not allow another beer. Louise counted this idea as being key to their happiness.

But life was more than fresh love and a new home. With the alimony payments piling up along with normal household expenses, money was scarce and Jon felt pressured. One of the results of this was that he began to neglect the novel. Things came to a head on April 22, 1940, when the couple decided they had to leave Ohio. They pawned or sold everything they had of value, put together a nest egg of almost one hundred dollars, and moved to St. Louis. They picked St. Louis because of an invitation from an acquaintance of Jon's, fellow true crime writer Harold Zimmer. Jon was doing well in placing articles in the detective magazines, and Zimmer hoped to learn how to be more successful. It was perhaps on their way to St. Louis that the newlyweds found themselves on July 11 at the Omar Hotel in Louisville, Kentucky. Jon watched Louise as she slept and wrote a long poem admiring her beauty and marveling at his love for her. Beginning "Sweetheart, I gazed upon your open / sleeping face / just now," the poem covered two handwritten pages and concluded:

Yes, sweet lovely sleeping face
Alluring, mysteriously still,
Like ageless gold,
Ancient, rare and thrillingly enchanting
Has opened in me a
Little door—
One I never knew was there
Always shut, I guess, before!

Jon and Louise stayed in St. Louis for about a month. By this time, Jon had decided Zimmer was milking him for information and giving nothing in return. Even though the Webbs had almost no money and certainly no plans, they knew it was time for a change. With only seventeen dollars to their names, Jon and Louise decided to move. Louise remembers the move being almost whimsical. "What happened was, we went to the bus station. Jon said, 'We've got to get out of this place.' And just then, a bus came by, called 'New Orleans Express.' We had never been to New Orleans. . . . Jon said, 'Do you want to go there?' I said, 'Sure, how much is it?' We had enough to get a cheap room on Cleveland Avenue in New Orleans. With that seventeen bucks, we got the bus fare and room-rent for a week." The rooming house wasn't fancy, but it did fit nicely with the couple's budget. The biggest drawback was that it only had "one bathroom at the end of a hall," Louise said. "Everybody in the place used it. And it was three dollars a week. So, he took it. That's all."

Jon's account to Anderson was somewhat at odds with Louise's. As Jon told it, he wrote some true detective stories "and a couple of idiotic editorials on crime" during their time in St. Louis before the two of them left to rent a cabin in the Ozark foothills, over one hundred fifty miles away. He was still working on the book that Harcourt had optioned in 1936 and spent a good bit of time trying to finish it: "In the six weeks that followed I wrote 16,000 words on the novel. Then we had to go on. Poison oak and ivy got both of us. We came down here to New Orleans."

The Webbs apparently moved from the Cleveland Avenue address in short order, because within weeks they were living a few blocks away at 139 South Claiborne Street, room five. The rent was three dollars and fifty cents per week, and the landlady was known for seizing deadbeat tenants' belongings if they got very much in arrears. Both Cleveland and South Claiborne were in a rough neighborhood, not far from the notorious Storyville red-light district. Jon assumed that the previous occupant of their room was a whore, "and before her a lot of other whores." Someone had begun repainting the room and made it around the dresser and two pictures on the walls, then quit. Jon decided the painter left off in disgust, "realizing the paint wasn't improving the room's looks." The room was infested with bugs, and Jon quickly identified seven different species.

After a few weeks in town, the Webbs were almost destitute. They were down to their last eighty-seven cents, behind in the rent and out of food. It was a desperate time, but Jon had one acquaintance he thought might be able to help. Sherwood Anderson had been good to Jon in the past. Now Jon wrote Anderson again, reminding him of their earlier association and telling him the story of how he and Louise ended up broke in New Orleans. They had been in town for a few weeks, pinching pennies and looking for a break. Jon had assignments for a few true crime stories, but he had sold his typewriter and could not even rent another without two business references. Without a typewriter, he couldn't sell the stories. "I know I have no right to be writing to you in this manner," Jon told Anderson. "Writers are always getting stranded and finding a way out without bothering people. I would, too, if I were traveling alone. But two of us makes it hard. We're just in a hell of a jam, that's all."

Around this time, an editor at the *Times-Picayune* somehow learned that an up-and-coming writer had come to town and sent a reporter to interview him. Jon had been writing in longhand through the night, finally collapsing at 6 a.m. When the reporter arrived at 10:30, he and Louise were still in bed. Jon answered the door naked from the waist up. Once the reporter was inside the room, Louise slipped behind him and "brazenly dressed, grinning at me in my wrinkly pajama bottoms." It was clear to both Jon and Louise that the reporter was ill at ease in the squalid room. He perched uncomfortably on the edge of a broken chair as he asked Jon his questions. Jon was uncomfortable, too. He told Anderson he was embarrassed to be interviewed, only thirty-five years old with no real accomplishments as a writer. If the novel were finished, that would be one thing, but anyone could have a large stack of unpublished pages. In Jon's mind, that did not count for much.

He thought a better story lay with the building's other down-on-their-luck tenants. There was the dignified old lady and her son who lived next door. The woman was sixty, her son, thirty-six. They were from Kentucky, where they once owned a horse farm. They lost the farm and one hundred fifty thousand dollars in the stock market crash and were left with only five thousand dollars. Now they lived in a New Orleans flophouse and drank a quart or more of sherry each day and slept in the same bed at night. Jon and Lou sometimes heard them through the wall late at night, drunk and talking in their sleep about the past.

In the apartment directly beneath the Webbs lived a man and a woman who fought three times a week, every week. The man came home late those nights, and Jon was sure he had a mistress with whom he kept regular hours. The nights he came in late, the woman he lived with would scream forty or more times, "Where you was at?," crying and sobbing. Later, they listened to her crying loudly as the man snored.

A ninety-five-year-old man lived down the hall from these people. The old man slept during the day and ate his breakfast on the corner at 1:00 a.m. He had a friend on the same floor, an eighty-eight-year-old man who worked during the day. Jon was sure that the older man purposely slept during the day so he would be able to spend more time with his friend. The men were veterans and drove Jon to distraction between 1:30 and 3:00 a.m., talking loudly about old wars and dismissing the war in Europe as small potatoes. Jon sometimes thought of shouting for them to shut up, but he never did: "That wouldn't make sense to them. Why should they shut up this late in life?" Jon told the reporter in detail about his neighbors, and if they were a better story than he was, there was an even better story right in front of him: "I would like to be honest with the reporter. Tell him what he should see about me he never could understand—Louise and me."

Before the interview progressed too far, the landlady stuck the Webbs' mail under their door. One of the letters was from an Anderson friend in New Orleans, a painter and interior designer named Marc Antony. Louise opened the letter and read aloud: "Sherwood Anderson has just wired about you and I would very much like to have an opportunity to talk with you. Please phone or come to above address." After that, the reporter relaxed, and the rest of the interview went smoothly. A giant cockroach and a horde of red ants appeared on the wall, and Louise served coffee. Everyone was happy.

FOUR STEPS TO THE WALL AND HOLLYWOOD DREAMS

ANTONY GAVE JON A TYPEWRITER and ten dollars, solving the Webbs' immediate problems. They paid their back rent and bought food to fill their makeshift pantry, a dresser drawer. Jon was able to complete his assignments with the detective magazines and generate income. Even better, Antony gave Louise a job sewing curtains for his interior decorating business. With this, the Webbs had a steady income for a while, until the damp atmosphere of Antony's store gave Louise respiratory troubles, forcing her to quit. As important as the money itself was that Jon was happy to know someone in town. Now, if things got terrible again, he at least had someone local to ask for help. Jon and Louise welcomed Antony's dinner invitation for the following Monday night. The food would be better than anything they had recently eaten, and it was good to socialize. Antony's other guests included writers Jon admired, including local novelist E. P. O'Donnell.

A few days after the dinner at Antony's home, the Webbs were exploring the area surrounding Jackson Square. Louise, used to the wide streets and more open spaces of Cleveland and the Midwest, was frightened by the close, narrow lanes and unfamiliar architecture of the Quarter. As luck would have it, they came upon O'Donnell and a young woman sitting on a grassy mound near the Mississippi River. O'Donnell recognized the Webbs and asked if they would like to sit down. It was the beginning of their first real friendships in New Orleans.

Edwin Patrick O'Donnell was "Pat" to his friends, "E. P." to the many readers of his successful and highly regarded 1936 novel, *Green Margins*. O'Donnell's companion was Mary King, an attractive dark-haired Texan with a pretty smile. King was O'Donnell's girlfriend and also a writer in the making. The two couples fell into conversation and discovered mutual affinities. Before the evening was through, O'Donnell and King had offered the Webbs their patio as a place to stay if they found themselves in need.

Pat O'Donnell, the son of a railroad man, was born in New Orleans in 1895 and lived there most of his life. A fourth-grade dropout, O'Donnell was an ambulance driver during World War I and also served with the adjutant general's office. He later worked his way from the assembly line to head of publicity for the New Orleans Ford Motor Company plant. Like Jon, Pat was a literary late bloomer, and the two men shared a benefactor. O'Donnell decided to become a writer at the urging of Sherwood Anderson, whom he met while touring Anderson through the Ford plant. Anderson was so taken with O'Donnell's vivid descriptions of the ins and outs of the factory that he suggested O'Donnell try his hand at writing. In an odd twist of fate, O'Donnell won the Houghton Mifflin Fellowship in 1936, the year that Anderson had backed Jon's entry.

O'Donnell published his first creative work in 1929. "Transfusion" appeared in the first issue of Charles Henri Ford's ambitious little magazine, *Blues: A Magazine of New Rhythms*. O'Donnell borrowed formal contrivance from the drama, with setting information, dialogue without description, and a curtain call, though the entire sketch is barely five hundred words long. *Blues* was a good place to publish. Based in Ford's small hometown of Columbus, Mississippi, the magazine attracted work from Gertrude Stein, Erskine Caldwell, Paul Bowles, and William Carlos Williams. Walter Lowenfels had a long poem mocking consumerism, "Antipodes," in the first issue. Regardless of this illustrious company, *Blues*, like most little magazines, paid its contributors only the prestige of being published. O'Donnell's first commercial success came two years later when *Collier's* published his story "Manhood." In 1935, *Harper's* published "Jesus Knew," which brought him to the attention of editors at Houghton Mifflin and put him in line for their fellowship, with its one-thousand-dollar prize. After O'Donnell won, he used fifty dollars of that money to buy a one-room shack in Boothville, Louisiana, a small town ninety miles south of New Orleans where he lived and wrote for a time.

A year later, Houghton Mifflin published *Green Margins* to good reviews and strong sales; the book was also a selection of the Book-of-the-Month Club. Both *Green Margins* and O'Donnell's second book, *The Great Big Doorstep*, were local color novels, richly describing the people and customs of southern Louisiana. The first was a drama, the second a comedy. After being out of print for decades, *The Great Big Doorstep* was reissued in 1979 by Southern Illinois University Press as part of their Lost American Fiction series. That edition had a sympathetic afterword by Eudora Welty in which she called the book a "triumph," and mourned the fact that she never had the chance to meet O'Donnell.

Mary King did not publish her first novel until 1941, two years after meeting the Webbs. *Quincie Boliver* examines the hardships of a young girl growing up in a rough Texas oil town. Her second novel came five years later. *Those Other People* is the story of a young woman searching the French Quarter for a red-haired sailor with whom she has had a brief affair. The story takes place during a single, hot June day in the 1930s. Mary's description of the Quarter mixes the happy bustling of a dynamic port community with the want and loneliness that lie beneath the surface. She wrote of Decatur Street, with its bars and small restaurants, its hotels and the Italian groceries fragrant with cheese and smoked herring, its prostitutes, sailors, tourists, and jukebox music, a bustling, lively street till late at night. But in the early morning, Decatur lay deserted, "except for a beggar woman feeling around in a garbage can that hadn't been emptied the night before; and one lone man with his hat crammed over his ears." Echoing Pat's success, Mary won a 1946 Houghton Mifflin Fellowship for *Those Other People*, with its dedication "For E. P. O'Donnell." Tragically, Pat was not around to see this. After a romance of several years, O'Donnell and King were married in late February or early March 1943. Pat died in New Orleans's Charity Hospital of a heart condition just six weeks later.

Being saved from ruin by a great author or striking up lasting friendships with writers sitting in the grass by the river might seem unusual in most places, but New Orleans, a city of contrasts, with heaping doses of what historian Herbert Asbury described as "glamour and spectacular wickedness" and "sin and gayety," was a town open to possibility. Louise later recalled one address where she and Jon lived where "Everyone living there then had talent of some kind. They were either artists, painting, or they were writers or poets or people trying to do plays. They were all talented, creative people."

Twentieth-century New Orleans certainly had its share of literati: Walker Percy, Truman Capote, Lillian Hellman, John Kennedy Toole, Anne Rice— the list goes on and on. These writers built upon a solid foundation. The first literary magazine in the city appeared in the mid-nineteenth century. This was the *L'Album littéraire: Journal des jeunes gens, amateurs de littérature Litteraire*, or *The Literary Album: A Journal of Young Men, Lovers of*

Literature. Its editors were free black men who were not shy about breaking with local custom. The magazine debuted in 1843 and regularly defied a harsh 1830 Louisiana law forbidding any reading material likely to breed discontent among the state's black population. The law carried penalties of three to twenty years' imprisonment or death, depending upon the judge's whim, but *L'Album littéraire* did not for safety's sake keep silent. Instead, it published a number of essays describing a corrupt New Orleans society and its toll on people of color. Not surprisingly, the magazine was attacked for fomenting revolution and ceased publication in less than a year. In 1845, the first African American poetry collection, *Les Cenelles*, was published in New Orleans.

Later in the nineteenth century, novelist George Washington Cable (1844–1925) achieved national acclaim for his fictive examinations of Creole culture. The city's first great literary light was thought odd for his progressive stance on American race relations and civil rights. With its examination of racial injustice, Cable's 1880 novel *The Grandissimes* is considered by many critics to be the first modern southern novel. Like his 1879 short story collection, *Creole Days*, this book was widely praised in the North, widely scorned in the South. In 1884, he published the equally controversial *Dr. Sevier*, which dealt with the problem of prison reform.

More often than not, the early writers who turned their attention to New Orleans were from elsewhere. In the nineteenth century, these writers included, among others, Walt Whitman, O. Henry, Mark Twain, and the Greek Lafcadio Hearn. Hearn is better known for his writings on Japanese culture, most notably *Japan: An Attempt at Interpretation* (1904), but before he became an expert on Japan he had already immersed himself in the French Quarter. Like his friend Cable, Hearn had strong interest in Creole culture and came to New Orleans in 1875 to learn more. He settled for a while at 516 Bourbon Street. In 1886, Hearn published two slight books, *La Cuisine Creole* and *Ghombo Zhebes: A Little Dictionary of Creole Proverbs*, and wrote a series of pieces on New Orleans life under the general heading of "Creole Sketches" for the New Orleans *Item*.

Whitman arrived in 1848 as a journalist for the *Daily Crescent*. This was soon after the Mexican-American War, and Whitman later recalled the city as a rollicking place with "the best news and war correspondents; it had the most to say, through its leading papers, the *Picayune* and *Delta* especially, and its voice was readiest listen'd to. . . ." Whitman drew a vivid picture of the French Quarter at mid-nineteenth century, similar in tone to King's take on the place a century later.

> One of my choice amusements during my stay in New Orleans was going down to the old French Market, especially of a Sunday morning. The show was a varied and curious one; among the rest, the Indian and negro hucksters with their wares. For there were always fine specimens of Indians, both men and women, young and old. I remember I nearly always on these occasions got a large cup of coffee with a biscuit, for my breakfast, from the immense shining copper kettle of a great Creole mulatto woman (I believe she weigh'd 230 pounds.) I never have had such coffee since. About nice drinks, anyhow, my recollection of the "cobblers" (with strawberries and snow on top of the large tumblers,) and also the exquisite wines, and the perfect and mild French brandy, help the regretful reminiscence of my New Orleans experiences of those days.

Whitman loved the "splendid and roomy and leisurely bar-rooms" of the city, especially those of the St. Charles and St. Louis districts, where he reported that all manner of business meetings and transactions were carried out.

In the late 1890s, William Sydney Porter, better remembered as short story master O. Henry, fled to New Orleans after being accused of embezzling money from an Austin, Texas, bank, where he had worked as a teller. He was later convicted of this crime and, like Jon Webb a few decades later, served time in an Ohio prison. During his stay in New Orleans, Porter lived on Bienville Street and worked as a reporter for several newspapers. He later used the city as a backdrop for a number of his stories, including "Cherchez la Femme" in 1903.

The French Quarter is divided into upper and lower sections, and Porter's Bienville address was in the Upper Quarter. The Webbs, over the years, lived in each. From some time in the 1950s through 1960, they lived at 638 Royal Street in the Upper Quarter, a few blocks from Porter's old address. This section occupies the area from Canal Street to the St. Louis Cathedral, with the Quarter proper officially ending at Iberville. Mark Twain visited his friend Cable in the Upper Quarter in 1882 and liked much about the area, though not Canal Street's architecture, especially the U.S. Custom House, which he said reminded him of a state prison.

In 1961, the Webbs moved to 618 Ursulines Street in the Lower Quarter, a neighborhood which encompasses an area downriver from the St. Louis Cathedral to Esplanade Street. A number of important figures either lived in or were otherwise associated with the Lower Quarter over the years, including John James Audubon, John Dos Passos, Truman Capote, and Tennessee Williams, who moved various times during his years as a New Orleans resident. In 1943, the neighborhood hosted the nuptials of John Steinbeck and singer Gwyndolyn Conger in the Madison Street home of novelist Lyle Saxon.

Two other transplanted Quarterites, Eugene and Maria Jolas, lived on St. Peter Street in the mid-twenties. Eugene was a poet and former expatriate, a veteran of the heady Parisian crucible occupied by Ernest Hemingway, Ford Maddox Ford, James Joyce, and other talented newcomers with an eye toward revolutionizing literature. While in Paris, Eugene met and married Maria McDonald, a Louisville, Kentucky, native who studied singing. The couple came to the French Quarter after tiring of the breathless Greenwich Village literary scene, where they had settled after France. Eugene found a job as a reporter for the New Orleans *Item-Tribune*. His beat didn't provide much excitement, though once Buster Keaton came to town for a movie opening, and Eugene had the chance to interview the great comedian at a party. Unfortunately, Keaton was a reluctant subject, and Jolas had to rely mostly on the witty remarks of several starlets in attendance to keep his story interesting. Another time, Jolas befriended Edmund Wilson, in New Orleans on a writing assignment for the *New Republic*. Jolas's most valued New Orleans acquaintance was the father of one of his colleagues at the *Item-Tribune*, Sherwood Anderson, of Bourbon Street. Anderson and Jolas sometimes took walks around the Quarter and talked about writing or the nature of the American character. The Jolases also met Julius Weis Friend and the other editors of the remarkable little magazine the *Double Dealer*.

The *Double Dealer*, long the most celebrated of New Orleans's little magazines, came about in part as result of a scathing critique of southern culture from H. L. Mencken, whose 1917 essay, "The Sahara of the Bozart," dismissed the entirety of the southern United States as a cultural desert: "Virginia is the best of the south to day, and Georgia is perhaps the worst. The one is simply senile; the other is crass, gross, vulgar and obnoxious. Between lies a vast plain of mediocrity, stupidity, lethargy, almost of dead silence." Mencken's essay was republished in 1921 when it came to the attention of a group of enterprising New Orleans writers and businessmen, led by Friend. The group refashioned a local interest magazine they planned to publish into the *Double Dealer,* which became one of the great literary magazines of the 1920s. The Jolases admired the *Double Dealer,* and discussed taking over the magazine, but in the end decided not to. Their true wish was to start their own magazine in Paris to serve as a bridge between European and American culture. It wasn't long before they left New Orleans for Paris, where they eventually founded *transition.*

In January 1925, William Faulkner moved to New Orleans, living for a time at 624 Pirate's Alley, where he wrote his first novel, *Soldiers' Pay.* He became friends with Anderson and the literary clique surrounding the *Double Dealer,* publishing several pieces in the magazine. These, along with essays he published in the New Orleans *Times-Picayune,* were later issued as *New Orleans Sketches.* Faulkner's second novel, the relatively weak *Mosquitoes,* satirized the New Orleans literary scene. If Faulkner failed to effectively capture the essence of the Crescent City, another Mississippi transplant, Tennessee Williams, did so splendidly. *A Streetcar Named Desire,* with its clash between brutish Stanley Kowalski and fragile, doomed Blanche DuBois, is perhaps the best metaphor we have for the powerful contradictions which run through the city. Williams used New Orleans again in *Suddenly Last Summer,* the story of a young woman under threat of a lobotomy so that she might forget her late cousin's homosexuality and death. It is a play rife with bad intentions, its characters on a path to doom.

Williams lived for a time with his grandfather, the Reverend Walter Dakin, at the Hotel Monteleone at 214 Royal, and there composed a portion of the experimental play *Camino Real.* He enjoyed the nightlife at spots like the Goat House, where patrons not only drank but ventured into exotic entertainments such as ether parties, and the more sedate Bourbon House on the corner of St. Peter and Bourbon. The Webbs met Williams at the Bourbon House one evening in the 1940s. According to Louise, "Everybody congregated there, all the people in the Quarter. [Williams] was there sitting with [his lover] Pancho [Rodriguez] at that time. I just started talking, just sat down with him. Then we went over to Pat O'Brien's. Then my husband came along and he met both of them. Then we moved across the street where I had my paintings hanging up, St. Peter Street, a building across the street, where he did *A Streetcar Named Desire.* I did a painting, after he left, called

'Streetcar Named Desire.' A crooked street, like going down Arnold Street. Maybe that's in there."

It was also probably sometime in the 1940s that Jon met Ernest Hemingway. Jon somehow learned that the author was staying at the Hotel Monteleone and called to introduce himself. The conversation went well and Hemingway invited Webb to his room. Jon told Louise he wanted to go for a little while, maybe have a couple of drinks. Louise gave her blessing, but became worried after several hours passed and there was no word from Jon. Finally, late in the night, she called Hemingway's room. When Hemingway answered the phone, Louise asked if her husband was still there. "Yeah," Hemingway replied. Louise asked if Jon was okay. When Hemingway said Jon was fine, Louise said, "Oh, all right" and quit worrying. "They got along," she said in 2003.

New Orleans must have been a heady place, capable, perhaps, of making newcomers forget they ever had a past life. But forgetting isn't the same as escaping, and Jon had ties to the past that could not be broken. One of these ties was to his son. In 1941, the twelve-year-old Jon, Jr., hitchhiked from Cleveland to New Orleans for an extended visit. This was in the dead of winter and the boy was half-frozen and starving for much of the trip. Once in New Orleans, he made money as a shoeshine boy, working all around the Quarter. "I shined shoes for the sailors and soldiers on Royal, Bourbon, Canal, Decatur, and hell I just can't remember all the streets. I always had a pocket full of change and a dirty face smeared with shoe polish," he later recalled. The Webbs socialized with Pat O'Donnell and Mary King, both of whom Jon, Jr., liked very much. There were good times in bars around Pirate's Alley, with Jon and O'Donnell smoking, talking, and drinking beer. Jon was fond of hats and sometimes wore a beret or a fedora. He held his cigarette in the corner of his mouth and tilted his head to the side so that, as the smoke rose, it curled over his cheek.

The thing Jon, Jr., remembered best of Pat O'Donnell was his "giant smile with the deep grooves lining his face." Pat loved to cook, and one viciously hot summer day, the Webbs came to eat dinner with Pat and Mary. The five of them took their meal on Pat's tiny patio, and Jon let his son sip from his beer. That was Jon's way: "Go ahead, have a drink. Go ahead, have a puff. Go ahead and masturbate, it won't cause you to go insane." The boy agreed with everything. "I was awed, not only with New Orleans, but with you and Lou and the French Quarter environment," he wrote his father, many years later.

"But especially with you. Man, the talks we used to have." Jon, Jr., eventually had to leave, but his time with his father and Louise remained a cherished memory.

The prospect of having a child in the house appeared again in the fall of 1941 when Louise learned she was pregnant. Both she and Jon were delighted. Each looked forward to having a child together, cementing their union as a family. Louise, nine months pregnant on May 4, 1942, was working at New Orleans's Office of Property Traffic while Jon stayed home, wrote, and took care of their apartment. When Louise arrived home from work that day, Jon had a spaghetti dinner waiting for her. She didn't want to eat, but Jon insisted and she gave in. Soon after Louise began eating, she became ill and vomited. Jon was concerned and called her gynecologist, Dr. Wilbur Moore, who came to their home and examined Louise. Dr. Moore determined she had a serious infection and needed immediate hospitalization. To make matters worse, Louise went into labor soon after arriving at the hospital. The situation became critical, and Dr. Moore had to use forceps to partially remove the baby from Louise's body. He had to use such force that the baby's skull fractured and he died. Jon was in the waiting room, frantic, and when told about the baby's death, said, "I don't care . . . save Lou . . . just save Lou." Dr. Moore did what he could, but Louise developed gangrene and peritonitis and fell into a coma. He told Jon that his wife was near death.

Jon became so distraught that his skin broke out in a condition resembling warts. Louise's mother and sister, expecting the worst, made the trip from Cleveland to be with her when she died and to arrange her funeral. To his credit, Dr. Wilbur refused to give up on his patient. He attended Louise during the day and set up a cot outside her room and slept there, in case she needed his attention during the night. Three weeks passed before she awoke and it was at last clear that she would survive. The family was overjoyed, but Louise was devastated at the loss of her baby. The trauma she suffered carried an even more terrible price: Louise required a hysterectomy; there would be no children from this union.

The child, a boy, had black hair and blue eyes and was given the name Tommy. Jon arranged that his body be cremated, but before this was done, he took a photograph of his son so that Louise would be able to see him when she awoke. When Louise recovered, she decided that Tommy's ashes should be scattered in the courtyard of the St. Louis Cathedral in Jackson Square, a place she loved. Though the church denied her permission to do this, Louise managed surreptitiously to bury a portion of her son's ashes in one corner of the courtyard. These were black days for the Webbs, and a despondent Jon suffered a major setback with his work. His contract with Harcourt fell through, and he and Louise were left to wonder if his writing career would ever be truly successful.

Jon did the only thing he knew how to do: he kept trying. Eventually, the pain of Louise's ordeal and Tommy's death began to dull and, after a time, Jon's career began to look brighter. He still wrote for pulp magazines, sometimes taking Louise with him when he covered a story. On one occasion, they found themselves at the scene of an airplane crash that had just occurred. Louise was horrified at the charred bodies, one of whose fingers snapped off as she watched when something brushed against them. Jon kept at his fiction, too. The novel he had worked on for so long was called "Hey Warden." It is unclear whether this manuscript was the same he was calling "The Glass House" by the mid-1940s, but both were based on his prison experiences. Either way, "The Glass House" finally brought success. Jon won a publishing contract with Dial Press in January 1946 and received a five-hundred-dollar advance. He finished the manuscript in December of that year and sent it to Dial.

The publisher ordered revisions, and the Webbs packed their belongings and headed for New York so that Jon could be near his publisher and his agent as he worked. As they had done when they escaped Cleveland, Jon and Louise raised money for their trip by selling or pawning everything they had of value, including "what petty jewelry we had, my best suits, phonograph, radio, etc." With that money, they were soon living at 11 Abingdon Square, a Greenwich Village rooming house about three blocks from the Hudson River. Dial provided an additional advance of two hundred fifty dollars soon after the Webbs came to New York, and an acquaintance agreed to loan Jon enough to survive until the book was complete. Jon soon realized the revisions Dial wanted were much more significant than he had thought them to be. After working on the revisions for six weeks, he decided that Dial's demands had caused the book to change so radically that it was leaning toward being "a sensational, typically corny prison novel." In order to avoid this outcome, he had to completely rewrite the final third. The book was scheduled for a spring 1947 release, but in late February Jon estimated that he still had three months of work ahead of him.

Money was tight and got even tighter after their benefactor learned that

Jon was an ex-convict and withdrew his support. By mid-February, Jon and Louise could afford nothing to eat but bread and coffee. After ten days of this, "dizzy and weak from not eating, a thousand miles from home, and expecting eviction at any moment," Jon hit upon a plan to enlist the help of popular gossip columnist and radio personality Walter Winchell (Anderson had died in 1941). Winchell was a long shot, because his stock in trade was celebrity news, and Jon was no celebrity. Still, it seemed worth a try; Winchell could make things happen. His column ran in two thousand newspapers across America, and his radio show reached an audience of fifty-five million listeners.

Jon was careful not to ask Winchell to tell his story to America. At the top of his letter, in screaming capital letters, he wrote: "THIS LETTER IS NOT A PLEA FOR PUBLICITY. PLEASE READ IT, AS WE'RE DESPERATE." After giving Winchell a history of his book, the dire circumstances in which he and Louise found themselves, and a vague and apparently misleading explanation of why he had been in prison—"Got into the jam while drunk, and have touched whiskey only twice since"—Jon asked if Winchell knew of anyone who might be willing to loan money with the book as security or against Jon's anticipated royalties. If not a loan, perhaps Winchell could arrange shelter. "[Y]ou may know someone who has a place they're not living in right now and could use a caretaker. I'd do that, anything so that I could write during the next three months and get this job done."

Jon had no illusions that his novel would hit the jackpot of a Book-of-the-Month Club selection, but told Winchell his contacts at Dial suggested the book might be chosen by the smaller, more prestigious Book Find Club. Regardless, Jon assured Winchell that "The Glass House" would "bring in at least several thousand dollars, so anyone who helps us out can't possibly lose." Jon urged Winchell to speak with George Joel, his editor at Dial, but cautioned: "I would be grateful if you did not embarrass me too much. They've been swell to me, especially on my not revising for spring deadline with the book scheduled." Emphasizing the urgency of his situation, he wrote that "we have a hall phone here, four flights down, so in case (miraculously) you want to contact me at once the number is Chelsea 3-9714."

Jon's pleas to Winchell went unanswered, but he and Louise managed to survive. In 1948 the Dial Press, a publishing descendent of America's first great literary magazine, the *Dial*, issued Jon's bleak and gritty look at prison life under the new title *Four Steps to the Wall*. The book carried the dedication "For Louise Madaio Webb" and received positive reviews. The *Mansfield*

News-Journal noted the book had been added to the local public library's collection, reminding readers with apparent pride that the author was a former inmate at the state prison there. Elsewhere, one reviewer wrote, "It is a grim tale, and the author, in this, his first book, has told it well." A more enthusiastic review by novelist David Davidson appeared in the *New York Herald Tribune*. Davidson, author of a well-reviewed 1947 novel about occupied Germany, *The Steeper Cliff*, praised the book in print and spoke highly of it to Dial editor George Joel after a chance meeting on a New York street. In his review, Davidson wrote, "In Jon Edgar Webb's first novel, *Four Steps to the Wall*, not one shot is fired. Yet it is hard, for me impossible, to recall anything in American prison fiction which matches this book for excitement. Mr. Webb succeeds in communicating the convict's feelings of confinement, aggressiveness and subjugation with such force and freshness that one might imagine him to be the first writer to take up such materials." Davidson acknowledged that Jon's terse prose could be confusing, but concluded that "these flaws are minor. *Four Steps to the Wall* is the work of a serious craftsman who has made a distinguished contribution to American writing." Not surprisingly, Louise, too, praised the book. Inside one copy, she wrote: "To my darling husband—more like this to follow—Your wife, Lou." Beside this note, she added, "Really terrific!," a phrase she underlined.

It was probably soon after Dial published his book that Jon returned to editing for the first time since his work on the *New Day*. Still in New York, he and Louise began a freelance business, doing final edits on novels and nonfiction books for about a dozen major publishers, including Scribner's, Farrar & Straus, and Dial. This was a lucrative venture, worth about twenty-five thousand dollars a year, by Jon's estimate, but he considered it to be hack work. It was also stressful, and Jon ultimately decided the problems were not worth the profit: "It was making nervous wrecks out of us, and I dragged Lou out of it, too," he later told Jim Roman. Besides, he had a successful novel of his own and if he could made a good living as a writer, so much the better.

Four Steps to the Wall sold well enough for Dial in a three-dollar hardcover edition to be reissued in paperback five years later by Bantam in paperback. On the advice of his friend, *Look* magazine photographer Sam Shaw, Jon decided to explore the possibility of selling his book to the movies. Shaw introduced Jon to Monte Proser, a would-be producer connected with New York's famed Copacabana nightclub, and Proser's friends, Charlie Weintraub and reputed gangster Frank Costello, a potential backer for the project. The meeting was successful and preproduction work began. Jon and Louise moved to Hollywood.

Proser hired David Goodis to translate *Four Steps to the Wall* into a screenplay. This appeared to be a good match. Goodis was a driven, prolific writer who published widely in pulp mystery magazines and wrote for a number of radio serials, such as *Superman* and *House of Wax*. He published his first novel, *Retreat from Oblivion*, in 1939, but poor reviews stalled his career. It wasn't until 1946, when the *Saturday Evening Post* serialized his novel *Dark Road*, that Goodis really got back on track. In 1947, the book was adapted to film by Delmer Daves as a popular vehicle for Humphrey Bogart and Lauren Bacall under the title *Dark Passage*. But *Dark Passage* was the high point of Goodis's Hollywood career, and his descent was swift and steep. "Goodis' career by this time—and this is truly strange in light of his dramatic gifts, his craftsmanship, and the peremptorily cinematic qualities of his writing—is curiously stillborn," observed crime novelist James Sallis. "He works at various for-hire projects, on an adaptation of Chandler's *The Lady in the Lake*, on an original screenplay which later becomes his last hardcover novel, with Jerry Wald on an epic film concerning the entry of civilization into the atomic age, none of these produced." Among these for-hire projects was *Four Steps to the Wall*, for which Goodis earned one thousand dollars per week.

Goodis had enjoyed a lucrative contract with Warner Brothers which stipulated that he would spend six months of the year writing scripts for the studio and the other six months writing novels, with the understanding that, as with *Dark Road*, these books might be reworked into screenplays for the studio. Goodis had a good deal with Warners but something, perhaps his eccentric nature, caused him to lose his contract. Sometimes his eccentricity came out in more or less innocuous ways, as when, rather than buying a house or leasing a bungalow, he rented a couch from a friend for four dollars a month. He drove a beat-up old Chevrolet, dressed shabbily in worn suits which he dyed rather than replace, and frequented seedy bars, often looking for women to abuse him. Part of Goodis's problem probably stemmed from an unhappy marriage. In 1942 or 1943, Goodis was living in New York, where he married a demanding redhead named Elaine. According to Sallis, Goodis felt a powerful sexual attraction to Elaine, and she used that attraction to control and humiliate him. Elaine was busty, and Goodis was completely taken by her large breasts. On at least one occasion, Elaine awakened her husband in the middle of the night and asked if he wanted to see her breasts. When Goodis told her yes, she sent him out for ice cream with the promise of showing herself to him when he returned. When he finally made it home with the ice cream, instead of finding a willing wife, he was met with insults. The marriage lasted only a year or so, though Sallis suggests that there may never have been a legal divorce.

Sallis notes that several of Goodis's novels share a common structure and a similar protagonist, a noble loser who once had everything. In *Down There*, for example, the 1956 novel which François Truffaut filmed as *Shoot the Piano Player*, Goodis writes of a former concert pianist who has become a lowlife musician in a cheap bar. *Street of No Return* (1954) is the story of a once-popular singer reduced to Skid Row destitution. Goodis put this formula to work on *Four Steps to the Wall*, but the script proved unsatisfactory to both Monte Proser and Jon. Jon was unhappy that Goodis kept nothing of his novel but the title, the names of the major characters, and the prison setting. The general disappointment with Goodis's script brought Jon back into the project as a writer.

By October 1949, Jon was faced with the difficult task of trying to fix Goodis's script, even as Goodis was still turning out pages. Jon worried that the best he could hope to do was bring more authenticity to the prisoners' dialogue and perhaps make some scenes more exciting. Since Goodis was not following an approved treatment, Jon could not predict the story line. He was convinced Goodis was making a hash of the job and wrote Weintraub: "From the beginning, in the story he's writing, Ditto is a softie and a dope, regardless of how much Goodis thinks he is making him a shrewd, cool character. So there's little I can do about rearranging Ditto's makeup—like all the rest of the characters in Goodis' script, Ditto is a B-picture stereotype. So, if I must stick to Goodis plot line, all I can do is to put a little life into these stereotypes. Like doping an old horse, or giving a dead man a transfusion." Jon saw Goodis's script as "corn from way back," suffering from a coincidence-driven plot in which it was impossible for realistically drawn characters to work. Jon aimed much higher.

Goodis's script appears not to have survived, but Jon gave a succinct, if sneering, synopsis in a letter to George Joel, his editor at Dial:

The screenplay has just been completed by David Goodis, a professional Hollywood hack. Maybe you recall his DARK PASSAGE, *Sat Eve Post* story.

With *Four Steps* he took only names of characters, little else. He did make Ditto an editor, but made him quite a mollycoddle, and an innocent man behind bars. Clara he made a glamorous bitch whose father is behind bars, in this prison, see? So she's digging a tunnel into the prison to get him out. He's digging a tunnel out of the prison and as the story opens they are coming together underground, only eight feet apart, but they hit a big rock. So that night Clara on leaving her tunnel near the prison is accosted by a road cop who says, 'Looka here, Miss, what you all doin in that there woods.' The prison is surrounded by a woods. 'Why officer, sir, I was—I was—' The cop snorts. 'That's no excuse, lady—get in your car and I'll foller you to the station.' So Clara gets in her car and he follows her. But the lady speeds up and the cop chases her. She turns a corner on the highway and there in front of her on the side road is a car. In the car sits John Ditto, an ex-newspaper man who pulled off the highway because he was drunk and couldn't go on. Clara just misses his car, but the dumb cop hits the curve going 100 or so and whams into the back of Ditto's car, jolting Ditto to soberness. The girl stops, Ditto gets out, they look down—the cop is dead. Just then a squad car comes along (on this deserted highway), and does not see the girl run to her car, get in and beat it. They find Ditto and obviously it was he who was being chased. Stopped his car so the cop would run into it. He gets seven to ten years for manslaughter. So that's how he's in prison. From then on all plot—the girl wretched with guilt for not coming forward, the father entreating her to keep quiet—Ditto finding out the father is in prison, etc., has a tunnel, etc.

Jon didn't like Goodis's work, but he had faith in his own novel and in the film that it could become. Once it appeared he might take Goodis's place, Jon made it plain he intended this script to be something special. "So what I definitely would prefer to do (despite the fact that it would be ten times harder work) would be to write a kind of prison *Snake Pit*, with accent on PRISON and not on a boilerhouse and tunnel." Jon was referencing the acclaimed 1948 film *The Snake Pit*, with its screenplay by Millen Brand. This story of a woman's descent into madness and her slow recovery won an Academy Award for sound recording and Oscar nominations for star Olivia De Havilland and director Anatole Litvak, as well as a best picture nomination. Jon was convinced that, properly done, *Four Steps to the Wall* could be Oscar material, too. He believed realism was the key to artistic success: "If only we could get a real prison for location, any old prison, no matter how small, we'd be able to do the job really right."

By November, Goodis was no longer with the project, and Jon had agreed in principle to replace Goodis's work with an original script of his own. The deal called for Jon to receive seventy-five dollars per week, plus "$5000 when shooting starts, $5000 after the picture is distributed, and finally 5% of the producer's share of the profits." The lump sum payments and percentage of the producer's share may have sounded good, but in practice this was a bad deal for Jon. Seventy-five dollars a week was well below the Screenwriters Guild scale, hardly enough for the Webbs to make ends meet. Jon's agent, after the fact, warned that he had settled for too little. At Dial, George Joel wondered how Jon had made a deal without a release from the publisher.

Even so, Jon remained optimistic. One reason was his faith in the material. Another was the faith of popular character actor Dan Duryea, who wanted to play Ditto. Jon agreed that Duryea was the right man for the role, and wrote him that "from the beginning I could see no other guy in Ditto's part but you. This is no crap. With a director who would not corn it up, the part is one in which you could let go with all you've got—and I see it as Academy Award stuff. But only with you bringing Ditto to life far better than I could on paper." Duryea kept busy, appearing in more than twenty films in 1941 through 1948 alone. Among these were a number of *noir* dramas, such as *Scarlet Street* (1945), *Black Angel* (1946), and *Larceny* (1948), that almost certainly convinced Jon that Duryea would make the perfect Ditto. The actor continued in a similar vein as the *Four Steps* saga dragged on. Between 1949 and 1951, Duryea appeared in another half dozen *noir* efforts, most notably *Criss Cross* (1949) and *The Underworld Story* (1950). Duryea knew his way around hard-boiled crime pictures, and his endorsement added cachet to *Four Steps to the Wall.*

Proser, by contrast, had no real Hollywood background and no ties to any major studio. He intended to film *Four Steps to the Wall* as an independent feature and had rented space at General Service Studios, a small contract studio located at 1040 North Las Palmas, to do the shoot. General Service was by no means a major player in the film industry, but it did have a decent history in the business. The studio was built in 1919 and owned, at one time, by James Cagney. Jean Harlow made her first film, 1930's *Hell's Angels*, there under the direction of Howard Hughes. Hughes shot part of the Jane Russell vehicle *The Outlaw* at General Service in 1943. Mae West, Harold Lloyd, Bing Crosby, Shirley Temple, and other notables filmed at General Service over the years. All of these connections suggest glamour and money, but Proser's operation proved short of both, as Jon soon learned.

Jon received his first contract for the *Four Steps* script in December and told Shaw he could probably complete the job in six weeks. Perhaps he could have if the only task before him had been writing the script, but Jon's prediction proved wildly optimistic and negotiations dragged on for weeks, as he and Proser wrangled over money. As poor as Jon's deal was, Proser was in no hurry to commit himself to it. Jon eventually signed the contract, but that did nothing to ease tensions. Jon was getting little writing done, and Proser was often late with his paycheck. Jon became progressively less satisfied. With little money available to cover their basic needs, Louise began visiting the studio regularly to ask for grocery money. Typically, someone there gave her "three or four bucks a day." Louise resented being put in this position and blamed Proser and his associates. She considered them thugs and was convinced they were not treating Jon fairly. One day, she went to Proser's office, where she found him in a business meeting. Proser had his legs on the table, clearly in command of the room. He acknowledged Louise with an impatient "yeah?" Louise told Proser that she needed money for food. He pulled fifteen dollars from his pocket and gave it to her, then made it clear she should leave. Louise, humiliated, felt like a beggar. By May, relations between the two camps had deteriorated to the point where Jon filed a complaint with the Screenwriters Guild. The guild found in Jon's favor and added Proser-Nasser Productions to its list of dubious operations writers should avoid.

As disenchanted as he was with Proser, Jon was desperate for the film to be made. He tried unsuccessfully to make an end run around Proser, attempting to entice Duryea to take over the film and pay him a living wage.

Still, the entire world of filmmaking excited Jon. He wanted to be a screenwriter, but was also fascinated by the potential of cinematography to function as art. He wrote Shaw that he was becoming more comfortable in Hollywood, reading screenplays and getting a feel for the art of screenwriting: "And I'm getting more and more fascinated in thought of the possibilities of what can be done with a camera. Dialog is swell and I feel at home writing it, but so much more can be said with a fresh bit of business displayed on a few feet of film than a thousand words of dialog. Being a photographer, you understand what I mean. Don't scoff at this, but I believe artistic photography eventually is going to merge with great art on canvas, and is going to supplant it. But let's not get into that."

Jon's enthusiasm eventually began to fade. He told Charlie Weintraub that money troubles forced him to accept a ghostwriting job to fix "an impossible novel" for an L.A. publisher which took from mid-February to mid-March. He also wanted better pay for his work. He and Louise had a room at the Crown Hill Hotel, a flophouse "filled with prostitutes, dishwashers, muggers, and the like" located at 1341 W. 3rd Street in Los Angeles. They took the room because Louise, destined now to be childless, had begun surrounding herself with pets. They were traveling with five cats, and only seedy places like the Crown Hill would rent to them. Jon was miserable in the hotel, though Louise liked the Crown Hill's managers, two prostitutes she thought were nice. The women, she believed, were "good people; they'd let you do anything." To make things more cozy, Goodis, too, had taken a room at the Crown Hill while he was working on the screenplay. On one occasion, Jon and Louise found themselves broke and hungry, so Jon asked Goodis if he could borrow a few dollars for food. "That's against my principles," Goodis told him. The Webbs were taken aback. "Imagine," Louise said years later. "Here was a guy getting one thousand dollars a week to do the screenplay of Jon's book. He couldn't afford a few bucks? Come on."

With all the distractions, Jon had trouble concentrating on his work. Charlie Weintraub seems to have been a go-between for Jon and Proser, and Jon hoped Weintraub could help get him a better deal: "I feel that I should get at least the minimum Screen Writers Guild weekly salary—but as I told you and Proser I'm willing to take less to get this done. I should get no less that a hundred a week, however—and be sure of getting that, so that I can move to Hollywood. I'd like to see you keep your composure after only a week in this dump—and I'm no more used to living in these places than you are. For ten years, until I took up novel writing, our minimum weekly income was 200 bucks (on up to 600). Lou's about ready to crack up too." Jon was also convinced that Proser intended not to shoot the movie, but to sell the finished screenplay to a major studio for as much as thirty-five thousand dollars. Among those interested in the script, Jon believed, was Howard Hughes. Later, when he was trying to break his contract with Proser-Nasser, Jon wrote George Joel he had heard his script might fetch as much as fifty thousand dollars. Joel cautioned Jon that such speculation was worthless and urged him to take whatever hard cash he could get and be happy.

The Webbs finally escaped the Crown Hill Hotel with a move to Portal, Arizona, a small town in the southeast region of the state near the Mexican border. They remained there from May through August 1950, while Jon worked on the screenplay. From Portal they bounced briefly to McNeal, Arizona, about eighty miles distant. Jon's effort during this time seems to have been divided between crafting the screenplay and, through his agent at the William Morris Agency, fighting Proser-Nasser for what he considered a fair deal. Along the way he found time to secure permission from a prison somewhere in the eastern United States to film part of *Four Steps*. Proser and his associates kept after Jon to send pages as he wrote them and, finally, the completed script, but Jon did neither. He was convinced that with script in hand, Proser would steal his ideas and leave him with nothing.

In the end, none of it mattered. The movie deal fell apart in October, a few weeks after Jon arranged for his agent to hold a completed copy of the screenplay in his office for Proser to read. If Proser liked the script, he was to accept it and pay Jon five thousand dollars. If he rejected the script, he was to pay Jon four hundred fifty dollars in back salary and void their contract. It seemed like a win-win proposition for Jon, but after repeated, unsuccessful attempts by the William Morris Agency to get Proser into their offices, the movie deal ultimately vanished. Jon chased that dream no further. The Webbs' western odyssey ended in October 1951, in the town of Douglas, Arizona, where, Jon wrote George Joel, "Lou and I and cats have been for several months." They decided to cut their losses and return to New Orleans.

OUTSIDERS IN NEW ORLEANS

AFTER THE HARD TIMES in New York and California, New Orleans offered a slower, more comfortable way of life. Jon and Louise had friends there and were happy to settle into life in the Big Easy. More than any other city, this was home. It was not without problems, however. Like much of America, New Orleans at midcentury was racially segregated, and the intersection between blacks and whites was often uneasy. In the Quarter, the broad expanse of Canal Street had long been considered neutral ground, with people of color living on one side, whites on the other. Bourbon Street was racially mixed, and Louise thought that the blacks seemed fearful of the whites. Regardless of this tension, she said, "I used to walk around any hour of the night. We used to walk around, Jon and I. We'd go into the black clubs and listen to music." One Christmas Eve in the 1950s, Jon told Louise that he wanted to wish their friend, singer Joe Hart, a merry Christmas. Louise remembered, years later, that Hart was a big man, adding, "Oh, could he sing 'Summertime.'" Hart was also an African American and a drinker and that meant that the Webbs had to visit bars in black neighborhoods if they were to find him. Louise dressed in black satin as the two prepared for a night on the town. It was early evening when they began their search, checking bar after bar with no luck. Sometime after dark, they found themselves, weary, on Rampart Street, where they tried again.

"You wait out here, honey," Jon said, going inside the bar. Before long, Louise heard Jon say, "Merry Christmas!" Jon soon returned with Hart, who wanted to say hello to Louise. Moments later, a white police officer came up beside them and thumped Hart's shoulder with his billy club. Jon became angry and confronted the officer.

"What's it to you?" the policeman asked. Jon answered that Hart was his friend. Louise later remembered that "he got mad, the cop. And of course Joe, he's just standing there, scared to death. And me, I don't know what the hell is going on. Jon had his own ideas."

"He didn't do anything to us," Jon said. "We came to wish him a merry

Christmas." The situation quickly deteriorated, and the officer called for a paddy wagon and ordered Hart inside. When Jon protested, he, too, was arrested. Louise, now alone and frightened, asked, "Can I go, too?"

"Yeah, you get in, too," the officer told her. The three were taken to the police station and booked. As part of the routine, each had to surrender his or her belongings. Louise didn't like giving the officers her money, and liked even less giving up her cigarettes. She was placed in an upstairs cell with an African American woman and was glad for the company. But the officer who put Louise in her cell didn't let the other woman stay. "He said to her, 'Hey, so and so—get out!' The n-word." Jon and Joe Hart were jailed on another floor, and Louise was nervous and lonely. Given her gregarious nature, it wasn't long before she struck up a conversation with prisoners in an adjacent cell: "There were two black guys in the cell next to me. We spoke, and I said, 'Oh, I wish I had a cigarette, honey.' And these two black guys said, 'Lady, would you like to have a cigarette? Go on over by the toilet, there's a little hole there. We'll pass a cigarette in through there.' I said, 'Okay!' I didn't sleep; I just sat there. Pretty soon the white cop came by, and he was saying something dirty, referring to me. He opened up his pants." The night was uncomfortable but otherwise uneventful. The next morning, Christmas, Jon, Louise, and Hart were released and Louise's money returned. She gave the clerk money to pass on to the men who had given her cigarettes. Though she had no real hope the money would get to them, it seemed like the right thing to do. They piled into a cab bound for the Webbs' apartment, where they spent the day and Hart stayed for Christmas dinner.

During their early years in New Orleans, Louise tried several jobs, including stints as a clerk typist for the New Orleans Office of Property Traffic, as a seamstress in Marc Antony's drapery shop, and as secretary to Larry Borenstein in his Royal Street stamp shop before she eventually began selling paintings alongside other street artists in Pirate's Alley. By the time of their Christmas Eve arrest, Louise was a Pirate's Alley fixture. She began selling paintings there before she learned how to paint, hawking the work of Charles Campbell, a friend of the Webbs who moved to New Orleans from California. Campbell was a good artist, but he needed someone with a magnetic personality to sell his work to tourists, and Louise fit that description. As Louise sold Campbell's paintings, she watched the other artists and learned their techniques. By 1952 she was painting and selling her own work. She sold the first painting she completed, a street scene of the

French Quarter, to a vacationing psychiatrist. Louise was excited by the sale and told Jon the first chance she got. When he learned what the man did for a living, Jon joked that it was no wonder he bought her work. The joke stung Louise, but she kept at her art. "I got better and better and then finally I quit selling for these other people and went on my own."

During her artist years, Louise acquired the distinctive nickname that became her trademark. A newspaper columnist, noting Louise's dark hair and penchant for colorful clothes, dubbed her "Gypsy Lou." The writer observed that Louise cut a striking figure: "She is perhaps the most startling of all the artists in the Quarter, with her full black cape, her beret or perhaps a gold-flecked bandana, and her metallic threaded slippers." A photograph accompanying the article shows Louise in a long, dark dress and black scarf, wide, leather wristband with large, triangular metal studs on her left wrist, and, though the picture is in black and white, an apparently dark red lipstick. She is surrounded by her watercolor street scenes. The effect is dramatic, and not greatly different from a stereotypical "gypsy" image of 1940s-era motion pictures. In addition to describing her clothing, the article gives what may be the best surviving general description of Louise Webb during those days. Louise spoke "in a low, clear voice which rises almost to a question as she finishes a sentence." She had "very wide, very black eyes."

"Gypsy Lou's Little Studio," as she called her art stand at the corner of Royal and St. Peter, became a neighborhood landmark. She hung a sign advertising "Watercolors with a Charm by Gypsy Lou Webb," and specialized in clown faces and French Quarter street scenes. The clowns sold for three dollars each, or two for five dollars. She encouraged passersby to post notes on a tackboard leaning against the wall. The tackboard bore the inscription "If You're Lost Or Want to Get Lost, Tack What You Wish On This Board." The board was Jon's idea, and some people took the invitation to heart, leaving messages like "Milton, waited three hours at Pat O'Brien's. Not Nice." Others left photographs or newspaper clippings. Louise posted a number of messages herself, the idea being that if she could get people to stop and read, she could make a sale. She also hung a sign: "Gypsy Lou Webb, painted by Every Quarter artist." The striking image she cultivated and her status as one of the few female street painters in Pirate's Alley probably contributed to her popularity as a model for the other painters.

Whether through wishful thinking on Louise's part or because a book deal had been made which eventually vanished, a reporter wrote that Louise's

novel of her childhood, "Black Olives," had been sold to Dial. She was sup-
posedly working on a second book, this one being dictated to her by one of
her cats. Louise playfully described the latter project: "Princess Bambi Loo
Toy Webb—she's a Siamese—is writing it, as told to me. Don't laugh, but
it's good, and it's almost done. It's in diary form—how to feed cats, how to
get along with humans, and Bambi's love affair with one of my other cats,
Prince Myshkin." She named the cat for Dostoevsky's hero in *The Idiot*. "He
sort of looks like an idiot," she said.

Jon and Louise now made their living through their respective arts. They
moved in artistic circles and enjoyed life in New Orleans. These were high
times for the couple: "For one thing, both of us used to drink—Gypsy a
little, me a lot," Jon later wrote. "Every day." Jon estimated they spent around
a thousand dollars a year on alcohol—not to mention buying drinks for
friends and all the little extras that a night on the town entailed. The couple
loved visiting nightspots like Larry Borenstein's famous Preservation Hall,
where they sat on the floor and listened to Dixieland jazz. Borenstein ran
a lively club and was an on-again, off-again friend from the Webbs' early
days in town. He owned an art gallery near Louise's art stand, and, when
she was rousted by police on several occasions for wearing "disruptive clothing," Louise believed Borenstein had put them up to it because she was taking business away from him. There is no question that she dressed the way
she did to attract customers: "I looked like a Coca-Cola truck going down
the street," she later recalled. Even with occasional friction between Borenstein and the Webbs, Louise periodically earned extra money working the
door at Preservation Hall. There was no set entrance fee, but patrons were
urged to make a small donation to support the club and musicians. As a
close friend later observed, "I bet not many got in without making a volun-
tary contribution with Lou at the door." Jon and Louise lived in Preservation
Hall briefly with jazz photographer Pops Whitesell as a neighbor. Eventually, they settled into the "oval room," a small apartment in a building also
on the corner of Royal and St. Peter streets. When their building went up
in 1857, it was the first four-story structure in the city and Quarterites still
knew it as "the skyscraper." George Washington Cable once lived there, as
did William Faulkner.

One of the Webbs' friends was Robert Cass, a painter and little magazine
editor-publisher who ran his *Climax: A Creative Review in the Jazz Spirit*
from the bar A Quarterite Place, at 733 Bourbon Street. On Mardi Gras day

in 1952, Cass and a theater full of spectators were arrested during rehearsal for a risqué "voodoo dance" review based on rituals a friend of Cass's had seen in Haiti. Jon and Louise came to the rehearsal, but got wind of the upcoming raid and left before the police arrived. Decades later, Cass remembered the Webbs as "stalwart people that I hope I helped to nudge a little bit into the publishing field. They took it one better than I did, with making books with original bindings that were really quite a kick." New Orleans was home to other little magazines, notably the quarterly *New Orleans Poetry Review*, which had a solid run from 1955 to 1958. Editors Maxine Cassin and Richard Ashman were puzzled by the lack of local submissions, though poetry arrived from around the United States, England, and New Zealand. Years later, Cassin conjectured that the *New Orleans Poetry Review*'s editorial policies might have adversely affected local submissions. "It's true that we did not represent the avant-garde as did Jon Webb with the *Outsider*," she wrote. Still, new writers like William Stafford, James Wright, Galway Kinnell, Maxine Kumin, and a young Sylvia Plath published there. The New Orleans Poetry Review Press launched in 1956 with Vassar Miller's *Adam's Footprint* and continued to publish books sporadically for decades.

In 1954, a priest alarmed Louise by telling her that her 1939 marriage to Jon was illegitimate, as they had been married outside the church. On July 9 of that year, the couple remarried under the auspices of a priest in a New Orleans church. As the years passed, Jon continued writing and Louise remained a fixture among the artists of Pirate's Alley. Jon made money as a ghostwriter and freelance editor and kept at his short stories. By 1955, he was well into a draft of another novel, this one about a man who surgically removes his own penis. He was contemplating names such as "The Saint and the Rock" and "Naked in the Womb," which Louise preferred. He decided finally on "Go Lieth Down South, Oh, Lover." Though Jon kept busy as a writer, his success was middling. His Hollywood adventure ended badly, and *Four Steps to the Wall*, well received though it was, had not established him as a literary force. Perhaps he came to understand that he would never achieve greatness as a writer. Perhaps he simply needed a new challenge. Whatever the reason, Jon eventually abandoned "Go Lieth Down South, Oh, Lover" and searched for a creative outlet that would allow him to flourish. He still wrote short stories, but needed something more in which to invest his energies. Around the end of the decade, he put into motion a plan to publish a literary magazine.

Jon knew that publishing a magazine was an expensive proposition and planned accordingly. For a year, the Webbs stopped going out for drinks, or even drinking at home, and managed to save a thousand dollars. Such a lifestyle change could have revealed serious flaws in some relationships that were covered by an alcohol haze. Not so for Jon and Louise. On June 15, 1960, Jon wrote Louise a note for their twenty-first anniversary. They had been together for more than two decades and remained devoted. "Doesn't seem a whole 21 years ago and I only wish to God I could have half as much as that more to go with you, you sweetest most beautiful girl in the world, and the most understanding and devoted and honest and clean. I love you love you more than ever and always will love only you darling."

Jon was fifty-five years old, Louise forty-four. It was an unlikely time for Jon to be in the midst of a career change, moving between his life as a writer and the life of a little magazine editor upon which he was about to embark. He was still writing short stories based around prison life and considering putting together a collection to shop to publishers. A letter from Norman Mailer suggests Webb had donned his "author" persona in dealing with Mailer. Mailer's letter was brief but collegial. Beginning "Dear Webb," Mailer continued: "Good to hear from you again. If you've written anything new about prisons, drop me a line about it letting me know where I can find the book." Mailer wrote Webb in care of *Mainstream*, where Webb had published a short story, "One of Them Heroes" in 1959.

Mainstream was also Walter Lowenfels's home base. In some ways, Lowenfels was Webb's literary conscience in the months leading up to the appearance of the *Outsider*. It would have been hard for Jon to team up with a more accomplished, generous advisor. Lowenfels was supportive to a fault and had a firm grasp of the emerging poetry scene. He knew who the good people were and understood that a famous name did not always mean quality work. Through Lowenfels, Jon got the support he needed to pick the right poets and the sage advice to shun inferior work, even from celebrated writers. Relationships such as this had long fueled the little magazine world. In the teens, Ezra Pound advised both Margaret Anderson at the *Little Review* and Harriet Monroe at *Poetry*. Such pairings were not always successful. When Harold Loeb decided to publish *Broom* in 1920, he had to woo Alfred Kreymborg, late of the respected *Others*, to come on board and help with the new magazine. Kreymborg took a position with *Broom* and shared editorial duties with Loeb. This partnership ended badly, with Kreymborg finally resigning after continued disagreements with Loeb over *Broom*'s focus. In situations more contemporaneous with the Webb-Lowenfels relationship, Douglas Blazek sought and received advice from Ron Offen of the *Chicago Literary Times* as he prepared to publish *Ole*, and Bob Fey, editor-publisher of *eikon*, helped mentor Diane Kruchkow before she launched *Zahir*.

Lowenfels's career spanned the decades between the golden age of the twenties and thirties and the publishing explosion which began in the late 1950s, an era some were calling a "mimeograph revolution," a reference to the inexpensive printing technologies many editors used to produce their magazines. He was an award-winning poet and anthologist, highly regarded among his peers. As a young expatriate in Paris, he was a frequent contributor to Eugene Jolas's *transition*, the first venue for James Joyce's *Work in Progress*, later known as *Finnegan's Wake*. In 1930, Lowenfels shared, with E. E. Cummings, the Richard Aldington Award for American Poets. In 1954 he won the Mainstream Award and, in 1959, the Longview Foundation Award. He was a member of the "revolution of the word" movement, with poets like Charles Henri Ford and Louis Zukofsky, and part of the Parisian literary scene inhabited by Henry Miller and Anaïs Nin. In 1930, with partner Michael Fraenkel, Lowenfels founded a curious enterprise known as the Carrefour Press to publish works of art anonymously. Their manifesto, *Anonymous: The Need for Anonymity*, argued that anonymity was the only way to bring harmony to the arts. Their plans were dashed after Carrefour published Lowenfels's play, *USA with Music*. A contentious lawsuit arose after Carrefour accused Irving Berlin of plagiarizing the work. The suit forced Carrefour to identify Lowenfels as the playwright. Carrefour continued to publish for a few years, though the anonymous movement was finished. Lowenfels returned to America with his wife, Lillian, and their three daughters in 1934. He had enough faith in the unpublished Miller that same year to advance him one hundred dollars toward the publication of his first book in the United States. As Lowenfels had no hand in publishing Miller, the advance was actually a loan, one which Miller and New Directions, his American publisher, eventually repaid. In his 1936 novel, *Black Spring*, Miller caricatured Lowenfels as the daft, drunken poet Jaberwohl Cronstadt.

Back in America, Lowenfels worked for a time in his family's lucrative butter supply business before leaving to become a writer for the Pennsylvania edition of the *Daily Worker*, eventually becoming editor. Lowenfels was a Communist, and the *Daily Worker* gave him a chance to be politically active and reasonably creative at the same time. Being a Communist in mid-twentieth-century America was dangerous, and eventually Lowenfels's politics led to his arrest on charges of violating the Smith Act, advocating the violent overthrow of the United States government. He described the ordeal in a *Mainstream* article appropriately entitled "On Trial." Though the trial dragged on for four and a half months—and the time between Lowenfels's July 3, 1953, arrest and his eventual exoneration was four years—Lowenfels only spent about a month in jail. He busied himself during his jail time writing poetry and translating sonnets by Baudelaire, Dante, and Guillevic into English, and made the observation that the prison population was made up of "insiders, outsiders. Guilt or innocence, assault or robbery, frame-ups or caught in the act—we all have one goal: to get out." This was a return to poetry for Lowenfels, who hadn't attempted the form since before becoming politically active almost two decades earlier. The result was his 1954 collection, *Poems for Amnesty*. Several years later, Lowenfels wryly suggested the claim to fame his incarceration had afforded him. Of the estimated hundreds of thousands of poets then working in the United States, "I am the only one with a court record and conviction to prove I am really dangerous. What an indictment of our craft."

Lowenfels had strong feelings about the nature of art in general and poetry in particular. He welcomed a progressive political stance in writers and artists, but not didactic writing aimed at the working class. Lowenfels believed that "we're writing for everybody who will read. The thing is to have the confidence that the working class will lead and, eventually, read us." He refused to engage in nostalgia for art of the past, preferring instead to look to new writers and to the future. Lowenfels believed that the poets of the 1950s and early 1960s had embraced a "voice of alienation" which was unavailable to earlier poets. He was also concerned with the potential audience for poetry, and believed that successful poets would do well to share his concern. "It's the new audience the writer must identify with—in the U.S. this audience is still in the process of being born."

Lowenfels understood that literary magazines played an important role in what he described as "a period of the greatest upsurge of poets and creativity in general—but particularly of poets—that there has been in this country since the poetry renaissance of 1915–1925." He took the burgeoning popularity of these magazines as a hopeful sign for progressive culture, making the remarkable observation that "[t]here are more poetry magazines being published here today than at any time in our history: there are at least 200, ranging in circulation from 300 to 3,000. I consider this part of the new Resistance, the new underground movement. It doesn't have the audience of millions that TV gets, but it's a very significant development." Jon did not share Lowenfels's political passions, but his support for good writing and little magazines was as strong as his friend's. The two men made a dynamic pair in launching the magazine Jon had decided to call the *Outsider*.

As Lowenfels observed, this was a boom time for little magazines in general and also for the literary underground, whose roots stretched back almost twenty years. Steven Clay and Rodney Phillips, in *A Secret Location on the Lower East Side: Adventures in Writing 1960–1980*, trace the origin of underground literary magazines to 1943, when William Everson published *The Untide*, a mimeographed newsletter of the conscientious objectors' camp at Waldport, Oregon. Everson also produced mimeographed books, such as his own *X War Elegies*, for Untide Press. By the time Untide Press closed shop, Everson had moved to letterpress printing. He printed his first letterpress book in 1945, Kenneth Patchen's *An Astonished Eye Looks out of the Air*. Everson later contributed to another important underground magazine, San Francisco's *The Ark*, which lasted only one issue, but contained the work of important new writers such as Kenneth Rexroth and Richard Eberhardt. A handful of interesting books and magazines appeared throughout the 1950s, among them *Suck Egg Mule* (1951), *Semina* (1955), and *Yugen* (1958). Nineteen sixty saw the debut of *Wormwood Review*, *Trobar*, and *Kulchur*.

Jon Webb was among the select literati who somehow learned of the new directions in literary publishing, and he wanted to be part of it. On July 13, 1960, before Jon even had a press to print his pages, he described to Lowenfels the kind of magazine he hoped to publish. It would be six by nine inches in format and contain at least thirty-two pages, perhaps forty-eight, done on good paper with a good cover. He also had an ambitious production schedule in mind, planning to publish the first issue by the end of the year. While it would be made up of "more poetry than prose," Jon hoped to include critical reviews of current poetry collections and thought Lowenfels was the right person for the job. Even better, Jon hoped to include a column from Lowenfels in each issue. He had no money to pay Lowenfels, or anyone else, for that matter, but Jon intended to publish a quality product: "I promise a magazine that won't be amateurish, and of course not slick either. I want to publish the emerging younger poets and prose writers, from here and abroad, and will accept name writers if they send something I like and is not a practice piece, nor for the wastebasket." In this attitude, Jon stood with many fine magazines of the past. Loeb and Kreymborg fashioned *Broom*, for example, as "a sort of clearing house where the artists of the present time will be brought into closer contact." Eclecticism was the guiding principle, with quality writing being the deciding factor on who published there. "Throughout, the unknown, path-breaking artist will have, when his material merits it, at least an equal chance with the artist of acknowledged reputation."

Jon valued Lowenfels's grasp of contemporary literature more than his own and asked his friend, in confidence, to name the "younger new poets" who were likely to become important. Webb designed a prospectus to send potential contributors, and Lowenfels made sure the right people were on his mailing list. Jon knew only a few poets in New Orleans, and most of these he didn't admire. He called them "passing-through 'beatnik' types" and questioned whether they were really poets at all, dismissing them as "scenery poets" who read their work in coffee shops, trying to shock listeners or "mangle even experimentation." Still, there was "some genuine interest in poetry among the shockers, which I appreciate whenever I find it." During a visit to a local poetry reading, Jon allowed a friend to read aloud a recent letter from Lowenfels on the subject of writing poetry: "[T]here was a genuine reaction, with exclamations to some of your lines, like: '. . . all you have to do is get burned alive and the poems float right off your teeth' . . . 'one has to learn about iambics in order to learn how not to write them' . . . 'I know what I have been after lately, a sort of skipped prose beat that slides you into the glass mirror we are always trying to slice' . . . 'you must destroy me, too' . . . 'not only what to read, but how to un-read.'" Jon prodded his friend to elaborate on the "you must destroy me, too," observation for the *Outsider*. Lowenfels was pleased with the attention: "The way you and your friends respond to my stuff is as close to the Nobel Prize as I'll get. So I accept." Hearkening back to his Paris days of the early 1930s, Lowenfels wrote that he, Michael Fraenkel, and Miller had mused that they had created their "own particular death school" of writing. They were writing, the three agreed, "for an audience that doesn't exist," because "the world is dead and the only way to be alive is to say it." Lowenfels said that Miller "cheated a little," though. "His books say 'everybody is dead but me.'"

Lowenfels agreed to help Jon with the magazine, though not with reviews. Had Jon been in New York, Lowenfels wrote, a sympathetic friend with a linotype machine might have been able to solve some of his printing problems. That not being the case, Lowenfels turned to the other half of Jon's dilemma, identifying promising new poets. His first recommendation was Leslie Woolf Hedley, a former American soldier who now wrote poetry and ran his own small publishing house in San Francisco, the Inferno Press. Jon liked Hedley's work, and his poem "Naked in My Century" appeared in the *Outsider* number one. Likewise, Jon later accepted work from Harland Ristau, second on Lowenfels's list. Lowenfels suggested that, for a prose submission, Jon might contact "the best beat writer of them all," Hugh Selby, Jr., of whom Lowenfels had written in his poem "Welcome Home to Cubby," which appeared in the February 1960 issue of *Mainstream*. While it is unclear if Webb contacted Selby, his work did not appear in any issue of the magazine. The same was not true for Selby's friend from Brooklyn, Gilbert Sorrentino, whose surrealist poem "ave atque vale" appeared in the *Outsider* one. Jon may have later regretted missing the chance to publish Selby, who achieved fame in 1964 with the publication of his novel *Last Exit to Brooklyn*.

The majority of the Webb-Lowenfels correspondence for the next year focused mainly upon editorial decisions and other nuts-and-bolts matters of publishing a literary magazine. By early August, Lowenfels was offering counsel on submissions from Lawrence Ferlinghetti and Allen Ginsberg. He did not want Jon saddled with second-rate poetry from famous writers and again warned Jon to demand the best. "Be choosy with everyone, including me," he cautioned. "Names do not make a mag—but content." Lowenfels was generous with his advice and praise, at one point writing, "Between us, you are probably the best editor since Homer (like Twain said—it was really somebody else who wrote the stuff and Homer just used his name)." A week later, Lowenfels asked Jon to write an article with the title "How to Start an Outsider," promising that he would try to get it printed. Lowenfels marveled at how Jon started his magazine from nothing and convinced people around the country to help him: "Is it because you tickle our vanity? Your title? Be a Horatio Alger and write the story of your success. And do it now! (I don't believe in waiting to analyze the election after the returns are in." Jon did not write the article, but he did acknowledge his debt to Lowenfels in the first issue of the *Outsider*, listing him on the masthead as "Consultant."

There was more. In Jon's mind, the issue's greatest asset would be a series of early letters he hoped to publish between Lowenfels and Henry Miller. The only stipulation Miller put on publishing the letters was that he see them first, "primarily to avoid hurting anyone still alive who might object to being mentioned." Miller was not sure Lowenfels's letters to him still existed. He suggested contacting the special collections library at the University of California at Los Angeles to ask about their holdings of such letters prior to 1940. Jon, in turn, asked Lowenfels to check with the university about the letters, suggesting that UCLA would be more forthcoming if Lowenfels made the request. He told Lowenfels that "this letter stuff would be a good splash." Lowenfels agreed Jon had "hit the jackpot," suggesting that the correspondence alone should sell enough copies of the *Outsider* to put Loujon Press in the black. He suggested publishing the letters as a book, possibly in conjunction with Jonathan Williams of Jargon Press: "Collectors, libraries, as well as Miller fans will have to get the stuff," he wrote. Jon also wanted Miller to contribute a piece of original writing, but Miller refused: "Everything I've written to date is placed and no time to do a new piece," he wrote.

As it turned out, the Miller and Lowenfels correspondence was of mixed literary value. The letters were sparse—twenty in all—and presented out of chronological sequence with little apparent thought behind their order. But they hinted at Miller's artistic development and provided his thoughts on such divergent topics as D. H. Lawrence and Duke Ellington. There were nuggets of real value, but, as the Webbs' longtime friend and patron Edwin Blair observes, "unfortunately, without guidance, only the most ardent Miller fan can fully appreciate what was transpiring." Even so, fortuitous timing helped add luster to the Miller material. *Tropic of Cancer* was released in the United States around the time the *Outsider* made its debut. The book caused a furor, with communities across the country calling for it to be banned and civil libertarians fighting against this censorship. The controversy almost certainly sold a few extra copies of the magazine.

CREATING A LITERARY NETWORK

APRIL 29, 1961, WAS LOUISE's forty-fifth birthday. Jon designed and printed a card, declaring his love for "the only human I've ever felt really comfortable with, and couldn't stop loving to save my life." His one complaint was that their time together passed too quickly. "But how much worse it would be without you . . . so I dare not complain, sweetest honey darling wife." Harmony was key, and not just for domestic bliss. The two had an enormous task awaiting them, and a less secure partnership would have cracked under the strain. Jon was eleven years older than Louise, and their ages may have worked in their favor. One did not, after all, have to be young to begin a literary magazine. Harriet Monroe was fifty-one when she founded *Poetry*. The Webbs were old enough to understand the value of patience. Each of them had long since learned that hard work was the basic element for survival. Success was never assured.

Before the *Outsider* could become a reality, Jon had to make his project known to potential contributors. One way he chose to do this was via an ad in the *Village Voice*, which had itself been in business only since 1955. The *Village Voice* styled itself "the newspaper of the trendmakers," and Jon seems to have had faith that this motto was well founded. In an August 4, 1960, response to Jon's initial rate inquiry, *Voice* advertising manager and photography editor Fred W. McDarrah, already known for his book of photographs, *The Beat Scene*, quoted ad rates of "4.90 per column inch cash in advance." McDarrah was taken by Webb's inquiry, remarking, "Your post card is a gas—thanks." He made a pitch for his own photographic contribution to the magazine. "If you use a photo for your cover or any photos inside I will be glad to supply—just about anything you need particularly New York scene."

Contact between Jon and McDarrah quickly intensified, as less than a week later, Webb received another letter from the *Voice*, again commenting on Jon's visually striking correspondence. McDarrah was concerned that the *Outsider*'s advertisement be as cost effective and useful as possible: "Jon

Edgar man, the next time you send one of those very hip post cards will you kindly put it in an envelope so it doesn't get chewed all to hell? Anyway, I have reservations about the ad you sent and herewith enclose a different version which may be more sedate but baby it's your bread and why waste it, unless of course you are planning a cooky magazine which it doesn't sound." In addition to redesigning the ad, apparently to make it less cluttered, McDarrah also offered Webb the *Voice*'s weekly contract rate, even though he suggested the ad run only once per month. The final third of this letter was devoted, again, to a pitch by McDarrah to have Webb consider using his photographs in the *Outsider*. No such deal was made, as McDarrah's photographs did not appear in any issue of the *Outsider*.

The *Village Voice* strategy worked well. About a month after the second McDarrah letter, Jon received a letter from Jack Fine, a jazz trumpeter with gigs around New York who worked as a *Village Voice* factotum. The business reason for the letter was to quote further ad rates, but Fine went out of his way to tell Webb his ad was generating excitement and to marvel that Jon planned to charge only a dollar per copy for his magazine. While Jon's general ideas for the content of his magazine were in place by mid-July 1960, he was still unsure about how to print it. He was hoping to purchase "a good second-hand 12 x 18 press" and was debating whether or not to set all of the type by hand. "If I can get printers' rates," he wrote Lowenfels, "may have all the prose matter linotyped and set only the poems and heads myself." This would mean an extra four or five hours of work for him each day, on top of his own writing schedule. He had begun writing poetry, but had no luck placing it in other magazines.

Jon's plans for the *Outsider*'s format changed by early October. He was recruiting well-placed individuals within the literary underground to serve as advisory editors, and he kept them informed of his plans. One of these people, Jory Sherman, noted Jon's plans to change his magazine's format and observed that, from the looks of things, the first issue was going to be hefty. "From the size of it," Sherman wrote, "this is going to be the size of *Botteghe Oscure* or the N.Y. telephone directory." *Botteghe Oscure*, a thick, biannual international literary anthology edited by Marguerite Caetani, an American-born Italian princess, was in publication from 1948 through 1960. Many important writers, such as T. S. Eliot, W. H. Auden, Conrad Aiken, and Robert Lowell, published there. The comparison, even if glancing, was a nice compliment.

Printing, however, not heft, was foremost on Jon's mind. He solved the printing problem when he managed to convince officials at Tulane University to give him an old Chandler and Price letterpress. Soon after, he hired a local typesetter named Wally Shore to set type at two dollars per page. Louise spent her days selling paintings, and often, when she got home, Shore would still be there setting type. According to Louise, "He was drinking a lot, this guy. He drank while he worked and he made a lot of mistakes." Louise didn't like paying two dollars a page for typesetting and she hated the mistakes, so she watched how Shore set type for a couple of nights and learned how he did it. She assured Jon that she could set the type and, after she set a page with no errors, Jon told her, "Hey, you're better than Wally." "Okay," Louise said, "let's fire him." They did, and Louise added several hours of typesetting each night to her already long days at the art stand.

Somewhere in all of this, Lawrence Ferlinghetti, making his way back to San Francisco after a trip to Cuba, paid the Webbs a visit. Cuba was a rallying cry for many young bohemians in 1960, and Ferlinghetti was among a wave of Americans who went to see what Castro's revolution was about. Before coming to the Webbs' Royal Street apartment, Ferlinghetti gave a poetry reading to a sizable crowd at the Preservation Hall. Louise and Shore went to listen, but Louise left before the performance ended. Afterward, Larry Borenstein passed the hat, but gave Ferlinghetti only five dollars for his cut. Ferlinghetti, nearly penniless and trying to raise money to get home, refused the cash. "Go get a gallon of wine with the five," Ferlinghetti told Borenstein. It wasn't enough money to matter. After the reading, the party moved to the Webbs' Royal Street apartment, Ferlinghetti in tow, where it lasted well into the night.

Playing host to a famous Beat poet was probably fun, but Jon knew that success required that he remain focused on his job. He printed the first page of his "Prospectus" for the initial issue of the *Outsider* on October 8, 1960, and kept the first copy off the press as a souvenir. In the upper left corner, beneath the date, he wrote, "To Honey Lou—This is the first approved copy of page one of the prospectus off the little pilot C & P press—on the magazine Lou & I are going to make famous in 1961—Love Jon." The press may have been little, as letterpresses go, but it was still heavy and awkward. Jon was a small man, and operating the press required effort. "It was a bitch," remembered his son, who helped print the first *Outsider*. "You'd ink it, pull it back, put a paper in, and pull it again. It was four pulls, I think, for one sheet. And this went on day and night." Running the press would have been a chore for most anyone, but Jon had the added problem of bursitis in his shoulder. He worked through the pain, frightening Louise, who thought that this would only aggravate the condition. After thousands of impressions, his discomfort actually vanished. "I would have thought it would have made it worse," she said. "I guess it just built him up." Gathering the pages and gluing them into covers followed the demanding presswork. Once they found their rhythm, this process took about seven minutes per copy, or over three hundred more hours of tedious, stand-up labor before the issue was done.

Through his prospectus, Jon marketed the *Outsider* as a "vigorous new, no-taboo Quarterly going to press now in oldest New Orleans with the newest in new poetry and prose, from writers in seven countries," a marriage of avant-garde literature and fine printing. The prospectus listed such contributors as Corso, Ginsberg, and Burroughs, while making a direct pitch to collectors of high-quality literary artifacts. He stressed that the *Outsider* would have a limited press run of three thousand issues, sold globally. This was a large run for any small press literary startup, the exact high end of what Lowenfels had calculated as the biggest circulation of any American little magazine, and enormous for a two-person, fine-printing operation. But Jon had faith. He urged collectors to preorder copies, as the issue was certain to sell out.

Jon told his readers that the *Outsider* favored fresh and experimental writing over established literary tradition. He admitted the magazine would print more poetry than prose, but promised that "an ever hopeful eye is being kept open for the new in all creative prose submitted. Prose, we believe, will never die—but ways of using it will." Jon was "bored to nausea by the prose of today, particularly the academic forms." But "new forms, new approaches, new creative uses by individual styles, new writing of any kind— all shall alertly and gratefully be appraised by OUTSIDER editors." He believed that what passed for avant garde within academic literary circles read as though it were "being written by English majors seemingly cut off from their privates," and was lacking in "fresh pitch" and vitality.

Not all in the academy were as stodgy as Jon suggested. One person who immediately grasped the *Outsider*'s potential was John William Corrington, a twenty-eight-year-old English instructor at Louisiana State University. Corrington was a poet who, as a young man, aspired to greatness as a trumpet player. He had been expelled from a Jesuit prep school in 1948 for smoking and having a bad attitude and, though the teenage Corrigan drank some and occasionally gambled, the reputation for wildness that hung about him was mostly self-grown myth. He was ever a nonconformist, an energetic mixture of piercing intellect, deviltry, and southern charm who was fond of referring to himself as "a redneck from Shreveport." With his thick, black hair and intense eyes, he bore a passing resemblance to a young Jack Kerouac. As he recalled years later in a tribute to Kenneth Patchen, Corrington found his first poetic touchstone as a freshman at Centenary College in Patchen's *Cloth of the Tempest* and had since remained in tune with nonacademic verse. He embraced the new literary climate and was a regular contributor to various little magazines. Corrington had a strong sense of self, and much of who he was came from being raised in the South. He understood himself as a southern writer and had little use for other southerners who resisted that label. As he once put it: "If nobody else wants to be, that's fine; then we would have only one: me."

Corrington thought Jon's prospectus was fantastic, and believed the *Outsider* might boost the Crescent City's literary community. In an undated letter, written sometime before the magazine debuted, Corrington wrote: "New Orleans is coming to life again. If you can keep it going we'll have another San Francisco right here." The allusion to San Francisco was high praise, a suggestion that Webb was on the cusp of creating a New Orleans renaissance, similar to what Kenneth Rexroth and the Beats had done in California. The comparison was particularly apt, as the San Francisco renaissance was also tied to a literary magazine. The *Evergreen Review*'s second issue appeared in 1957 with the banner "The San Francisco Scene." The issue contained work by Josephine Miles, Rexroth, Brother Antoninus, Ferlinghetti, Kerouac, Ginsberg, Miller, and others who were making noise. *Evergreen Review* editor David Allen later chose a number of these poets for his influential *New American Poetry* anthology.

Not everyone who learned of Jon's plans for his magazine was as supportive. Jon told Lowenfels that Denise Levertov refused an invitation to submit work because she disliked Colin Wilson, a contributor to the first issue. Wilson was author of the best-selling nonfiction work *The Outsider*, which was making a stir in the world of literary criticism. Levertov assumed the magazine's title signaled an allegiance to Wilson's ideas. But plenty of other writers were delighted to publish in the *Outsider*, and its pages bulged with their work. Though not, as per Sherman's prediction, the size of the

New York telephone directory, the first *Outsider* was substantial. Issue one, printed and bound in the Webbs' tiny apartment at 638 Royal Street, appeared in the fall of 1961. The cover sported a striking, close-up photograph of Louise, chin on fist, staring into the camera. As in each of the following numbers, Jon was listed as editor and Louise as associate editor. For this issue, Lowenfels was a "consultant," and there were a number of advisory editors, including Marvin Bell, Margaret Randall, and Jory Sherman for the United States; Edwin Morgan for Scotland; Melville Hardiment for England; and Sinclair Beiles for "France, Etc." Most of these individuals also appeared in the magazine as contributors. Subscriptions cost five dollars for six issues within the United States and six dollars elsewhere. Nationally prominent magazine distributor B. DeBoer of Bloomfield, New Jersey, handled newsstand sales.

Newsstand sales were only one part of Jon's distribution plans. What with the middleman fees and the possibility of the distributor not paying at all, he realized it was unwise to build a business around a distributor. Jon made individual subscriptions a bargain and marketed nationally to libraries. At least twenty-six university libraries subscribed right away at a cost of five dollars for a one-and-one-half-year subscription. Purchase orders arrived from a diverse mix of universities, ranging from Ivy League institutions to state universities and small, liberal arts colleges. As important as subscription sales were to his success, Jon initially turned down at least one such sale, a three-year gift subscription for a nun. He shot back a letter reminding the person wishing to give the subscription that the *Outsider* was a "no taboo quarterly" of contemporary literature and that "today's literary efforts pull no punches in word usage, for there is no obscenity in four-letter words when used without obscenity in mind—besides, there is a trend to take the dirtiness out of four letter words in the literary quarterlies that are not academic by using them as casually as one would any other word in a piece of valid writing. At any rate, we do not believe a convent sister would quite understand our stand in this direction, nor be able to appreciate the nuances embracing honesty in writing in our magazine."

As things turned out, the nun in question held a Ph.D. in English and chaired the English department at Mount Mercy College in Cedar Rapids, Iowa. It is probable that, learning all of this, Jon finally honored the subscription request. If so, the first issue she received set a high standard. It was perfect bound and encased in lightweight, beautifully designed card covers.

The issue's weakest element was the paper it was printed on. Jon and Wally Shore scavenged a good deal of the paper and much of what they found was of poor quality. Otherwise, the magazine was substantial. It ran a hefty 101 pages and was a solid mix of poetry, fiction, and nonfiction prose from both well-known and emerging writers. On page two, Webb ran a detailed illustration of a ragged man emerging from a tunnel into a prisoner's darkened cell. A caption set in large, bold type read: "Bravo, another escaping Outsider . . . enter, man, and be calmed!" This was Jon's refuge for readers and writers disaffected by mainstream literature.

It was a place for people like Charles Bukowski. The L.A. poet was a heavy drinker, a horseplayer, and a loner whose tough, honest—sometimes funny, sometimes brutal—poems were often snapshots from his life. Here was the realism Jon had always coveted, unflinching glimpses of society's fringes. He had plenty of raw material to draw from: years of living in cheap rooming houses, horrible relationships with women, uncounted drunken escapades, and more. He used these in his art, always with an eye toward building the mythic Bukowski persona.

Things were beginning to happen for Bukowski. After publishing short fiction in *Story* and Caresse Crosby's international journal *Portfolio*, Bukowski remained relatively silent for about a decade, when he switched to poetry. By 1960, he had made a name for himself in the literary underground as a regular contributor to many little magazines with names like *Matrix, The Willie, Blow,* and *The Anagonic & Paideumic Review*. His first standalone publication, a broadside of his poem "His Wife the Painter," was published by E. V. Griffith in early August 1960, to be distributed as an insert in the first issue of Griffith's magazine, *Coffin*. Griffith was also working on a Bukowski chapbook, *Flower, Fist and Bestial Wail*, that the poet anxiously awaited as the summer dragged on. These publications were major events for Bukowski, more important, it seemed, than a friendly contact from an unknown New Orleans editor. Still, it was nice to be courted. On August 17, 1960, the day after his fortieth birthday, Bukowski wrote his friend Jory Sherman to tell him "thanks for word on *Outsider*. Finally got card from them through *Coastlines*. Asking me for contributions. Ah, well."

It wasn't long before Bukowski came to suspect his good fortune. He was impressed with Jon's aggressive marketing in the *Village Voice*, and delighted to see his name listed in these ads with famous poets. In November, he wrote Jon that "I believe right now you are the most famous lit mag in America, although you have yet to issue." Jon was happy with Bukowski, too. He admired Bukowski's writing and even this early seems to have been considering publishing a chapbook of his work. Before Bukowski wrote Sherman to tell him of contact from the *Outsider*, Sherman had already written Jon to say, "Chapbook for Buk sounds good. Hearse been sitting on one of his for long time, and he's getting pretty shook waiting for Griffith to get on the ball. They're all late this summer, though . . . editors slow in reporting, gone on vacation . . . out cold, or something. It is slow slow slow." The chapbook as such didn't pan out, though Jon did print ten copies of a brief, eleven-poem "Charles Bukowski Album" as a stand-alone publication prior to running the album as a Bukowski showcase in the *Outsider*.

Bukowski was in good company. The contributors' list for issue one was a veritable who's who of 1960s outré literary talent, with some unknowns and a few old heavyweights such as Millen Brand, Curtis Zahn, Walter Lowenfels, and Langston Hughes. Rising stars Charles Olson and Robert Creeley represented the Black Mountain poets. Cid Corman, editor of the respected *Origins*, provided a poem. Colin Wilson's contribution was an essay. Going against the grain of the magazine's otherwise bohemian sensibility, Wilson's piece dismissed Beat Generation writers as childish revolutionaries. As if to demonstrate the catholic nature of the *Outsider*'s selection policies, issue one also featured Gregory Corso, Diane di Prima, Allen Ginsberg, William S. Burroughs, and Gary Snyder. Wilson's presence was controversial, and, like Levertov, Jack Kerouac took offense. Though he published a poem in the second issue, Kerouac wrote Webb to dismiss Wilson and the "anti-christ poets" he did not like in issue one.

Corrington wrote Bukowski that the magazine was "full of wild jazz, and if somebody doesn't find something to like, it's cause he's dead. And there you were with the biggest spread of all! I already had all the poems in the little album Jon had sent a couple of months ago, but they still read new." Lowenfels had two poems in the issue, "Welcome Home to Cubby," reprinted from *Mainstream*, and "Good-bye Jargon," subtitled "Elegy for a Small Press." All the more ironic because of Lowenfels's help with launching the *Outsider*, this poem took a bleak view of poetry in the age of the atomic bomb. Lowenfels imagined hundreds of thousands of poets, many of them lauded beyond reason, and almost no one reading their poems. "You can realize what a vacuum our non-readers are creating," he lamented. Instead, "In the great silence even Tiberius no longer asks 'what song / the sirens sang' because what the Emperor of Today hears / is the mushroom screaming. / And that's the song." Jory Sherman contributed an angry poem to an ex-lover, "Dear Liz," and Corrington offered up "Hard Man," a brief meditation on a ragged womanizer "who loved so bad so many / (once upon a time) till / a deft gash cut him down."

Corrington liked his work appearing with Bukowski and suggested Bukowski send poems to "a blah little mag out of Madison Wisconsin" edited by a longtime friend of Corrington's, Marcus Smith. "The only reason it's blah is because he hasn't gotten any swingers yet," Corrington said, adding, "You don't need to mention me, dad: he knows you." It wasn't unusual for Corrington or Bukowski to make such suggestions or to praise one another's work, and though Bukowski sometimes dismissed Corrington in letters to other people—an unfortunate habit that he often fell into when writing about any given person to a third party—there was a genuine respect between the two men. Corrington felt like a shareholder in Bukowski's poetry "because, without trying, and for no reason except respect, I can recite some of your dolls (which I can do with none of mine). This is why carbons and why respect for the work. Writing is for the man writing first—but it's for the man reading, too."

Corrington often mulled over the nature of writing, considering, by his lights, both the good and the bad. His ideas were not generally in tune with the prevailing wisdom of his university colleagues, perhaps a reason he was so passionate about them. He and Bukowski had different styles, but Corrington was convinced that Bukowski was a true poet, and important. He believed that Bukowski's power came from his poetry's imperfection and once explored this idea by contrasting Bukowski to John Ciardi, poetry editor for the *Saturday Review*. Ciardi was a formalist who nonetheless worked to make his well-polished verse accessible to the common reader. His *How Does a Poem Mean?* (1959) was already becoming a standard text in many high school and college poetry courses. One August night in 1961, Corrington wrote Bukowski that "I got to thinking about you because I had been thinking about Ciardi and wondering why I hate his guts enough to cut off his thing."

After some reflection, Corrington realized the answer was that Bukowski made mistakes: "You make all kinds of mistakes when you write: not grammar or that jazz . . . I mean sometimes you pity yourself, sometimes you get maudlin, sometimes you fall on your prat. Ciardi never makes mistakes. He writes poems like a hathaway shirt ad is conceived. It may not sell everybody, but it don't alienate a soul." Corrington saw Bukowski's true self shine through in his poems. Their lack of polish was their greatest asset. Corrington could not bring himself to trust a poet like Ciardi whose work was rubbed clean of all humanity: "Men make mistakes: they marry ugly women and beat up strangers for laughing at the cruddy bitches. They go nuts for God and sometimes slice off their peckers. They booze and bleed and their lumpy hearts pump off rhythm, and they die for forty cents or for the flag. Of they rot like a hog in the sun, or they sleep for eleven years and wake up sane, or they scurry to a racetrack and bet the nags and then go home boozed like a cracked floodlight and make big songs." Corrington cautioned that "Ciardi could kill you at poker. Not in one hand, not in ten—but sweetie he bets with the house, and you know, you absolutely know the house can't lose on the average unless somebody feeds 'em a queer deck."

If Bukowski was an antidote to the tidy writing of the Ciardis of the world, he was not alone in the *Outsider*. Along with the poems and stories, there was an excerpt from William S. Burroughs's then-unpublished experimental novel, *The Soft Machine*, now considered a classic of its kind. Jon asked Burroughs to contribute to issue one, and Burroughs responded with a packet of material, including a "statement of Our Position from recent press interview. Statement of and illustrations of The Cut Up Method Of Brion Gysin." Burroughs solicited other cut-up writers to send material and suggested an issue of only cut-up material in the future. A week later, Burroughs wrote Jon again, this time sending material from Gysin. Jon apparently felt the connection with Burroughs was progressing to the point where he might call upon Burroughs to help with distribution in London. Burroughs tried to help by telling people in his circle about the *Outsider's* needs. His friend and sometime collaborator, Sinclair Beiles, a South African expatriate and outspoken apartheid critic, soon assumed the duties of European editor.

Through Beiles, Jon sent word to expatriate American Paul Bowles, asking for an essay on kif, a hallucinogen smoked in the Middle East and India. The idea was to examine "kif smoking abroad . . . effects of it on intellectuals, bums, etc." Bowles, a spiritual precursor to Beat Generation writers such as Kerouac, Burroughs, and Ginsberg, demurred that he would not be able to write such a piece because, in the areas he frequented, "Morocco, the Sahara, Tanganyika, Ceylon, and India," there were few if any bums or intellectuals smoking kif. "It's just the ordinary citizen who smokes in my territories, not the exception as in Europe or America." Bowles instead sent a "kif dictionary," listing and explaining terms used in conjunction with the drug. Jon rejected this submission, but sent it on to the editors at *Kulchur*, who accepted it. Three months later, Bowles wrote Jon to thank him for forwarding the manuscript to *Kulchur*.

Jon's associate editors showed a passion for the work that belied their unpaid status. Writing from his room at the so-called "Beat Hotel," at 9 Rue Git le Coeur, in Paris, Beiles suggested Webb do an advertisement swap with the French literary magazine *Two Cities*. This would help get the word out about the *Outsider* in conservative French circles and in India, where *Two Cities* was also distributed. *Two Cities* editor Jean Franchette could be helpful in distributing copies of the magazine in France. Still, Beiles was protective of the *Outsider*: "I don't intend handing distribution here over to him entirely. Shall do some myself and see how he goes first. Really want to make very sure *Outsider* is not ditched in any way." Jon apparently had complained about his health and other problems associated with printing the first issue of the magazine, because Beiles chided him not to work so hard as to overstrain himself, finishing the letter with the cryptic exclamation, "Jesus! Sounds like you suffer deliberate sabotage!"

For all his enthusiasm, Beiles ended up being less useful to Jon than he at first appeared. In July 1960, Beiles wrote Jon a long letter explaining that he had not been able to attend to his duties because he had "gone mad" on separate occasions in Paris and Germany. In a matter of weeks he wrote again, this time hinting broadly that he wished to come to America and, at the very least, pay a visit to Jon and Louise in New Orleans, perhaps settle there. Even with his instability, though, Beiles remained loyal. He went so far as to suggest that the magazine could be an agent of change in the literary world. "I have the feeling that the 'Outsider' marks the end of literature and I'm glad you are making a big volume of it and taking your time to bring it out," Beiles wrote. Later, he added, "But you're putting up a great and real fight Jon and I admire your courage and the 'OUTSIDER' is postbomb literature (I hate the word literature). I hope the whole of OUTSIDER is sung by our post-bomb primitives."

British poet Melville Hardiment served as advisory editor for England. Hardiment was well connected in literary and media circles, and was associated with Beiles, Burroughs, Corso, Ginsberg, Gysin, Irwin Shaw, James

Jones, and a number of other less-well-known figures of the late 1950s and early 1960s. Hardiment had published a volume of poetry in the middle 1930s and later served in the Second World War. Like Beiles, he became an advisory editor for the *Outsider* at Burroughs's behest and took his duties seriously. He had already contacted Burroughs regarding a piece Burroughs had read on the BBC's *Third Programme*. Hardiment believed Burroughs "will let you have it and I expect to post it off to you next week." He recommended work by Piero Heliczer, a poet, musician, and filmmaker whom Jon did not publish in the *Outsider*, but who later achieved some notoriety for his poetry and for his short film *Venus in Furs* (1965) examining iconic rock band the Velvet Underground. Then there was Clancy Sigal, an American in England who had already published one novel, *Weekend in Dinlock*, and later published several others, including *Going Away*, whose theme was "the myth of the road." As was the case with Heliczer, Jon never published work by Sigal.

When midwest advisory editor Marvin Bell came on board, he was a promising young Chicago poet who had had "work accepted/published by some three dozen little magazines, including *Arbor*, *Descant*, the *Coercion Review*, *Odyssey*, *Quicksilver*, *Nomad*, and *Prosidia*, and [had] done literary and photographic reviews for *Trace* and *Contemporary Photographer*." At the same time, Bell was awaiting word on a fellowship from the University of Iowa that, if awarded, would allow him to attend the university's prestigious Writers' Workshop. Like Beiles, Bell became an advisory editor after Webb accepted several of his poems. The trigger for Bell's close involvement probably came at the end of a cover letter he sent with his first batch of poems: "I'll be looking forward to the *Outsider*, and, of course, let me know if I can aid in some small way."

Bell's enthusiasm grew when he saw the contributors' list for issue one. One Saturday, after receiving Jon's prospectus, he declared that the *Outsider* was "the most significant and worthwhile collection of contemporary poetry" yet published. "Do you know your publication is going to give heart to a lot of fine poets, cringing in obscurity with fears of the groups who threaten to control presses for contemporary stuff?" Bell was struck by the flexibility of Jon's selection policies. He suggested that the *Outsider*'s value lay in Jon's success in presenting a collection of poets more diverse and relevant than those gathered in Donald Allen's landmark *New American Poetry*. Bell compared the *Outsider* to issue four of the controversial little magazine *Big Table,* which, like Allen's collection, sought to give respectability to Beat Generation and Black Mountain poets. Jon also managed to gather together a number of poets who not only did not fit in with the Beat and Black Mountain sensibilities of Allen's collection, but, as with Langston Hughes, G. C. Oden, and Robert Sward, represented other traditions entirely: "Now, the *Outsider,* with a concern not for one or two schools or who knows who, but for individual voices. With a concern for broad coverage, irregardless of name-fame, with an appropriate disregard for irrelevancies. And with a promotional effort that just might help crack thru the conservative editorial facades of current presses."

Bell backed up his praise with action. Already on the staff of a start-up little magazine, *Choice,* he arranged for an exchange of advertisements between *Choice* and the *Outsider.* He got permission to write a column for *Choice* that would center, at least in part, on the *Outsider.* Finally, Bell offered, with no apparent expectation of payment or other consideration on Jon's part, to serve as a proofreader, and Jon sent proof sheets for issue one in June 1961. These pages included a brief fable by Russell Edson, which Bell enjoyed, about a defecating horse and a group of pretentious intellectuals trying to find a message in the horse's actions. He wrote Jon of how he might arrange distribution in Iowa City, primarily through sales to friends, before trying to place copies in retail outlets. This would mean that the Webbs could keep more of their profits.

Bell assured Webb that "It's going to be a terrific magazine, Jon." He hoped to mention the *Outsider* in *Choice* number two, but, "If not, there will be other issues of both, and plenty of places to say the name loudly." If other editors shared Jon's poetic sensibilities, Bell wrote, he would submit his work more broadly: "But it's so terribly hard to find an *Outsider,* that I generally pile the poems in the corner—why should I pay 8 cents to own a rejection slip from some academic hole? Or, on the other hand, a nasty note from some phony clique. Tell me, Jon—would they believe that you responded, first of all, to a sonnet by me? Why are so many editors incapable of seeing both sides of each fence? Corso writes good poetry; Sward does too; J. B. May, Creeley, Crews, Ferlinghetti also; etc.—but yours is the only magazine to recognize this fact." Bell decided that the array of styles Jon picked for the *Outsider* made it a throwback to the golden age of little magazines. Galleys for the first issue reminded him, "more than anything recent I can think of, of the magazines of the 20's, etc.—with their blasting, varied and hodge-podge (therefore interesting, as a Greenwich Village street will be more in-teresting than a neat wide highway) formats. A good issue, with lots in it, and a wide selection."

Jory Sherman, like Bill Corrington, was from Shreveport, Louisiana, though the two did not meet until both were grown and living elsewhere. In Sherman's case, that elsewhere was San Francisco, from which he served as advisory editor for the western United States. Sherman was also the ini-tial contact between Jon and Bukowski. The twenty-eight-year-old Sher-man was the poetry editor for an alternative newspaper, the *San Francisco Star*, for which he once conducted an exclusive interview with Nobel lau-reate Linus Pauling. He was also a poet and a literary translator, and his translations of Federico García Lorca were published in the little magazine *Quixote*. Sherman had published poetry in many little magazines, including *Epos, Quicksilver, American Bard, Scimitar and Song, Poetry Digest, Galley Sail Review, Simbolica,* and *The Prairie Poet* and was an established figure in San Francisco's artistic counterculture. He was a member of the North Beach Artists Association and socialized with people like Ferlinghetti and Bob Kaufman. Sherman regularly read his poetry to audiences in such San Francisco venues as the Coffee Gallery and the Cellar and was a skilled or-ganizer, having "thrown three benefits here and handled the poetry reading at annual Grant Ave. Street Fair with 40,000 people coming to stare."

Sherman echoed Lowenfels's earlier advice that Jon reject inferior work from Ferlinghetti. He told Webb that Ferlinghetti had said the first poem he submitted "was written in a shithouse in Big Sur." Sherman asked Ferling-hetti to send the *Outsider* a "good substantial poem." Perhaps due to Sher-man's urging, Ferlinghetti sent a much longer poem with the irreverent title "Underwear." Jon's reluctance to accept second-rate work from Ferlinghetti paid quick dividends. Before the issue appeared, New Directions publisher James Laughlin asked for reprint rights. "Underwear" would be included in Ferlinghetti's next collection, *Starting from San Francisco*, with an acknowl-edgment to the *Outsider*. Jon responded quickly with proof sheets and a copy of what Laughlin described as a "fascinating little circular you have gotten out about your progress on getting out the magazine." The change seems to have pleased Ferlinghetti, too. With a poem he clearly valued included in issue one, Ferlinghetti wrote Jon an enthusiastic note: "Congratulations on No. 1. It looks good! Please send City Lights Bookstore 100 copies (at 40% discount?) Thanx! LF."

Sherman maintained contacts with many poets and little magazine editors, including James Boyer May of *Trace*, Carol Bird of the *International Review*, and Anthony Linick of *Nomad*. His letters included gossip about editors and poets and occasional requests for information: "Think Ginsberg pulling out of Chile," he wrote, after asking for Corso's address so that he might "drop line" to him. Sherman's networking probably benefited Jon, as many people Sherman suggested eventually published in the *Outsider*. Jon, Jr., had joined the army in 1947 and was stationed at Ford Ord, California, near Monterey, when, in early December 1960, he met Sherman and his wife during a visit to San Francisco. The trio visited Ferlinghetti's City Lights bookstore, then stopped for drinks at a nearby bar. The younger Webb liked Sherman, who was energetic and open, drank screwdrivers, and wore worn-out tennis shoes. He described Sherman as a man who served as rent collector in his apartment building and had an attractive young wife with "black long hair, dark eyes, sweet disposition" who was expecting a baby in the coming weeks. Sherman talked a great deal about Jon, Sr., and the *Outsider*, convinced the elder Webb was a genius. Grateful for Sherman's help with the *Outsider*, Jon, Jr., himself almost broke, considered giving Sherman money: "I would have slipped him a few bucks . . . but felt there would have been some embarrassment if I had so didn't."

Some time later, Jon, Jr., and Sherman were scheduled to meet again, this time for dinner at Sherman's 616 Broadway apartment in San Francisco. Jon, Jr., was late, and Sherman spent the time waiting for his arrival by writing a letter to Jon, Sr. Sherman assessed the current poetry scene and, for the most part, his observations were not flattering. Like Bell, Sherman groused about Donald Allen's *New American Poetry*, calling it "a daisy chain affair with every snotnosed poet running to him with hardon, and ms. clutched in crotch." Among the people Sherman discussed were Ron Lowensohn, with whom he seemed to be feuding, and Leslie Woolf Hedley, who would appear in the *Outsider* one and was a "great guy, and very hated here" in San Francisco. Sherman also took the measure of Robert Duncan ("swelled head, but I like him and consider him one of the best poets around"); Jack Spicer ("a cynic, but likeable because he doesn't give a damn . . . yet I can't accept him as anything major . . . he has been sweet to me, since I had some publicity . . . but that again, is all that counts with these creeps").

Sherman was convinced he was the victim of unprovoked attacks from San Francisco newspaper columnist Herb Caen, who had referred to Sherman sarcastically in print as a "Half-Beat Poet." Sherman believed Caen and other columnists had used their newspaper forums to ridicule him: "These columnists having ball with me, and I am tired of it. Their readers like it, but I can't see the sense in it. A poet is fair game in S. F. tho . . . all the notorious ones quiet now, and they have turned their sights on me." Not all of his publicity was negative. Columnist Dick Nolan, of the *San Francisco Examiner*, "has been okay with me," Sherman wrote. He told Webb that Nolan had written nothing about any other San Francisco poet.

Sherman and the other advisory editors were part of a far-reaching network Jon was creating around his magazine. He understood the value of such networks and took advantage of a time-honored custom in little magazine publishing, the building of synergistic networks through the trading of advertising space. Jon threw the *Outsider* into this mix, trading ads with more than a dozen other magazines. Advertisements for these journals were not, as a rule, sent already designed and ready to be printed. Indeed, the technological limitations of Jon's and most of his colleagues' printing processes did not allow for camera-ready copy to be of much use. *Epos* editor Evelyn Thorn described the general practice when she told Jon, "Of course, the arrangement of typography for our ad is for you to decide, as we will arrange yours." In a splendid show of solidarity, *Migrant* editor Gael Turnbull, a contributor to the *Outsider* one, sent his magazine's mailing list along with the ad copy.

With everything now in place, the Webbs stayed busy; Louise set pages and Jon printed them on their old Chandler and Price press. In late June 1961, Bukowski wrote Corrington that Jon was "still cranking away, reaching a near end, counting up the number of days it's been since he's had a drink. I don't see why he has to have 4,000 copies or what he's going to do with them. He could have turned out 20 mags of 200 copies with the same effort, but, well, he's the one turning the crank." Though Bukowski exaggerated the *Outsider*'s press run by a thousand copies, his question would likely have remained, even with the actual number Jon was printing. It was an enormous undertaking.

Jon introduced himself to his readers in this first issue through his column, Editor's Bit. There was a long tradition of such columns, stretching back at least to Harriet Monroe and *Poetry*, though many of the quickly produced publications of the mimeograph revolution era did not bother with them.

Monroe's editorial comment, As It Was, in the inaugural *Poetry*, took the form of a heroic fable. Monroe wrote of an ancient king who forged a society through battle and wisdom. When death was upon him, the king grieved that all he had created would vanish with him. His son comforted the old man, assuring him that he would tell his father's story and that all generations to come would continue in the telling. Thus, poetry began.

Margaret Anderson ran the occasional column in the *Little Review*. She said what was on her mind, tending often toward giddiness and an almost spiritual adoration of art. Anderson was an iconoclast and proud of it. As a motto for her magazine she chose "Making No Compromise with the Public Taste." What Anderson really wanted was to publish "the best conversation the world has to offer." According to a 1944 *Time* magazine review of *The Little Magazine in America*, "for some years she pretty well succeeded." Anderson found other creative ways to editorialize. Once, frustrated with poor-quality submissions, she published ten blank pages and challenged writers to send work worth filling them. Another time, she ran a series of ads for businesses that had not paid for them, hoping to shame the proprietors into coming up with money after the fact.

Blues, published in Columbus, Mississippi, by the young Charles Henri Ford, was also sporadic in publishing editorial columns. The first issue offered For a New Magazine, penned by associate editor William Carlos Williams to justify the magazine's existence. *Blues* was needed, Williams argued, because all other literary magazines were "thoroughly, totally, completely dead as far as anything new in literature is concerned." Being open to broad experimentation, even the inevitable failures that came with the successes, was William's prescription for a vital magazine.

Jon's Editor's Bit was as personal as Anderson's columns, but almost opposite in tone, alternating between braggadocio and bleakness. His opinion of little magazines, as proposed in the *Mainstream* symposium, was in harmony with Williams's, and he did sometimes argue for experimentation in his column, but his concerns tended to be far more personal. In future issues, the column offered a running account of the ordeals he and Louise experienced in ushering the current issue from planning through printing. This first time, however, he used the space for a short story about a man just released from prison. His protagonist finds himself in Cleveland, Ohio, falling into conversation with, among others, a wise, cynical blind man and a pretty young woman. Other than being free, the character is at loose ends. He has no job and nowhere to go and compares himself to a bird with a broken wing. He is a double outsider, out of jail and out of step with the world.

Jon provided nothing else which might connect him with the newly released convict, and anyone lacking personal knowledge of Jon's past would have no reason to believe the story to be more than a complete fiction. He was revisiting the days he described in his letters to *Story* magazine in the mid-1930s—not just the simple fact of being free, but the dangers of letting people know about the jail time. More than twenty-five years had passed since Jon's release from prison, though, and his life had changed dramatically. He had a longtime marriage to a woman he loved, a successful, critically praised novel, and a number of stories published in respected journals. Money was always a problem, but by most any other measure of artistic and domestic success, Jon had made it. But now he was on a different path and he knew this was a gamble. The Webbs' investment in time, money, and labor was high and if the *Outsider* failed, all would be wasted. With everything depending upon the magazine's success, perhaps he was taking this chance to say, quietly, "This is who I am."

As the weeks before the magazine's debut crawled by, Corrington awaited issue one "on the verge of panic." He became even more enthusiastic after he actually saw the magazine and read of Jon's hope to upgrade to a motorized press: "I got it and it's too much to talk about: everything: contents, layout . . . worth every minute of the time it took (though I hope to God you can get the press . . . for which I will send ten as soon as I get paid by this dump). If OUTSIDER does not sell out, we all may as well hang our dream of a literate nation on the nearest American Legion flagpole and entrain for Brussels." It would be easy to dismiss Corrington's praise as excessive, but similar comments arrived from all quarters once the *Outsider* hit the stands. As did a number of others, Corrington offered his services to help promote the magazine: "When you've disposed of all the copies already taken, let me know so I can push a few. I have at least five friends who will absolutely want one, and I have a very close friend at Wisconsin U. who can get a bookstore to handle for you. Also a friend at Oklahoma, and possibly one at Kansas U. who would scour the bookstores for an outlet. This would beat the distributor out of his unearned pound of flesh, huh?" Corrington and Webb's relationship was quickly cemented.

Corrington made plans to visit Webb two weeks later and wrote that he would wait until that time to get Webb's approval to begin pushing his friends to help distribute the *Outsider*. Certain the magazine would be a success, Corrington wrote, "Man, with a product like this, you can't miss." A letter from Bukowski to Webb was equally enthusiastic in its way: "There were a whole bunch of *Outsiders* down at the newsstand at Hollywood and Las Palmas, then it went down to one, and now you are sold out. The other mags still there, covered with dust. Thought you might be interested in this oddity because as editor they are your babies."

❖ 5 ❖

THE *OUTSIDER* FLOURISHES

SOMETIME IN 1961, poet Kay Johnson, or "Kaja," her occasional pen name, decided to quit her Ursulines Street apartment and move to Paris. Johnson was a longtime friend of the Webbs', and her move was lucky for them, as they now planned to move into her apartment, with its solid cement floor, a good foundation for their press. The apartment's most charming feature was a patio with banana and fig trees and a mimosa, which, in May, "explodes like fragrant cottony moonlight all over the place." The patio held a chair and picnic table, and Johnson loved to sit outside with her dogs, admiring the trees. "I sure hope you can enjoy that patio and the chair out in the yard and the picnic tables as much as I did," she told Jon. The Webbs also had dogs, Gypsy and Lady, with whom to enjoy the patio.

Johnson's destination was the "Beat Hotel," an aging relic at 9 Rue Git le Cour, which served as unofficial home to the international Beat movement for much of the early-to-mid-1960s. Gregory Corso had a room there, and Johnson, who had fallen in love with Corso through his poetry, was excited about the prospect of being near him. Besides, she was angry with New Orleans. The previous Mardi Gras, she had been arrested for participating in the segregated Zulu parade and still harbored resentment. The move to Paris seemed ideal for both Johnson and the Webbs. Jon apparently considered Johnson an agent of the Loujon Press in much the same way that he did the advisory editors he used for issue one and also a source of information about the writers living in the hotel. Johnson was happy to oblige. She told Webb of a young Greek poet she had met named Spiros, suggesting that she might send samples of his work. Johnson met Harold Norse, a figure of growing notoriety who had been living in the hotel but recently moved to Africa, and asked Norse to send Webb poems. She planned to check with two Paris bookstores, the Mistral and the American Bookshop, about late payments for sales of issue one.

Johnson kept loose tabs on Burroughs, noticing him on the stairs and "downstairs having coffee" and assured Jon that he could reach Burroughs there if he wished. Another time, she noted a positive change in Burroughs's demeanor: "Yes, Jon, Burroughs is here . . . oh what a change—from a sick old man of last year when he first returned, i look in his face and now see a jubilant spirit of age 20—he is beautiful in his soul—and young and eternal— he doesn't like women; well, i don't blame him—so i told him i was Henry Miller (actually i do think i look like Miller in the mirror a bit . . . altho some kids here say i remind them of Allen Ginsberg)—well the next time we met, he said "HELLO, MILLER . . . and we shook hands warmly—and now he smiles at me on the stairs . . . and asked if I'd heard from you." Even with the romance of the place and the famous faces in the halls, Johnson wasn't especially happy. She pined for Corso, who was on an extended trip to England, and lamented in an undated letter that "everyone loves what I write for Gregory but Gregory."

The second issue of the *Outsider* arrived in the summer of 1962 and was sent to a growing list of individual subscribers and libraries. The little magazine movement was getting stronger, and the *Outsider* was joined by new titles like *Burning Deck; Poor. Old. Tired. Horse; El Corno Emplumado;* and *Fuck You: A Magazine of the Arts.* Johnson received her new *Outsider* and "read avidly standing swaying on subway—you should have seen me—all caught up in it." She was especially taken with "Oldest of the Living Old" and recommended that Webb contact Bob Cass, "as he is for the old jazz, and he writes a new old-time ballad anti-poem like in the jazz days—it might be just what you need to tie-in poem and old-time-jazz, if you haven't gotten in touch with him already on it???" Like Corrington, Johnson thought the *Outsider* would do great things for New Orleans. "I think you will put New Orleans on the map again," she told Jon. Johnson was enthusiastic about Bukowski's poetry, especially "sick leave": "How do you pull the guts out of Bukowski, i mean, how do you do it? you are really an editor. how did you get it out of him so whole? So perfect? Cesarean operation? did it come in a poem or in a letter? . . . anyhow you can sure pull the poems outa him. and this 'sick leave' is right from the guts. i think i try to make him too lyrical like me. he is really like you a very gutty guy."

Back in New Orleans, the *Outsider* had gained a following, and this was sometimes a problem. Jon worried that the wrong kind of attention could cause trouble. According to Ed Blair, "It freaked him out when young followers were dropping off marijuana as gifts through his door on Ursulines and Royal. He knew that cops might arrest him due to ex-con status if they found anything in his apartment." Still, a new issue of the *Outsider* helped ease the tension. It was sold in a few well-placed bookstores around the United States, a few outlets in Europe and, from her little shop on St. Peter Street at Royal, by Louise Webb. Jon and Louise approached production of the *Outsider* two the same as they had done with issue one. They worked seven days a week, sixteen hours a day. Setting type and printing pages had a predictable outcome: do the work, see the results. Keeping a healthy cash flow was a different matter. A strategy to sell enough $12.90 lifetime subscriptions to keep the *Outsider* alive had not been particularly successful, and the Webbs remained chronically broke.

There was a successful precedent resembling Jon's basic idea, but when Harriet Monroe used a similar financing method for *Poetry* in 1912, she was more financially astute. Monroe was as broke as the Webbs when she started out, but took the advice of her friend H. C. Chatfield-Taylor to solicit one hundred people to take a five-year subscription at fifty dollars a year. In theory, after five years, the magazine would be self-sustaining. Monroe's plan worked, for one reason, because she didn't give her patrons lifetime subscriptions. They paid a sizeable subscription fee, but when five years ended, the patrons knew they were entitled to nothing more. In the *Outsider*'s case, a lifetime subscription meant subscribers could expect Loujon materials in perpetuity for a relatively small amount of money, which the Webbs spent almost as soon as they got it. This created a built-in burden which increased with additional lifetime subscription sales and only got worse the longer Loujon existed. Perhaps Monroe's plan worked also because she appealed to the better angels of her subscribers' natures. These people understood up front that they were acting as patrons for the magazine. Jon marketed his lifetime subscriptions as bargains for his readers. A bargain is often a strong incentive to buy, but maybe for a cultural product as fragile as a literary magazine, it is not quite enough. Still, the Webbs had to take heart that the *Outsider* was considered worthwhile by members of the cognoscenti. Among the handful of individual lifetime subscribers listed in the second issue, for example, was the great Langston Hughes. Webb had more success selling lifetime subscriptions to university libraries and made a point to mention, in his Editor's Bit, the names of several of the more famous of these libraries—Harvard, Yale, Duke, Notre Dame, Swarthmore, Chicago, Cornell, Colgate, Brown, Princeton, Oxford—"and some who said not to mention it."

Louise again graced the cover. She was photographed in profile, her gaze directed upward at the *Outsider* logo snaking around her head, and beyond to a photograph of Punch Miller blowing on his clarinet, a teaser for an article on New Orleans jazz, "Oldest of the Living Old," which anchored the issue. Jon's pride in the appearance of his magazine was clear from the care he took in its construction. In a special note to other editors, he brashly described the effort it took to get the cover just right: "The outside cover was made with 110-screen plates, took 12 hours to do on a fast Miehle vertical. I went to Bill Grammer who operates one & told him the special effect I wanted on my Impact coated cover paper, and Bill, with incredible patience, stopped & started the press 3,200 times, double-rolling for each impression, and between each wet, very wet, piece coming off I tossed in 2 sheets of telephone-book paper (slipsheeting). Try to find the screen."

As in issue one, Jon spoke directly to readers through his column. This time the voice was unmistakably his own. He wrote of money troubles and hard labor, the demands of little magazine publishing. He also wrote of his need to replace the worn type Louise used to set the issue, and emphasized that the *Outsider* needed good prose submissions. Webb now broadened his role as editor-publisher-printer to include, in a much more overt way than before, the aspect of public relations manager. With this column, he found his voice as a total literary magazine producer.

The lifetime subscription plan hadn't worked out, but newsstand sales in the United States and abroad and annual subscriptions were strong enough to keep the magazine going. This combined income enabled Jon to sell Loujon's old hand press and purchase a motorized, secondhand Chandler and Price press from Tulane. Dissension in the university's drama department caused its *Tulane Drama Review*, considered by many to be the world's premier theatre magazine, to fold, and they no longer needed the production equipment. Webb paid just under five hundred dollars for the press; installation and delivery was another three hundred dollars, which took much of their savings. As always, the Webbs were sustained by money Louise made selling her paintings. All of the cash she brought into their home went to promoting the second issue, to paying rent and utilities and buying food. Money from sale of their first press bought eight cartons of six-by-nine paper, a good amount, though not enough to print the 3,100 copies of the 113-page second issue. The Webbs repeatedly ran out of money, but when new subscriptions arrived, "we'd go over to the paper companies to scavenge thru the 10c-a-lb. scrap heaps until we found the paper we needed, or its next best facsimile." Ink was also a problem, though there was plenty on hand to get the second issue started. The Tulane purchase included enough ink to print eighty pages of the complete press run.

Their most serious problem was worn type. Again and again, Louise had to reset pages because much of their type was too worn to properly ink the paper. She was forced to find replacement letters in the case and reset the type for Jon to make new proof sheets. They repeated the process until each piece of type printed crisply. This took time and effort and could be frustrating. Also, even with their new press, they could still only print one page at a time. Thus, the time problem translated into a volume problem, which led to a money problem. A slow printing process meant that fewer copies could be printed and sold, and Webb had hoped to increase his press run to five thousand copies by issue four, ten thousand by issue five or six; but that now seemed unlikely. A press that could dramatically increase production would take money the Webbs did not have.

Along with increased production, Jon remained concerned with the quality of work he published. He wrote that he had followed a deliberate strategy for the magazine's first two issues. Issue one was designed to include a broad sampling of current literary trends, being "a provocatively divergent assemblage of fifty-some 'voices' representing interrelated schools of creative action today, chiefly in poetry." Roughly the same selection process held for issue two, though with fewer contributors there was "less of a hodge-podge," and "rather more from less than a little from a lot." There were forty-three contributors in issue two, not including the brief passages assembled from a number of jazz experts for "The Oldest of the Living Old."

Kenneth Patchen made his first *Outsider* appearance in this issue with a series of abstract drawings, introduced by a brief, handwritten letter of January 1962, reproduced in holograph: "Dear Webb—Certainly appreciate your patience and persistence and interest in getting things of mine for your magazine. Past months I've been in and out of hospital, more dead (at times) than alive. 5 photos of paintings & 5 drawings enclosed. Please return when done with them—only copies I have. I might use them in book later on." As his letter indicated, Patchen had a serious health problem. He had suffered for years with a chronic, debilitating back ailment, and was trying to arrange for an operation that might offer some relief. This appearance in the *Outsider* was meant to alert readers to Patchen's plight and elicit financial support. Patchen's letter was followed by a brief note from Jonathan Williams, his longtime friend and advocate who, through his Jargon Press, had published Patchen's collection *Poemscapes* in 1958. Williams told readers to "[r]eassure yourself, if you must, that he 'deserves' because he is a great imaginative poet, that any page of his may contain the line you have been waiting to hear all your life, as Denis Saurat says of Blake. After all the data and feed-back are computed, do something!—or stop reading magazines like this one and rejoin the hydraheaded sons of bitches who always oh love poetry so." Jon added an editor's note, directing readers who wished to contribute to the Patchen Surgery Fund to send their contributions directly to Patchen at 2340 Sierra Court, Palo Alto, California.

Like the Webbs, Patchen was a native Ohioan. He came from the Mahoning Valley, a region of steel mills and coal mines about seventy-five miles southeast of Cleveland. His father, Wayne, was a steelworker, and Patchen worked in the steel mills, too, for a time, trying to earn money for college. In 1928, when he was still in high school, Patchen published his first poems in school literary magazines. That same year he published two poems in the *New York Times*. He attended the University of Wisconsin for one year and Commonwealth College in Arkansas for another, before abandoning higher education for a life of wandering and odd jobs. Patchen met Miriam Oikemus on Christmas Eve of 1933 and married her in June 1934. His first poetry collection, *Before the Brave*, was published two years later by Random House, beginning a prolific career that saw publication of dozens of books. He was adept at both fiction and poetry, and his distinctive "painting poems" blended Patchen's considerable skills with the paintbrush and his often mystical, pacifistic verse. His highly regarded antiwar novel, *The Journal of Albion Moonlight*, appeared in 1941. Another novel, *Memoirs of a Shy Pornographer*, came out in 1945. Each of his books carried the dedication "For Miriam."

An impressive group of poets joined Patchen in the second issue of the *Outsider*. Among the names that remain well remembered at the beginning of the twenty-first century—though some were not especially famous in the summer of 1962—are William Burroughs, Gregory Corso, Howard Nemerov, Marvin Bell, Jean Genet, Jack Kerouac, Henry Miller, and Charles Bukowski. In what was a fairly common practice among little magazine editors, work by Jon and Louise Webb also appeared in this issue. Louise's effort, a brief section from her still-unpublished novel, "Black Olives," appeared under her maiden name, Louise Madaio. Jon printed his own short poem, "suddenly over":

who is this stranger
who comes into
my wife's bedroom,
mine too,
looking about as if
she owns both me
and the mare in
the meadow?

For a long while, Corrington believed he would not have work in the second issue. By late September 1961, he had yet to interest Jon in any new poetry, but remained enthusiastic in helping with the magazine. He had sent a copy of the *Outsider* to a publisher in Washington, in hopes of finding a small distribution outlet there, and was on the lookout for other distribution opportunities. Corrington noted that the local Shortress bookshop had sold all of its copies, and he planned to ask if they needed more. He was also trying to interest a Houston bookstore in carrying the magazine. "You don't sell mags by playing fadeout," he wrote Webb. "We gonna sell 'em all, and sell 'em to people who'll read 'em." Corrington also maintained close ties with Bukowski and didn't keep his esteem for Bukowski secret. Probably as a result of Corrington's efforts, Corrington wrote Webb that admiration for Bukowski was developing among LSU students: "O Lord, a bunch of grad students got hold of OUT #1, and . . . Bukowski is getting him a fan club here. I would have figured the Black Mountain puffs or maybe Hedley could catch on, but Chaz? I guess they're just making a better class of grad student nowadays. Probably sick to their guts of KENYON & Co."

A few days later, Corrington wrote to tell Jon that Bukowski claimed to have won a large sum of money at the track: "Letter from Chaz. I think the Schlitz finally got to his brain: he says he bet eight races in a row to win . . . and came home on *all* of 'em. I don't say you can't do it, but man you can just as quick roll ten passes with the dice. Of course you can't drop a nag in water to see if it's loaded. No, you got to test the horse's water. Therefore dice are the opposite of nags. Anyway, Chaz says he won so much loot that his wallet wouldn't bend. Now he never shitted me in all the letters I've gotten from him, but this sounds awful hairy."

Healthy skepticism aside, Corrington was an important friend to both Bukowski and Webb. With a word of encouragement here, help with distribution there, Corrington pitched in however he could. In early February 1962, Corrington delivered the good news that Bukowski's brief manuscript *Run with the Hunted* had been accepted by Rob Cuscaden, editor-publisher of the Midwest chapbook series. Bukowski's popularity was growing fast and Corrington felt vindicated: "As each day passes, our judgment is being seconded by slower eyes & ears. Had we been around, we would doubtless have spotted Mozart's potential at the moment of his conception. It is no small thing, amidst the welter of current works & names, to have spotted the genuine article amongst the pyrites and dung." He deferred to Webb with a gracious, "Accept my congratulations," but his pride in helping to launch Bukowski's career is clear.

Corrington spent time thinking of how he and Bukowski each manifested a distinct writing style. "The difference between us parallels the difference between Dante and Byron on one hand, and Shakespeare and Joyce on the other," he reasoned. "Bukowski is always on stage in his work. He is actor-observer in nearly everything, and he has the power to make you understand that this is right, the way it should be; the proper stance for this voice. Corrington is a born lurker. He picks and pokes and sings a bar from the wings, maybe even chisels by using an 'I' which is patently not himself, writes poems with sentiments as far removed from his own heart as a mind can hold—and is in no way concerned with affirming any sonofabitches' dorctrine or notion, but only with an honest to god bird in it."

Corrington was often on Bukowski's mind, and Bukowski was cool and steady in his praise of the Louisiana poet in his letters to Webb. In October 1962, Bukowski compared Corrington's poems unfavorably to his letters, but added, "When the letters catch up to the poems (and I think they will)—I mean when the letters become the poems—they can't catch them, being past them, Corrington will be a poet to listen to." Corrington's letters "make the Miller letters look like burnt apple pie," Bukowski told Webb.

Some time earlier, Corrington and Bukowski began supplementing their correspondence with reel-to-reel audiotapes. Bukowski initiated the exchange, and so Corrington was the first to observe the nuances he had missed in Bukowski's letters. After scrambling to find a tape recorder to play the tapes Bukowski sent—tapes that broke several times while Corrington listened—Corrington considered yet again what made Bukowski a poet:

"Nothing clearer. Bukowski has the classical ailment: it killed Alexander sure as fever (no his mother died of self-sodomy; his father died of himself), it made, believe it or not, Baudelaire a poet: ennui. Humdrum. Tedium." When Corrington sent a tape in return, Bukowski called it "a thing of astute beauty," and told Corrington "there is some Southern sticking out of you but it is in the delicate tradition, without cotton."

Along with the novelty of the tape exchange, Bukowski and Corrington had a new area of significant mutual interest. Corrington's friend Marcus Smith wanted to move into chapbook publishing and hoped to publish a Bukowski-Corrington volume: "Now look, this is no idea of mine. He hit me with it like a herring in the face of a hazy Sunday morning. He says it will be offset, with colors on cover and all that crap, and that he can sell 500 copies, and that he'll split any profit three ways." Bukowski agreed to do the chapbook, with the caveat that nothing in it be a repeat of work from his previous chapbook, *Flower, Fist and Bestial Wail,* or the upcoming *Run with the Hunted.* He reminded Corrington that he didn't keep carbons of his poetry and that much of his work was under consideration by various magazines, some of which he couldn't even remember. The idea of Bukowski sending out poems to perhaps be lost horrified Corrington, who chided his friend that he should be more careful, "not for vanity or the Big Time . . . least of all for Marc's convenience, but because you say things, and maybe one of these things gets lost, and never said that way again." Smith soon contacted Bukowski, and the chapbook seemed more and more like a sure thing. Over the next few weeks, Corrington and Bukowski tried out various titles, such as "Double Shot," "The Professor and the Horseplayer," and "Buried with a Mouthful of Cherries," neither of them happy with the suggestions.

Though the chapbook was good news, Corrington was still having no luck placing work in the *Outsider* and had come to believe that Webb was simply too demanding: "He has this frame in his mind, and if my stuff doesn't stretch across the frame like the hide of his own private critter, I don't make it. Nuts. This is no detraction. I dig him plenty, and he puts out a real scary magazine. I'm just afraid I won't be too much in it. But I expect both of us can stand that." Corrington was correct that Webb took being an editor seriously. Unlike many of his peers, Webb went beyond simply accepting or rejecting manuscripts. He occasionally changed the text of work he accepted, sometimes radically. An example of this occurs in Jack Kerouac's "Sept. 16, 1961, Poem." In manuscript, a line reads: "This is an attempt at the easy lightness of Chinese poetry." Webb circled the word "Chinese" and scribbled, "use alternate word," which he did over Kerouac's express instructions. A handwritten note from Kerouac to Webb asks that the poem be printed exactly the way it was written, down to Kerouac's idiosyncratic line indentations. Beat Generation scholar Dave Moore later discovered that Webb did a strange thing with Kerouac's poem. Rather than make a single substitution for "Chinese," he made different substitutions in different copies of the magazine. Moore has identified at least seven variations, including "Ciardi," "Ciardian," "civilized," "chamber," "Beatnik," "drawing room," and Kerouac's own, "Chinese."

Kerouac only became aware of the change in late 1964 or early 1965 after he received a copy of *Poesia Degli Ultimi Americani*, an anthology of new American poetry published in Italy and edited by Fernanda Pivano. After Kerouac read his poem there, he wrote to ask Pivano's help in solving what he described as the "great mystery" of how the poem became altered. He remembered that it had originally appeared in the *Outsider* and wondered if that were where Pivano got her copy. As Moore observes, since Kerouac didn't know of the change before this time, there is a good chance Webb sent Kerouac a copy of the magazine with the word "Chinese" intact. A piece of art in the *Outsider* deepens the mystery. Beneath a striking woodcut of a sailing ship coming perilously close to a vulture-dominated, rocky coastline is this odd caption: "So what if Kerouac is on board? You can't believe everything Ciardi says." In a February 6, 1960, *Saturday Review* piece, Ciardi wrote, "Whether or not Jack Kerouac has traces of a talent, he remains basically a high school athlete who went from Lowell, Massachusetts, to Skid Row, losing his eraser en route."

What Jon did to Kerouac's poem was nothing compared to his editing of a submission from William Burroughs entitled "Cuts from 'Word Line' William Burroughs for Hassan i Sabbah." The piece was done in Burroughs's distinctive, jumbled, "cut-up" technique and had no easily discernible narrative flow or quickly grasped meaning. Perhaps for these reasons, Webb heavily edited and retitled the piece, casting it as a poem which bore little resemblance to the original. On Burroughs's manuscript, Webb wrote that he had condensed and rearranged the submission into "wilt caught in time," the title under which it appeared in the magazine.

Such behind-the-scenes work was, by its nature, invisible to the magazine's readers. They responded to the literature that made it to the *Out-*

sider's pages and probably didn't give much thought to the potential for significant editorial changes from Jon; the issue was the thing. This certainly seemed to be the case with Bukowski, who, soon after receiving his copy of the second *Outsider*, wrote Webb to offer his critique. Johnson caught Bukowski's eye, and he assured Webb that, though Johnson admired Corso, Johnson was the better poet. As to the other poets in the issue, Bukowski reserved real praise only for Carolyn Stoloff. Others, such as Joel Oppenheimer, Howard Nemerov, Russell Edson, Gloria Oden, and Jean Genet, he damned with faint praise or dismissed entirely. Bukowski told Webb he had been uneasy about Louise appearing in the magazine, but that his fears about the quality of her work, and Webb's editorial judgment, were put to rest after he read her story. Bukowski again wrote about the issue in late July. As before, he pointed out the poets he disliked in the magazine and praised Johnson's work: "[B]ut then it is always the unknowns who come on while the others grow fat under their names."

Twice in letters of late September 1961, Bukowski had praised Johnson as a developing writer. By the middle of October, however, his estimation of her work had cooled perceptibly. In a three-page letter concerned primarily with Johnson's poetry, Bukowski wrote: "ah, well, I have gazed lightly upon the enclosed kaja and found its temper did not bid me to cast coins upon the air. I will give it a fuller reading now, try again. This girl lives in a walkup room in paris, 6 up, and she watches wharves and tugboats or what on the Seine and she quit working to become a saint, and all this breathes good intent, but sometimes intent is disinfected by lack of proper talent." He concluded, sadly, that "I know that sitting here sweating this afternoon, naked, October 15th., 1961, that these words written by a girl who is in Paris and has to walk 6 flights up, are not the words for me." To Bukowski, this criticism was simple honesty. "It is a hard thing to say because I know kaja from her letters, but she would say the same of me if I failed her."

Bukowski shared his thoughts on Johnson's poetry with Corrington, who agreed about her work. "Kaja is real abstruse," Corrington wrote. "I like her, but the work is just work. I read stuff she gave me, and it is not bad like *Kenyon Review* is bad, but it don't smell like dynamite and taste like a glassful of almighty. I guess we've seen too many things done with words, and too many hearts exposed on the table of print to get moved by anything except the unbelievable."

Closer to home, both men were becoming concerned about the chapbook

Marcus Smith had proposed. Things were beginning to look bad. Bukowski wrote Corrington that Smith was considering selling ads, suggesting that perhaps Smith was actually planning to do a magazine instead of a chapbook. Either way, the whole thing was taking longer than either Bukowski or Corrington expected, and each finally asked Smith to pull several poems because they had been accepted elsewhere. Corrington admitted that their work would probably be more widely read if it were published in magazines, but he wanted the chapbook and had faith that it was forthcoming. It was frustrating to wait, "[b]ut Smith will materialize," Corrington assured Bukowski.

Corrington finally succeeded in placing a poem in the second issue of the *Outsider*, though this was not a complete victory. As he had done with Kerouac and Burroughs, Jon intended to change Corrington's poem to suit himself: "Jon has taken one for #2 (wants to hack it all up, and insists on removing the first line: 'Three niggers smiling could not reproduce/the tumult of that kiss')." Whether Jon took moral offense at the racial epithet or just thought his editing could make for a better poem, Corrington was unhappy with the changes. Bukowski liked Corrington's line, but reminded him that there may have been a whiff of jealousy in Corrington's response. He saw, correctly, that Jon was making Kay Johnson into a special project and that Jon had to look out for himself. "For all we know, the mag's his only income. By doing the work himself, enough dollars to carry on. This is a bad time. People are frightened of doing any wrong." The line change aside, Corrington was even less happy that Jon was not backing his career the way he was Johnson's. "I reckon Jon has a right to make him a crusade once in a while. Maybe he thinks we're already too far along to require pushes. For my part, that's some crap. I could use an album or something in one of the *Outsiders*, but I never push."

Corrington had glory on his mind when he wrote Bukowski, jokingly, that if Bukowski became famous first, he could expect Corrington to turn on him. He asked Bukowski to do the same if the situation were reversed: "I will need it. Crow is eaten by the wise famouses. Always prepared by friends." Corrington was convinced Bukowski would achieve fame through his poetry; as for himself, he hoped to do well with a novel. Corrington had sent dozens of pages of a civil war novel to Harper & Row, and they were interested in seeing more. Better still, the publisher was talking about a decent royalty. But real financial success as a writer was rare, and Corrington knew this. In May, Corrington learned he had been accepted into a Ph.D. program at Sussex University in Brighton, England. If he were to advance in the academic hierarchy, a doctorate was essential. This would mean a more secure future, and Corrington had a family to consider. He calculated the degree would take two years to complete, and he told Bukowski that "they will let me have a Ph.D. without a lot of shit if I write a good dissertation—which I can do. No classes or exams—which I can no longer do." He asked Webb, perhaps tongue in cheek, about becoming "your roving European correspondent."

As it turned out, Webb did not publish the poem that caused Corrington so much consternation. Instead, he took "surreal for lorca," an antiwar statement set amid the horrors of the Spanish Civil War. The poem demonstrated not only Corrington's own power as a poet but also his sharp eye for good lines in the poetry of others. Near the end of his poem, Corrington speaks of "god / no taller than a scream," echoing a line from Bukowski, who made a similar comparison of "god, no taller than a landlady," in his poem "The Sunday Artist." Bukowski caught the apparent homage, writing Corrington that perhaps they were developing similar styles, or "maybe we both write like Synge."

Bukowski had been coy about publishing with the *Outsider* so soon after the "Charles Bukowski Album" of issue one. Jon asked for poems several times and Bukowski refused, but his refusal wasn't consistent. Bukowski told Jon, more than once, that he had new poems that he would like Jon to consider. Whatever Bukowski really wanted, Jon was intent on including him in the second issue, and Jon prevailed. Bukowski's poem appeared in a section Jon introduced as "An album of definitive anti-poems on love not written with expectation of being detoured into such unresolved a label via editorial whimsy . . ." Joining Bukowski in the sixteen-poem album were Genet, Bell, Johnson (as herself and as "kaja"), Jon, and others.

In Jon's editorial decisions he continued to rely heavily on advice he received from Lowenfels. For issue two, he used what was originally a personal letter from Lowenfels as "A Letter to the Editor Editorial." Lowenfels's letter was in response to a request by Jon that he elaborate on an earlier statement that "What is really revolutionary in contemporary art is a new relationship with a new kind of audience." Jon prefaced Lowenfels's piece with a statement declaring that the initial idea behind the founding of the *Outsider* was a connection with "a new kind of audience." With Lowenfels's strong influence on Jon, this piece can almost be read as the *Outsider*'s manifesto. Lowenfels drew upon ideas from Mexican muralist David Alfaro Siqueiros (1896–1974), a leftist, social realist artist, who taught Lowenfels that "Mural art is a relation between a painting on the wall and a moving audience." From this observation, Lowenfels extracted the foundation for a theory of art based upon the movement of an audience in three spheres: space, time, and social class. A work of art was to be judged not only by its contemporaries, based upon their experiences, attitudes, beliefs, and so on, but by future audiences existing in different social structures. Lowenfels observed, by way of illustration, that "the feudal lords and ladies are no longer with us; the kind of epics medieval society produced are not being produced today." Lowenfels wrote that the new audience the artist should seek is "not audience in a practical sense of immediate cash, but the audience you, too, help to create as you write for it." In Lowenfels's view, artists have the duty to continually seek to express new and genuine revolutionary ideas grounded in "the way the world is moving." While admitting that such a creature did not exist, Lowenfels insisted that "the perfect contemporary artist is the one who continually kills yesterday's self."

Lowenfels's good will toward Jon extended beyond his work with the magazine. In early 1962, when Jon was trying to quit smoking, Lowenfels tried to help him concoct a workable strategy to give up tobacco. Lowenfels was a former smoker who, ten years earlier, had published an essay on smoking cessation in *The Worker*. Lowenfels told Jon he had been able to give up cigarettes only after he realized the political and psychological dimensions of smoking. He sympathized that the smoking habit revolved in large measure around conditioned response, "but the psychological thing I finally licked by making a study of the rise of the cig industry, its monopolization, finding the great growth of cig smoking paralleled the rise of US imperialism, 1900–1950, and arriving at a slogan: DOWN WITH YANQUI IMPERIALISM and cigarettes. . . ." Two weeks later, Lowenfels wrote again about Jon's health, this time in response to an apparent complaint Jon had made about his prostate. He wrote whimsically of a plan to subtract decades from one's age and concluded with the admonition that Webb should "tell yourself every day—old age is a bourgeois disease!"

With Jon perhaps in the doldrums over his prostate troubles and his attempt to quit smoking, it is not surprising that his friend would seek to find ways of cheering him. On Valentine's Day, Lowenfels wrote Webb a letter lavish with praise. First relating a dream in which he flew by private plane to visit Jon in New Orleans, Lowenfels switched to reality, writing that some promotional materials from Jon had arrived. Lowenfels called the materials "poetry." He assured Jon that his work was of value by adding, "I can see generations of doctorates being written on The Inside Story of the *Outsider*." He would not predict how the *Outsider* would be ranked among the great little magazines of history, but praised the physical beauty and the care Jon took in crafting it, "which is certainly a real treat for poets who never before have ranked with the stock market pages."

The second issue of the *Outsider* was announced to the French Quarter by a local newspaper, the *Vieux Carré Courier*. The notice bore the standard conceit about the *Outsider* being the first important literary magazine to be published in New Orleans since the *Double Dealer*, the Webbs' long hours at the press, and their money problems. For all its hand wringing, the story ended with hope for the magazine's future: "The third issue of the *Outsider*, Mr. Webb asserts, is already being printed as issue number two is sold. While he indicated that the going is not exactly smooth, considering the laborious work of editing, typesetting, printing and distribution, the promise is good and there is reason to believe that the *Outsider* may outlive a few life subscribers." Jon and Louise were the only editors listed, the "advisory editors" having been dropped from the masthead. Louise's drawing of two Royal Street buildings dominated the title page. Beneath her illustration was a legend speaking of the *Outsider*'s place in the continuity of New Orleans's literary life. "In building on left[,] above[,] the renowned DOUBLE DEALER, which helped introduce Hemingway, Faulkner & Sherwood Anderson to a world unlike today's, was first published in 1921. In building on r., in a room Whitman wrote in, THE OUTSIDER was born in 1961."

As the magazine reached its readers, congratulatory letters began filling the Webbs' mailbox. Burroughs sent congratulations from Paris. On the home front, Bell wrote from Iowa City that this was "another terrific issue." Bell assured Webb that he had heard "nothing but enthusiasm and good words for both issues from all persons I've shown them to, and from those who have subscribed or bought via newsstands as a result of my suggestions." Bell's only complaint was with the postal service in Iowa City, which delivered his copies in poor condition. Jon doubtless took pleasure in a note he received from the editor of *The Raiford Record*, an inmate-produced magazine at the Florida State Prison, seeking to initiate a regular issue exchange.

"There are many men in this institution who have a desire to write for free-world publications; some have already had the good fortune of being published. Needless to say, the self-respect and dignity these rare instances engender in the rest of the would-be-writers here is something to encourage." Jon agreed. He sent them issue two straight away.

As always, Jon and Louise wanted the next issue to be their best yet. To this end, they came up with an idea to bestow an annual Outsider of the Year award to a deserving poet. The award would be done in high style, comprise several pages of accolades, and serve as an anchor for the issue. They hoped it would generate excitement for the magazine and perhaps give the recipient's career a boost. The first award, they decided, should go to Bukowski.

❖ 6 ❖

A FOCUS ON BUKOWSKI

BUKOWSKI'S FIRST KNOWLEDGE of the Outsider of the Year award came in mid-September 1962, and it was an honor like nothing he had ever known. Never one to hide his emotions in his letters, Bukowski apparently had been giving in to his darker impulses in correspondence with Jon. Things seem to have come to a head with Jon's receipt of a "special delivery" of some sort from Bukowski, which made Jon believe that Bukowski was seriously considering suicide. Attempting to help, Jon told Bukowski that suicide "would be pretty stupid." Jon admitted that he had also contemplated suicide, attributing this to the onslaught of "male menopause." Suicide might give license to unscrupulous publishers to rush out inferior collections of "The Best of Bukowski," Jon warned. Bukowski should be more judicious with his death: "Better wait until you've made arrangements for the rights to your estate of poems, and better keep turning them out so the estate will be bigger."

If anything were likely to wash away Bukowski's thoughts of suicide, it was the shining offer Webb made him in this letter: "But this is a quick letter this moment to make last mail here—to say it occurs to me you ought to get our first Outsider Award. We'd been thinking of starting this: declaring at the end of each year our choice of OUTSIDER-OF-THE-YEAR. And since we will come out end of 1962 with issue #3, thinking why not you?" The award was contingent upon Bukowski's acceptance and was to include the publication of several photographs of the poet and some of his letters to Webb. "The issue is tragic-comic on the sardonic side, and believe this would fit with accent on the tragic."

Bukowski accepted. The bulk of his undated acceptance letter was devoted to the story of how he began writing poetry after being near death in a hospital charity ward, only to survive and be thrust back into hard manual labor days after being released. He told of a hospital visit from a drunken Jane Cooney Baker, a chronic alcoholic who was his first true love, and of a young Mexican woman who flirted with him as she changed his bedsheets. Baker was now dead and the young woman was long gone, but the Outsider of the Year award was a balm. "Mr. Webb, to close this thing before it runs into weeks," Bukowski wrote, "I kindly accept your award."

Soon after, Jon telephoned Bukowski in California. During the conversation, which Bukowski cut short out of fear that Jon and Louise could not easily afford to pay their phone bill, Jon told Bukowski some of his plans. He intended to send a photographer to Bukowski's apartment to capture him relaxing and at his typewriter, to ask other little magazine editors for brief tributes to Bukowski, and to highlight Bukowski's checkered past. Assuming Jon meant for him to ask the editors for their comments, Bukowski made it clear in an undated letter that he was uncomfortable with the idea of personally contacting the other editors, but was fine with Jon putting the spotlight on his past and its place in his growing reputation. Bukowski claimed not to understand, though, how the gritty life he had led could be the basis for what Jon apparently called a legend. "I don't worry about legends. The judge didn't know I was a legend. Neither did the cops who arrested me. The landlady doesn't know I am a legend. She wants the rent. My car doesn't know either. It wouldn't start when I got in it today." Such protestation aside, Bukowski assured Jon he considered this award to be a high point in his life. Being named "Outsider of the Year" was something to cherish, though he doubted that it would change his fate: "I can see myself looking at this magazine in years to come, say in some small room, myself very old, feeble, sipping on a small glass of port wine, come home from my dishwasher job, and maybe some old woman across from me, and myself saying, 'See, Helen, that's me, By God, YES, I was ALIVE ONCE, old woman!' And she will say, 'Will you please put that magazine away? You've shown it to me a thousand times!'"

In another letter, Bukowski commented on Jon's plans for testimonials from magazine editors and a proposed critical article from Corrington. In a section from this letter, which Webb used to help introduce the Outsider award in issue three, Bukowski admitted that testimonials from twenty editors would be wonderful, but he knew some people would second-guess his selection: "Some will say . . . why that fuckoff Bukowski? There may well be somebody dying of cancer and writing immortal poems on the backs of pieplates with charcoal. Who the hell knows? Then there's always Patchen, a great writer and artist, who is smashed everyday, not by the bottle and foolishness and madness as I am smashed, but by something he cannot control. Then, there's W. and then there's X. and then there's M. in New Haven, and don't forget G. Still, I feel pretty much OUTSIDE, as about as OUTSIDE as you can get." Bukowski began the letter with a litany of his personal troubles: "Bad weekend. Face cut. Suit ripped and torn. Knee smashed. Horses sour. Money gone. Back to bottom." He closed it with the admonition that "the act of creation is still the important thing," and that preparations for the award were intruding upon his creative life: "with all the g.d. photographs I have written less than a snail."

It was Corrington's idea to include a critical article on Bukowski as part of the award. After he had completed a draft, he assured Jon the piece was "damned good," dealing with "the theme of damnation and escape" in three of Bukowski's poems, "The Tragedy of the Leaves," "The Priest and the Matador," and "Old Man, Dead in a Room." Corrington wrote that he had composed the article for his own purposes, mainly "to see if I can still make the critical bit." Less than a week later, Corrington submitted a complete draft. This version was somewhat shorter than the original ten pages he had promised, because he had cut discussion of "Old Man, Dead in a Room." Corrington suggested this would be the first truly scholarly examination of Bukowski's poetry to appear in print, an earlier essay by R. R. Cuscaden notwithstanding. While Corrington dismissed Cuscaden's earlier article as being "too general," he insisted his own would be of real value. "It might, I hope, be the beginning of a serious examination of Chas' work. Therefore it seems to fit your tribute to Chas." Corrington had seen proofs of the *Outsider* three by this time, and mentioned an eviction notice Bukowski had sent in lieu of a particularly memorable rejection slip, which Jon had requested. Corrington noted that the eviction notice was part of a pattern in Bukowski's work that revolved around landladies. "I want to do a Buk article on THE POET AND THE LANDLADY. Chas has a fixation on landladies. They appear over and over again. Like snakes or guns or falling from high places."

By early December, Corrington had revised his article and reinstated his discussion of "Old Man, Dead in a Room." He wrote Jon that Bukowski had not only endorsed the idea of the article, but he had also offered an epigram to accompany it in the *Outsider.* " 'Old Man, Dead in a Room' is my future, 'The Tragedy of the Leaves' is my past, and the 'Priest and the Matador' is a dawdling in between." Corrington was so eager to do Bukowski justice that he became overwhelmed. "This is the first time I've had so much to say that I get lost trying to shape it up," he told Jon. "Buk is so there that you keep remembering things that need saying and that of course you'll not have room for. We must make an outline of things that have to be said." Corrington saw Bukowski as representative of a tradition of literary outsiders stretching back to Villon and Rimbaud: "I may lean on that 'outlaw' tradition, because the almost prophetic quality of Buk (which has not the hysterical mutterings of Ginsberg) fits well with his ancestors: men who knew the world from having seen it through the portal of its asshole. BUT, unlike Ginsberg, again, Chas does not blame classes and institutions and the rest. (Unlike Rexroth, too) Buk does not know who or what is to blame for the agony; he suspects that, in Hemingway's phrase, 'there are no remedies for anything in this life.' And he lives and writes with the strength and grace of a condemned man who is too large to try to buy his freedom by fingering someone else, or share the agony by spreading it to others."

To Corrington's eye, Bukowski's best work showed that art was the only hedge against doom: "The final cheap room opens, through its door, into the same dark hall where the landlady and matador, priest and penniless tenant move in the unending rite of their doom. But there is another way out. The passage lies somewhere between pen and paper and the escape consists in creating an artifact, a substance, an illimitable fabric richer and more meaningful than the life from which it has been spun."

Corrington and Jon's efforts delighted Bukowski, and he took pains to convey this to Jon: "That Willie would bother to write about my work is good enough, however, and shows a selfless, clean gesture on his part. That someone writes about me as a poet, it's a lift, especially on morning like this . . . when I am beaten, bereft and worn." As good as all this was, Jon soon had even better news for Bukowski: Loujon wished to publish a substantial book of his poetry. Bukowski, of course, was delighted.

Jon planned a hands-on approach to all phases of this project, down to helping choose its title, though Bukowski resisted his title suggestions. Bukowski specifically did not like "Naked in the Womb," which Jon had at one time considered naming "Go Lieth Down South, Oh Lover," his own unfinished novel, nor did he respond well to a title which played off of the prison Alcatraz. Bukowski was toying with titles such as "Beer and Frog Legs"; "I Can't Stand the Sunshine When People Walk Around in It"; "For Jocks, Chambermaids, Thieves and Bassoon Players"; "Tonic for the Mole"; and "Minstrels Would Go Crazy Singing This." He was searching for the perfect title and told Webb, "I will strictly be dreaming titles from here on in." The dreaming lasted only one more day: "Another letter, but, I think, a necessary one. I have been walking around thinking of titles and either letting my head work with it, and when only slices there, listening to conversations or reading newspaper headlines and articles, then going back to titles, mostly to self and writing them down and then crossing them out. Then, by chance, tiring or what, I picked up an old collection of Jeffers and began reading and then . . . there was the title—at least for me: IT CATCHES MY HEART IN ITS HANDS (selected poems 1955–1963)." The title was a paraphrase from "Hellenistics," a long poem by Robinson Jeffers, the California poet Bukowski often credited as a primary influence. Bukowski was careful to note that Jon and Louise were "the editor and the editoress" and that he would defer to their judgment if they found the title unsuitable. He acknowledged, also, that a title such as this carried weight. "I realize this is a serious title, but some of my work is serious in its way, and even when I affect the comic . . . hell, I would say it fits. You know my work. I won't try to pressure you."

Bukowski was also concerned with how his tribute section in the *Outsider* would turn out and how it would be received. He worried that the photographs of him were not especially flattering, and that unhappy readers might complain about his star treatment. But he knew how important all of this might be to his career and continued to show his gratitude, and in more tangible ways than before. He promised to send "50 bucks Thursday or Friday unless I get run over by a truck and killed." The money was a gift, with Bukowski hoping that it would take "a little of the pressure off the book."

Corrington wanted to write an introduction to the book, and Webb quickly agreed. Corrington maintained his fast-paced correspondence with both Bukowski and Webb, and kept Webb abreast of Bukowski's feelings about the book. "Several letters from Chas; he is in good shape and excited about book (naturally) says he's glad I'm to do intro: he must figure youth and small reputation offset by depth of friendship. He figures right." Corrington was also helping choose poems for the book. The plan was to select Bukowski's strongest work written over the past eight years, when he had begun placing poems in little magazines. There was a great deal of poetry from which to select. Ever the scholar, Corrington kept everything he received from Bukowski. His personal archive, which included dozens of old magazines and many letters from Bukowski, came in handy as the book began taking shape. Some of the poems Corrington thought deserved consideration were from Bukowski's letters: "I'm sure they're off the cuff and might have gotten dumped in garbage except I hold on to all things of value like a packrat. I reckon you've already gone through your letters looking for such? I expect that between us we have the bulk of this kind of thing— thank God. I get shakey when I think of the poems he's mailed out without keeping copies and then never gotten back from some stinking rag. OLD MAN, DEAD IN A ROOM could have gone that way. That we lost some Greek tragedies I have finally gotten used to, but to lose stuff of value to-day is grotesque."

Corrington eventually read every available Bukowski poem and agonized over which ones should be included in the book. "I had to grit teeth to junk many: all had interest even when not good." Corrington soon wrote again, this time commenting on Bukowski's growing reputation in the scholarly community, where people were complaining that Bukowski's work was not easily available. He assured Webb that, on his own, he could sell ten copies of *It Catches My Heart in Its Hands* and jokingly suggested the alternate title "The Potable Bukowski," playing on Bukowski's well-earned reputation as a heavy drinker and on books such as Viking's *The Portable Faulkner* and *The Portable Hemingway*.

By January 28, Webb had approved Corrington's introduction, "Charles Bukowski at Mid-Flight." Preproduction was well under way and, as usual, Webb pushed himself hard enough to worry those around him. Corrington wrote Webb that he felt "good about both #3 and the Chas. book," adding, "If you don't put yourself in the hospital or in the ground, you've got it made." As for Bukowski, Corrington believed the attention helped "when he gets butcher knife moods." Not everyone agreed. Jory Sherman warned Webb that the attention Loujon was paying Bukowski might be bad for him. Corrington countered that, even if Sherman were right, he "could be so neurotically pissed that he can't restrain himself. I think he believes what he wrote you. But that cuts no ice." Corrington believed Bukowski's writing was his anchor and that he benefited from knowing that Corrington and Webb thought his work important. "If that destroys him, I guess it will have to. Men have been wrecked by love, by hate, by envy, by autos. But we all end wrecked and dead."

In fact, Bukowski seemed energized in the months leading up to publication. His zeal for the project extended to contacting friends in an attempt to sell copies. In early July 1963, Bukowski wrote Sherri Martinelli, editor of the mimeographed *Anagogic & Paideumic Review* to update her on the project and nudge her toward buying a copy of the two-dollar book. Bukowski had seen a dummy copy and was effusive about Webb's craftsmanship: "[E]ven without the poems the book would be worth 2$ because of the paper and the way he's hung it together, the design, the love, the taste of good steak and avocado, he has put his gut into the work and it is like a bell ringing or water running or stretching out on the bed and looking up at the ceiling." When Martinelli received her copy a few months later, she was equally impressed: "Gotcher book & you must be unconscious with love—it is a bewt, babe & I thank you with my heart."

The general excitement surrounding *It Catches My Heart in Its Hands* did not mean that Jon could ignore the new issue of the *Outsider*, which was still in press and already causing a stir. A member of a Greenwich Village literary group wrote to say that the last issue had gotten the group so excited that they had been "talking it up all over the place." This would-be editor was trying to start a magazine called *Reject* and looked to the *Outsider* as her exemplar. She hoped Jon would give her some tips. Elsewhere in the underground landscape, the *Censored Review* came into being, as did *Wild Dog* and *City Lights Journal*. In Cleveland, Jon and Louise's hometown, a young poet named Darryl Allen Levy, who went by the pen name "d. a. levy," bought a letterpress and began publishing books and the magazine *Renegade*. Jon barely had time to notice any of this, his attention focused sharply on getting out his own magazine. Four days before Louise set the last page of the *Outsider* three, Corrington wrote Bukowski, whose face was to appear on the cover, with an update on the magazine's progress: "Still sweating OUTSIDER #3 with the son of Frankenstein on the cover. Man those cow eyes of yours. To look, nobody would know you're the mad rapist. You will be a full fledged celebrity when it comes out. I will write an essay comparing you to Frost & Sandburg, drawing conclusion that you are worthy to follow in their footsteps."

Beneath Corrington's enthusiasm lay the hint that production was moving slowly. Jon had planned to publish issue three on or about January 1, 1963, but by February 7, there were still at least fifteen pages left to typeset and print. If the pages were set in numerical order, this number was significantly higher, as Jon's update on the printing schedule appeared on page 96, and the issue finally appeared at a hefty 138 pages. Regardless, another full month of production work lay ahead before the issue was completed.

On March 6, page 138 was finally set and all that remained were the pages of contributors' notes. Jon took an ad in the *Village Voice* to announce the new issue. The ad contained a list of all contributors and touted a special "27 pages on the poet who received The Outsider's 1st Annual Outsider-of-the-Year Award," without giving away who the winner was. In the list of contributors, one name was misspelled: Bukowski became Bukawski.

If Jon had found his voice in issue two's Editor's Bit, in issue three that voice became more eloquent. In essence, this Editor's Bit was a continuation of the column in issue two, building upon the themes introduced there. He wasted no time in getting to the point. "We need help, and on bended knee, compositor's stick in hand composing as we handset this ragged typeface into spontaneous (& dizzily tired) articulation, we're about to beg some." Jon wrote of his now-abandoned goal to publish the *Outsider* as a quarterly, scuttled because there simply wasn't enough money to do it. The revised plan called for the magazine, in its current format, to fold. It would be replaced by a "Biannual Book Periodical," which would sell for $1.45 per copy, rather than the $1.00 per copy price for issues one through three. Subscriptions would increase to five dollars for four issues. Jon admitted that raising prices was risky and even that the end result would not be more profit, "just less loss." He reminded readers that he and Louise did all of the production work and claimed the job was better suited to a staff of between five and twenty workers. With just the two of them doing everything, each worked between twelve and sixteen hours a day. Jon typically remained on his feet for ten-hour shifts, feeding pages into the press. He was exhausted and suffering dizzy spells.

He again wrote of Louise's role as breadwinner via her Pirate's Alley art shop, but described her work in much darker terms than before. Since they had no patrons or grants to rely on, their "only survival income (we haven't a cent in reserve) is from a small sidewalk art gallery (surrounded by competitors) selling $1 to $3 souvenir French Quarter scenes to tourists. Gypsy, who paints them, goes out each morning at 8:30, 7 days a week, to this outside job, in zero cold in the winter and 100-degree heat in the summer, sometimes netting as low as 50 cents in the nine to 14 hours she stays there; then home to hand-set type for me to make into a page for next day's printing— often going to bed at two or three in the morning." It was practically impossible to survive on Louise's income from her paintings, and publishing a magazine to Jon's exacting specifications was expensive. The first *Out-*

sider ended up five hundred dollars in the red. To make up the difference, they began selling their belongings. Jon described these things as jewelry, hi-fi equipment, cameras, and other luxury items they had acquired when he was making money with his writing. They sold more of their possessions to help finance the second issue, and were helped by strong subscription and newsstand sales. For issue three, "the toughest" one yet to finance, "We had to part with everything negotiable (or so we thought) left in the house. . . ." Jon admitted that, even with the price increases, Loujon stood to lose about two hundred dollars on issue three, which he concluded was "not bad at all." But there was no money left to begin work on issue four: "Number 2 brought in another heap of university subs, and a few more Life Subscribers, but that incoming cash went out for bills fast as it came in." He asked readers to help any way they could, from buying extra issues or subscribing to making outright contributions.

Jon's declarations of poverty aside, the new issue generated tremendous excitement. The little magazine community came together in force to honor Bukowski as "Outsider of the Year." Editors from twenty magazines, including Margaret Randall of *Plumed Horn*, Marvin Malone and A. Taylor of *Wormwood Review*, and James Boyer May of *Trace*, sent congratulations. Either because of Jon's exacting editorial standards or because of a desire to say exactly the right thing, *Renaissance* editor John Bryan appears to have tried at least twice before his comments were finally settled for the tribute. Bryan wrote Jon in mid-October 1962, describing his first meeting with Bukowski. He wrote in detail about the poet's wretched, dirty apartment, his garbage can filled with empty condom wrappers, his medicines to treat athlete's foot, the hemorrhoid cream containers scattered about the room, and the antique plumbing snaking along the walls. All of this, Bryan wrote, left him depressed. The description was leavened with a portrait of Bukowski as a gentle, generous man, eager to share his poetry and beer. Bryan's published tribute is much different. The lowlife imagery is replaced with a brief note built around the idea of Bukowski as prolific poet unconcerned with the details of the publishing business. Beginning with the congratulatory words "Most tickled to hear of OUTSIDER'S award to Outsider Bukowski," the tribute concluded with a prediction for the poet's longevity. Bryan wrote, "[W]e here think he's going to out-burn most of the magazines who've published him, and those who are going to before and after he kicks off."

These endorsements were solicited, but spontaneous praise came from

Left: Jon Webb at work, 1950s. Photo courtesy of Jon Webb, Jr.

Below: 638 Royal ("the skyscraper"). This house is one of the most important landmarks of New Orleans's Spanish Colonial Period. The Webbs lived here in the late 1950s and early 1960s. Photo courtesy of Ed Blair.

Above: Lou Webb at 638
Royal, New Orleans,
printing the *Outsider*
one. Photo courtesy of
Ed Blair.

Right: John William "Bill"
Corrington, c. 1960.
Photo courtesy of Joyce
Corrington.

Above: Jon Webb in New
Orleans. Photo courtesy
of Jon Webb, Jr.

Right: 1109 Royal Street.
The Webbs lived here
from May 1964 to June
1965.

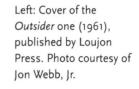

Left: Cover of the *Outsider* one (1961), published by Loujon Press. Photo courtesy of Jon Webb, Jr.

Above: Lou and Jon Webb in Las Vegas, Nevada. Photo courtesy of Ed Blair.

Right: Jon and Lou Webb in the studio of 1109 Royal, New Orleans. Photo courtesy of Ed Blair.

Above: Ed Blair and Jon Webb at 1109 Royal. Photo courtesy of Ed Blair.

Below: Lou Webb, Ed Blair, and Jon Webb at typesetter Wally Shore's home and studio, New Orleans. Photo courtesy of Ed Blair.

Above: Lou and Jon Webb
read bindery pages of the
Outsider. Photo courtesy
of the *Tucson Daily Citizen*.

Right: Cover of Charles
Bukowski's *It Catches My
Heart in Its Hands* (1963),
published by Loujon
Press. The book was the
first major collection of
Bukowski's poems. Photo
courtesy of Jeff Weddle.

Left: Jon Webb and Charles Bukowski. Photo courtesy of Ed Blair.

Right: Jon Webb and Charles Bukowski in Santa Fe, New Mexico, October 1965. Photo courtesy of Ed Blair.

Left: Charles Bukowski and Lou Webb reviewing a copy of Bukowski's *It Catches My Heart in Its Hands*, published by Loujon Press. Photo courtesy of Ed Blair.

Above: Charles Bukowski and Lou Webb in Tucson, Arizona, July 1967. Photos courtesy of Ed Blair.

Left: Charles Bukowski and Lou Webb. Photo courtesy of Ed Blair.

Lou Webb at the New Orleans School of Glassworks, making "Two for Jon" print, 2001. Photo courtesy of Ed Blair.

readers such as Diane Wakoski, then a little-known New York City poet struggling to make a name for herself. Wakoski had kept a running correspondence with Jon as she tried to interest him in publishing her poetry. Her poem "The First Day" finally broke through in issue three and Wakoski wrote to congratulate Jon for the new issue. After comparing his "beautiful, fat magazine" favorably with *Trobar* and *Nomad*, which she called "the best on the scene," Wakoski turned her attention to the Bukowski tribute: "I was also surprised and pleased to see such a spread on Bukowski. He is making it this year—and well deserves to." Wakoski admitted she had once sent Bukowski a fan letter. "Sometimes his work is inexpressibly vulgar and I do not like it then. But despite this, when he writes about his experiences (especially with love) a kind of pure, almost ballad-like tone is set and he achieves beautiful moments. There is something fresh about his poems."

Harold Norse sent his congratulations from Paris. He praised the new issue, especially the Bukowski section: "The real kick of the issue is Bukowski—whose letters get me right in the pit of the stomach, even more than his poems. He comes on powerfully, the martyred poet in isolation (how I identify with that!), and writes damn well of his personal trials & tribulations." Apparently as an afterthought, Norse decided to make a pitch for Webb to consider him as Loujon's next great discovery. In a handwritten note scrawled along the margin of his typed letter, Norse wrote: "The Bukowski story can only be matched eventually by the Norse story. I'm the OUTSIDER of all time, the way I feel." Norse wrote that he had several book-length manuscripts, which he would be happy to send Webb for his consideration. Unfortunately for Norse, Webb's plate was full and he had other ideas for future projects. Specifically, he remained interested in publishing Kenneth Patchen.

Though Bukowski was the star of the new *Outsider*, Patchen was present, both in the reference by Bukowski and through material supplied by him and Miriam. Bukowski's acknowledgment of Patchen's literary status and health problems was powerful in its own right. More powerful still was a series of six letters from Miriam which accompanied an original painting poem by her husband. The text of Patchen's poem, handwritten over a background which included an elephantine creature standing before a flower and beneath what appears to be the sun, read: "What do you say / we let it shine / for a bit longer." In contrast to this allusive, hopeful poem, Miriam's letters were direct and dark. She wrote of the terrible pain Kenneth suffered from his back trouble and the dead ends the couple had reached in trying to get him medical treatment. The last letter in the set contained a grim hope: "How we're going to get out of this punitive action against us, just because some doctor made a mistake, I can't figure. We're stuck, I guess. It's most frustrating to feel stupidly useless. Kenneth's been in hellish pain for weeks— we're just worn out. There'll be a *day* though." As in issue two, publication of the letters was transparently calculated to elicit sympathy and financial help from readers of the magazine. The ploy worked. Miriam later wrote Jon that the *Outsider*'s help had produced "a sweetening of the pot."

Only marginally better off than the Patchens, Jon and Louise struggled to keep their business afloat. Producing the magazine was a continuous battle. There was Loujon's chronic cash flow problem, and the policy of paying for each element of production as it arose, so there would be no debt on a particular issue when it was eventually published. Then there was Loujon's one-page-at-a-time Chandler and Price printing press and the enormous demands in sheer physical labor required to design, typeset, print, and collate the magazine once all of the submissions were received, evaluated, accepted, or rejected. Things always took longer than it seemed they might, but finally the issue was finished. Jon put aside a copy and inscribed it to Louise, his "angel co-editor & backbone."

As difficult as it was to produce, issue three, published in spring 1963, is beyond question the most famous number. Even from a casual glance, there was no mistaking that this was Bukowski's issue. Unlike issues one and two, which featured cover photographs of Louise, this sported a close-up of Bukowski, "cow eyes" and all. Bukowski's tribute was the centerpiece of the issue, but otherwise the *Outsider* was much like the two earlier issues. The poets continued to be literary outsiders; many, however, were becoming familiar to readers of the magazine and, indeed, to readers of many other literary magazines. Among the thirty-three contributors were Robert Creeley, Kenneth and Miriam Patchen, Kaja, Genet, Norse, Miller, Snyder, Mike McClure, Diane Wakoski, and, of course, Bukowski.

This issue contained the only literary feud in which the *Outsider* ever indulged, as Jon published Creeley's work, but also took this opportunity to attack him. Referring to a letter of Creeley's he published in the issue, Jon wrote that Creeley had insinuated that the magazine was falsely advertising a "new" type of poetry in its pages. Jon declared that "new" as it applied to poetry in the *Outsider* meant poetry that was freshly written, as opposed to poetry of a new school. For Jon, the main criterion for good poetry lay not in its adherence to emerging styles or technique, but simply in his personal reaction to it. In other words, if Jon liked a poem, he took it. Jon considered Creeley's comments not only wrong, but also boorishly elitist. Jon attacked Creeley for almost a full page, referring to him repeatedly as a snob or as a member of a "snob-clique," probably meaning the Black Mountain group. Jon chose to single out Creeley for his strongest venom, but lumped Cid Corman, Paul Blackburn, Ron Loewinsohn, and Denise Levertov in with him as "clique-elected greats" who had criticized the *Outsider* for publishing lesser talents along with first-rate work. Creeley was not amused and sent a scathing reply: "You are free to misunderstand me again, and again—which I cannot, of course, do more than object to, as now. But another time I wish you would pay me the simple courtesy of being open in your own feelings and of not asking me to contribute to a magazine where I am present only to be misread by you and to serve as that punching bag for your splenetic assumptions."

The seeds of Jon's attack may have been planted during correspondence with Corrington, who had no love for the Black Mountain poets, particularly Creeley and Levertov. Corrington told Webb that he had already written articles criticizing the two: "Well, if we are going to take on the Black Mountain and all its rocks, I guess I'm ahead of you. The Denise Levertov critique in the next MIDWEST is pretty rough; and the Creeley thing in NORTHWEST REV. is a hard bit, too. In both cases, criticism is easy to sustain: neither of these people are talented writers. They are better, surely, than the amateurs like Sherman, Hedley, etc. But they do not make it up against the best of Ferlinghetti or Corso—not to mention Buk."

Echoing the language Jon would use to criticize Creeley and the others in the *Outsider* three, Corrington suggested that engaging in a critical battle with the "cliques" posed no great danger: "The worst they can do is keep you out, and since I don't want in, what's to lose? I've got fine relations with a dozen editors of honest magazines, and that's all anyone needs." Corrington shared all of this with Bukowski, assuming a southern drawl as he assured Bukowski that "Jon is ready to take on the shitkickers. He got some crud notes defending Creeley, but they were very few and I reckon he can weather them. They all come from Yankees anyhow, and we don't none of us set no store by that kind of opinion." One such note came from Gary Snyder, who wrote that he could see no justification for the attack. Snyder cautioned Webb that "Editors, etc. should avoid creating antagonisms and schisms where they needn't exist, or there will never be any hope of a 'community of poets.'"

The Webbs were not especially interested in the abstract "community of poets" that Snyder suggested. They were more concerned with their own work and with publishing the best writing they could find. To this end, they maintained their correspondence with the Patchens. Many of these letters, especially those from Miriam, dealt with Kenneth's affliction. In a memorable letter of July 1963, Miriam wrote of a lawsuit Kenneth had brought against the physician he believed responsible for his condition. To their horror, the suit had been dismissed. This "cause of the pogrom against the Patchens . . . ignominiously concluded without Kenneth's having had a chance to be able to do at least the one thing for which he was willing almost to be killed: confront them with their lies. 'Our lawyers' postponed his appearance for several days, then called him for a Friday afternoon. This meant getting a registered nurse, ambulance gurney, wheel chair and getting to a doctor who was willing to tape his back to give some support. When we got to the doctor's, half-way to San Francisco, eighteen miles, there was a message from 'our' lawyers that we were to return, that Kenneth would be called 'sometime next week.'" Legal fees cost the Patchens the hefty sum of seventy-two dollars a day. After the judge dismissed the case, ruling that Patchen—finally called to testify—hadn't proven his allegations, Miriam ruefully noted that it cost the Patchens their daily seventy-two dollars for the jury to hear the dismissal.

Jon, deep into production of *It Catches My Heart in Its Hands*, was unable to craft an immediate response to Miriam's letter. He and Louise had begun work on the book in June, a hot and steamy month in New Orleans. Rats and exotic bugs provided some annoyance as they worked, but bigger problems came with rainwater seeping into their apartment and ruining stacks of printed pages. Fuses blew, electrical wiring in the walls caught fire twice, and the press broke down repeatedly. The humidity was brutal, causing composition rollers to burst and preventing finished pages from drying. More troubling to Jon, however, was the fact that he was quickly running out of paper and did not have money for enough to finish the book. Help eventually came from an unexpected source, a young oil executive named Edwin Blair.

Blair was a recent Yale graduate when he came to New Orleans in January

1963 as an employee of the Kerr-McGee Oil Company. In the spring of that year, Blair attended a dinner party at the home of Haywood Hillyer, a leader in the Louisiana Republican establishment. Another guest at the party was Ben C. Toledano, a young attorney and former English teacher at the McCauley School, a rigorous preparatory academy in Chattanooga, Tennessee. Toledano was well schooled in modern literature and was friends with writers Cleanth Brooks and Robert Penn Warren, both of whom taught at Yale. The men fell into conversation, and Toledano was delighted to learn of Blair's Yale connection.

Blair had not studied with Brooks or Warren, but he was fascinated with Toledano's stories of these men and a little magazine they founded with a group of friends during their student days at Vanderbilt University in Nashville. The magazine was called the *Fugitive*, and the young men who published it styled themselves the Fugitives. The group had a local connection, as many of the Fugitives had published in the *Double Dealer*. Blair was taken with the idea of the *Double Dealer* and wondered aloud if anything similar were currently being published in New Orleans. Toledano admitted that he knew of a magazine published by a husband and wife in the French Quarter, though this magazine wasn't to his taste. Still, if Blair was interested, Toledano would gladly take him to meet the publishers, Jon and Louise Webb.

About a week later, Toledano and Blair drove to the Quarter and found Louise at her art stand at the corner of Royal and St. Peter, where she sold her paintings and copies of the *Outsider* number three. Blair was charmed by Louise's "wild and colorful regalia," and it wasn't long before he and Toledano asked Louise if a visit with Jon could be arranged. Louise left for a moment to call Jon from a nearby telephone and alert him that company was coming. A few minutes later, the two men found themselves ringing the bell at the carriage entrance to 618 Ursulines, then standing face to face with Jon Webb, who met them at the door.

Jon led Blair and Toledano along a path of plank-covered brick, the three of them careful not to step off and into one of the ubiquitous piles of dog waste that covered much of the floor. The apartment was a disaster, old and unkempt. Much of the room was taken over by the Chandler and Price printing press. As the tour proceeded, Jon kept talking about his current project, a book by a California poet Jon was convinced would achieve great success. The only problem was a lack of money. As things stood, Webb just didn't have the cash to finish the job. Blair thought the book sounded worthwhile, and, since he was in a position to help a little, he told Jon that he would try to do so. Blair and Toledano left soon after and returned to Louise's art stand to say goodbye. They found her in tears: "She told us that she had gotten a call from Jon and that money was on its way to pay for the paper needed to finish the printing of *It Catches My Heart in Its Hands*." Rather than being put off by Jon's presumption, he was delighted. Many years later, Blair admitted that Louise's outburst was a turning point for him. He was hooked. This was the start of a lasting friendship. Blair respected the older man and was moved that Jon always responded to him as an equal. "Jon treated me as a special friend," Blair later wrote.

With the book progressing well, Jon found time to write Miriam in mid-August, telling her that the Patchens' troubles "saddened and keep saddening us." But, with what they were up against, there was little the Webbs could do to help. They were hard at work on "the monumental, the daily tasks, for we're sandwiching in this gorgeous Bukowski book between *Outsider* issues." One thing he could do, though, was offer to publish Kenneth. Jon sent samples of the fine, heavy paper he was using for *It Catches My Heart in Its Hands*. After describing the care and attention to detail with which they were crafting this book, Webb promised to send a dummy copy, which he was sure would delight the Patchens. He was determined that the next Loujon book would be written by Kenneth Patchen, "and we want you and Kenneth to see how we'll do it. A completely new idea in format, we hear, and completely non-profit. That's the trouble. How to pay the author. We're giving Bukowski fifty of the books, which is all he wanted—in fact not even that many, but we insisted. On the second book we plan or hope to give 100 copies to the author, and it would certainly be 100 if only a way could be found to do such a book." Jon understood that Patchen might have other commitments, or might not have material on hand for a new book. Still, "we'd love our next book to be his. A limited edition too of 777 copies. You'd surely be able to get at least 7.50 a copy."

In the same letter, Webb demurred, "But we won't maybe irritate you with talk of a Patchen book right now, for we don't know what the situation is there right now. It's a dream which only you and Kenneth can discuss and think about and let us know." After also broaching the subject of "a big Patchen section" in issue four, Jon asked forgiveness if he were "writing this at a very moment when you couldn't be less interested, with Kenneth perhaps very very ill and all this just nonsense to you. But we are sincere as can be, and love him, both of you, and want to make much bigger show of recognition for Kenneth than was made in #3." Jon and Louise's efforts on behalf of the Patchens did not go unreciprocated. With as tough a spot as the Patchens were in, they wanted to help the Webbs financially, something that the Webbs resisted. Miriam wrote: "You two are appalling! The checks came right back. Don't you dare. Wait till we scream." Miriam wrote that she and Kenneth were "happy about your tremendous plans—will try to do all we can."

Jon had been ambitious with each item he published, but he had bigger plans for Patchen, surpassing what they had done on Bukowski's "Outsider of the Year" tribute. He and Louise were on a fast timetable for the next issue of the magazine. He wrote the Patchens: "We want to be printing #4 by Oct. 1. Months of work there, but we want the #4 our best issue. We figure between 40 and 50 pages in the Kenneth section—if we get the responses we need. And we hope you have an album of photos from early days till now. We plan it as a homage to Kenneth from his creative early days till now. We'll soon let you know how you can help, and you can help a lot on this section, especially with helping us make contacts with writers who might give us a short piece on Kenneth, or just a paragraph or two."

Miriam provided an annotated, five-page, handwritten list of friends and literary acquaintances. Archibald MacLeish was on the list, with the annotation "Knew each other since the late 30's." Miriam suggested Webb contact Lawrence Ferlinghetti, describing him with the note "Bookstore, publisher, reader(!)." She suggested that James Laughlin, whose New Directions had published a number of Patchen's books, might be willing to contribute material. Longtime Patchen friend Mrs. E. E. Cummings was on the list, as was Rexroth, described as an "acquaintance—might be good—sometimes very acute." Jazz great Charles Mingus, Miriam suggested, "might be prevailed upon to write the tale of Charlie Parker's reading aloud Patchen's novel, *The Journal of Albion Moonlight* to a group of jazz musicians." Also included on the list were Malcolm Cowley, James Boyer May, Henry Miller, T. S. Eliot, and others of lesser fame.

Jon set about contacting these people. Ferlinghetti, Cowley, Miller, Mingus, May, and several others sent material. Others did not. Poet James Broughton sent his regrets, noting that he admired Patchen, but had only met him once and thus had nothing personal to contribute. Miller, through his secretary, Gerald Robitaille, wrote that he felt "a block," which kept him from writing anything on Patchen. Miller did give Webb permission to print a section from his previously published "Patchen: Man of Anger and Light," however, in which he called Patchen "the living symbol of protest." A few, such as Laughlin, who pleaded a lack of time, seem to have simply refused. Eliot presented the problem of already being dead.

This was a good time for Loujon. *It Catches My Heart in Its Hands*, after months of hard labor, was almost finished. The Patchen issue seemed assured, and prospects for a Patchen book looked strong. The third *Outsider* was a success, and the Webbs were now book publishers. Letters of praise came from readers across the country, among them John K. Martin, the manager of an office supply company in Los Angeles: "I've had a chance to sit down and read through the several issues of your magazine, and Jon, my feelings go out to you and your good wife. It certainly hasn't been easy for you. But the two of you have managed to accomplish miracles; your magazine, despite the birth pangs, has come forth whole and perfect. Really, every issue is a work of art, and each one a step forward." Martin urged Jon to make a list of supplies, which he would send at no charge. He also wanted to help Loujon's star poet: "By the way, if you think it would help Bukowski out, I'll be very pleased to send him all the paper, envelopes, typewriter ribbons and so forth that he might need. He's a good gutty poet. And deserves a decent living and some recognition from his work. All he has to do is get in touch with me and rattle off a list. I'll see that he gets the supplies he wants."

Jon solicited endorsements for *It Catches My Heart in Its Hands* from the heaviest hitters he could find. Blurbs came in from Lowenfels, Miller, Genet, New Directions editor Roy Miller, Margaret Randall, and others. Genet gushed, "Beau livre, belle poesie!" Ferlinghetti wrote that the book was the "most beautiful printing of poetry I have ever seen in this country." Kenneth and Miriam Patchen offered equally lavish praise: "The book is perfection—looks, job, contents. Tell Bukowski we love his baby."

In a stroke of good fortune, Kenneth Rexroth reviewed the book favorably for the *New York Times Book Review*. The review was marred only by Rexroth's swipe at Loujon: "Charles Bukowski suffers from too good a press—a small but loudly enthusiastic claque. Down in New Orleans, where they publish a magazine called the *Outsider*, the local advance guard seems to consider him the greatest thing since Homer. He is not. However, if you put aside his volunteer public-relations experts, he turns out to be a substantial writer." After placing Bukowski in the "small company of poets of real, not literary, alienation, that includes Herman Spector, Kenneth Fearing, Kenneth Patchen and a large number of Bohemian fugitives unknown to fame," Rexroth moved Bukowski above these others: "His special virtue is that he is so much less sentimental than most of his colleagues." Rexroth went out of his way to suggest Bukowski was a serious artist in a way that escaped the more celebrated Beat poets: "Unlike the beats, he will never become an allowed clown; he is too old now, and too wise, and too quiet. More power to him."

This review was a remarkable event for Loujon and Bukowski. The poet was essentially unknown and only 777 copies of the book were printed. Rexroth's positive review gave standing to Loujon and Bukowski that they might never otherwise have achieved. Blair came across Rexroth's review by chance. He was visiting family in Connecticut and, sitting on the beach, casually picked up a copy of the *New York Times Book Review*. "I couldn't believe it," he said. "I went crazy." Blair understood that very few books get reviewed and the fact that this one did was a small miracle. Jon must have been pleased with the review, but his response to his own work was more primal. As far as he was concerned, the book was "written in blood . . . and printed in blood." Publishing it was an enormous undertaking, but "we've nothing to complain about. The experience was unforgettable, one that could not be bought for gold—nor sold to the devil." Bukowski was ecstatic: "Never such a book! Where? Where?? In all the libraries, in all the cities I have never seen such a book put together in such a way, inventiveness, creativeness, and love. Where have the publishers been for centuries? You've done it." He inscribed a copy to Jon on June 19, 1963, and his gratitude was clear: "To Jon Webb, who makes Mencken, Burnett, and the rest look like rusty shivs in an old alley and who does it the hard way and asks nothing in return but to continue to live in order to create the miracle of the love of his work."

7

MEETING BUKOWSKI

THE WEBBS KEPT AN EYE toward their next project, whatever it might be. Jon hoped to be printing the fourth issue of the *Outsider* by October, with the Patchen section occupying between forty and fifty pages. Even better, Patchen had given his blessing for a Loujon Press book of his work. There were basically two ways to go with a Patchen book. It could either be a fairly standard text, not much different from *It Catches My Heart in Its Hands*, or it could be a far more ambitious collection of painting poems, a form that Patchen had made his own. Jon wanted to do a collection of painting poems. He wrote Miriam that "It'll be great fun working on Patchen book, and we're already visualizing the format—most elegant." Webb intended to use the profits from *It Catches My Heart in Its Hands* to finance the next issue of the magazine, and planned on saving money to use for production of the Patchen book. By November, though, it seemed that Loujon's Patchen plans were finished. Miriam wrote that "Kenneth doesn't want to try to do the book. He doesn't want the Patchen issue—things are bad here and I'm not able to keep things going now. So—I can't say it—after all you've done and hoped—forget it—us etc.—will try to clarify later—but I can't get anywhere with the situation now—forgive." Less than two weeks later, the situation again reversed. A Western Union telegram signed by Patchen contained the brief message, "Full steam ahead on Patchen issue and book our blessings."

A letter from Miriam soon followed, giving a more complete explanation of the recent roller coaster of events. Miriam wrote, "I'm so glad, for I wanted the OUTSIDER to be us and us to be it, but at the time there was nothing to be said or done." Apparently, Patchen's decision to disassociate himself from Loujon had been the result of acute depression caused by a combination of severe pain, a bleak prognosis from his doctors, and Miriam's decision to pursue studies in dental assistance as a hedge against total financial ruin. This combination of events "tore the lid off. Horror set in for Kenneth," wrote Miriam. "However, the main fact of this moment in history is that we are still very interested in THE OUTSIDER and most touched by your willingness to do the Patchen pages, Patchen book. Somehow we will try to pay you for the nasty weeks Kenneth's now-cancelled action caused you. That was about the only thing in the last four years which has made me react angrily against him. Now *we* have it all clear, if you are still willing to have anything to do with us."

On April 26, 1964, Jon telephoned Patchen to discuss details of the tribute. Patchen agreed to sign ninety-nine copies of a page printed in holograph which Jon would tip into the magazine, making the copies collectors' items which Jon could sell for a higher price. He also suggested a theme for the tribute, having well-known writers share their memories of Patchen. Miriam wrote a letter afterward to expand on Kenneth's ideas. She warned that Jon's hope to get material from famous writers and artists might lead to disappointment. The Patchens had never been particularly social, focusing their energies instead on the two basic realities of Kenneth's life: his work and his pain. "The few close friends in the arts from 'way back' are dead: John Wheelwright, Paul Rosenfeld, E. E. Cummings, Kenneth Fearing, Maxwell Bodenheim . . . so many others. We've known most of the others, of course, but only slightly, not as intimately as these." Kenneth, through Miriam, suggested that Jon ask other writers what his body of work meant to them. "Then," Miriam explained, "people who have either/or both friendly relationships to record and/or purely literary ones can do so without artificiality." Miriam promised to explain each person's relationship with Patchen when she provided their contact information. "Personal reminiscences are possible," she wrote, "but not terribly likely from 'names.'" Miriam also worried about the Webbs' demanding work schedule. "No impatience here, just concern about the Webbs driving themselves. Don't push yourselves to an early old age, or to such a weariness that joy becomes too much for the tired being to experience. There's time, it says here."

As time passed, it became clear to Jon that a Patchen book was not going to be easily done. Publishing a collection of Patchen's painting poems would require expensive color plates, and this would take money he did not have. He had developed a taste for book publishing, though, and a compromise between publishing what he wanted to publish and what he could afford to publish was heralded by a new poem from Bukowski called "A Letter from Paris." Jon was so taken with the poem that he decided to publish another collection of Bukowski's work. While no Loujon publication was simple or cheap to produce, another Bukowski book would eliminate most of the thornier problems a Patchen book presented. Of course, Jon could always have dropped the idea of a painting poem collection and pursued a more standard Patchen book, but that would have meant settling for a project he only half wanted to do. Plus, experience proved that it was difficult to get momentum going from the Patchen camp. Bukowski, on the other hand, was eager and appreciative of Jon's attention. He was thrilled when Jon suggested a new book.

Bukowski was quick to share the good news with Corrington. "I have just heard from Jon—ANOTHER BOOK, BABY!! How much luck can one old beero like me have??? They're already planning format and running around for paper and running wild, and it's great, it's hard to believe that while I sit here in Los Angeles kind of like a dumb animal, sullen, dismal, fattening around the middle, they are down there putting me together like a king with reverence and joy and love. You can't ask for a better world." Bukowski's only concern was that, for the new book, there would be less than a year's worth of new poetry from which to choose. *It Catches My Heart in Its Hands* contained his best work, painstakingly selected by Corrington and Jon. Bukowski wanted this book to measure up.

He might also have been concerned with the stability of his publishers if he knew of the manic wanderlust that was about to seize them. Even with a new book in the offing, Jon and Louise were unsettled. They had been relatively stable in New Orleans since returning from their Hollywood adventure more than a decade earlier, but now Louise was getting restless. She had sold her paintings from the same art stand at the corner of Royal and St. Peter streets for thirteen years, talking, by her estimate, to perhaps four million tourists over the years. Louise liked people, but she had had enough. She began coming home at night and taking her frustrations out on Jon. After a doctor told her that moving her stand might make her happier, she and Jon scouted new locations in the Quarter. They came up empty. Their new plan was to leave New Orleans altogether.

They had heard good things about Santa Fe, so after reading up on the history and culture of that city, asked New Orleans Mayor Victor H. Schiro for a letter of introduction to the mayor of Santa Fe. In early May 1964, "We packed our stuff—3,000 pounds of it: mostly manuscripts, books, files and the printing press and type. And sent it all Will Call to Santa Fe by motor freight," Louise recalled. Jon and Louise and their dogs, Gypsy and Lady, shared a berth "and the four of us were both sad and happy as we looked out the window and waved goodbye forever to old New Orleans." Louise wrote that the minute New Orleans was out of sight, "an immense relief came over me—over Jon, too. We'd finally made it—we'd cut the cords binding us to one spot on earth."

The Webbs stayed in Santa Fe about a week before deciding that this wasn't the place for them. Their freight hadn't even made it to town before they knew they were leaving, so it was a simple matter to tell the moving company to return everything to New Orleans. The homecoming lasted about two weeks before Louise again became unhappy with the city, and so they moved again, this time back to Cleveland, where they stayed four days before alerting the moving company once again to turn around and ship their belongings back to New Orleans. On their trip back south, Jon and Louise made stops in Chicago and Memphis, thinking these might be places to settle, but neither city felt right. Their old apartment was no longer available when they returned, so they took a tiny apartment at 1109 Royal Street. But the urge to leave New Orleans was still strong, and soon they were traveling again. They visited Tucson, but didn't like it. On the return trip, they passed through El Paso without stopping. By the time they reached New Orleans, the Webbs were already unhappy that they had not gotten off the train to spend a day in El Paso. They decided to visit El Paso by way of Albuquerque, but after Albuquerque, they went instead to Santa Fe, then to Taos, back to Santa Fe, and finally to Los Angeles for a week with Bukowski before returning to settle back into life in the Quarter. Louise found a corner across the street from where her old art stand had been and, with this small change in scenery, was suddenly happy again. A chatty article she wrote describing their adventures, "Gypsy Lou Lands," made the front page of the local news paper, the *Vieux Carré Courier*. They were probably on the road on June 15, 1964, when Jon gave Louise a card in celebration of their silver wedding anniversary. "I thank God for those 25 years & pray there will be many more, sweetheart wife & angelflower," he wrote. Jon usually printed his own cards to Louise. This time, the card was from American Greetings.

In the midst of their travels, Jon entered into discussions with New York–based publisher Lyle Stuart about forming a partnership based around the *Outsider*. The Webbs would still be responsible for content, design, and printing. Stuart would become publisher, assuming the financial risks for the prestige of publishing a respected literary magazine. Jon was ambivalent about the deal. The partnership would mean that the *Outsider* would continue, in one form or another, but Jon believed that it would likely scare away any potential "angel" inclined to donate a large sum of money, no strings attached. Jon thought he had found a way out of the Lyle Stuart deal when his friend Jim Roman floated the idea of a foundation to support, but not interfere with, his work. Jon was quick to respond. "I wish you'd quickly as possible let me know what the chances are of your bringing in some investors on an *Outsider* Foundation, and how soon it could be done. I feel I'd rather work with you than with Stuart," he wrote. But a foundation wouldn't necessarily spell the end of Loujon's troubles, and Jon needed to know how Roman's plan might work. "Would a foundation give Lou and me a decent salary, or would it be a lump sum to work with? I know there'd have to be books, and I wouldn't mind; we'd keep them for the record—but we'd have to have survival money, and the costs of producing, plus some things like a cutter and maybe a better press."

Time was against Jon. By the time he learned of Roman's foundation idea he had already sent Stuart two potential scenarios for a partnership. If Stuart agreed to one of these arrangements, Jon felt obliged to sign the deal. In that case, any hope for a foundation would vanish. One of Jon's proposed arrangements called for the *Outsider* to remain in publication essentially as before, but with a definite biannual publishing schedule instead of Jon's dreamed-of quarterly schedule. The other was for "an annual—a documentary annual of contemporary poetry & prose—from existing schools and cliques of writing, favoring no one clique." Jon remained convinced that the magazines focused on a particular "clique" tended to fail quickly because it was impossible for them to maintain a steady supply of quality submissions.

It is ironic, then, that they were in the early going of a project which would make them best known for publishing nothing so broad as a clique, but rather a single person: Charles Bukowski. The reason for the Webbs' Los Angeles visit at the end of their whirlwind moving spree was to finally meet Bukowski. Bukowski's companion, Frances Smith, was expecting their baby in September, and, after a series of letters and telephone conversations, all agreed the Webbs should visit before the baby arrived. Jon and Louise arrived in Los Angeles on August 22 and took a room in the Crown Hill Hotel, the same flophouse where they had lived years before while Jon pursued his dream of Hollywood success. Now he was following a new dream and Bukowski was currently at its center. The couples got along well and, as they had done in many of their stops along the way, the Webbs briefly considered moving to Los Angeles. After five days of drinking, late night storytelling, and bonding, Jon and Louise left for New Orleans, convinced that a new Bukowski book was the correct decision, and they commenced production right away. They financed this book through a deal with Stuart. Roman's foundation idea had not worked out, and there was no other way to begin a new project. Jon could live with the deal because they made it a one-shot affair, leaving Loujon free to accept the help of anyone—foundation or otherwise—who might wish to donate money. It also meant that far more copies of this book could be printed than were of *It Catches My Heart in Its Hands*. Jon chose the title, *Crucifix in a Deathhand*, from one of the poems in the collection.

Marina Louise Bukowski, her middle name in honor of Louise Webb, was born on September 7, 1964, and joined her parents in their small De Longpre Avenue apartment. The demands of family life and his hated job at the post office took their toll on Bukowski. His writing became more sporadic. Both he and the Webbs worried that this might bode ill for the new book, and, after repeated letters and telephone calls between Los Angeles and New Orleans, Bukowski decided to pay Jon and Louise a visit. There was no room for him in their cramped apartment, especially now, as every available space was covered with pages from *Crucifix in a Deathhand*. Even the bathtub was filled with pages, prompting Bukowski to ask Louise how they bathed. "Sponge baths!" she answered.

Jon and Louise arranged for Bukowski to stay with their friend Minnie Segate, owner of the Cajun Kitchen restaurant in the Quarter. Minnie gave Bukowski his own room and cooked his meals. It was a chance for him to write in peace, and he began taking a sheaf of poems to Jon each day. Jon accepted some, rejected others. Louise later remembered Bukowski saying to her, "He sure is tough on me!" Another time, frustrated with the growing stacks of pages, Louise got angry and complained about the clutter and about Bukowski himself sitting in her home drinking beer. "I hate the son of a bitch," she screamed. But this was from frustration, exhaustion, and the claustrophobia of living in a home filled to bursting. There were no lasting hard feelings. The stacked pages were tangible evidence of Jon's fierce dedication to this book. Aside from Bukowski, he eventually cut off all outside visitors except Ed Blair and Marcus Grapes, a Tulane undergraduate and developing poet who had recently begun dropping by for talks with Jon and critiques of his poems. Both men had set times when they could visit. "I don't know when Grapes was allowed to come but my visiting hours were late Sunday afternoon. This was the only day he told me he allowed himself to have a beer," Blair later recalled.

One evening, Jon asked Lou to buy some beer because Bukowski was coming by. She soon returned with twelve cans of Bukowski's favorite, Miller High Life. When Bukowski arrived, it was with a sheath of poems, and Jon, on doctor's orders not to drink, wanted to go to work on them right away. He suggested that Louise and Bukowski drink a beer in the kitchen while he worked. This suggestion was fine with Bukowski. He liked Jon and admired his dedication and skill, but he preferred Louise. Jon was filled with nervous energy, and Bukowski thought him flighty. He also thought Jon sometimes purposely made him angry, just to see what sort of man he really was. But there was none of that with Louise. Bukowski believed there were no games with Louise. She was a natural. The two of them settled themselves around the kitchen table and each opened a beer.

They drank and talked and enjoyed the evening. By the time Jon returned, Bukowski and Louise had finished all twelve beers and Louise had matched Bukowski drink for drink. Bukowski seemed unaffected by the beer, but Louise, not a heavy drinker, was very drunk. She excused herself, telling Jon she needed to lie down. Jon and Bukowski helped Louise into bed where she quickly passed out. The two men fell into conversation and time passed. When it became late enough for dinner, Jon tried to wake Louise, but to no avail. To his horror, it appeared she was having trouble breathing. Jon and Bukowski pulled Louise out of bed and managed to get her into a taxi and to Charity Hospital, where she remained through the night. Fortunately, Louise was fine the next day and ready to go home.

There was more excitement during Bukowski's stay in New Orleans. One memorable night, he and Corrington finally met face to face at a party at the Webbs' apartment. Two years earlier, a drunken Bukowski had telephoned Corrington and invited himself for a visit, to which Corrington had quickly agreed. A day or two later Bukowski, contrite, wrote to apologize for the call: "You needn't worry about my knocking on your door in Baton Rouge. This was simply more of my vague buffoonery. Yet I am touched with your response of welcome. Southern hospitality among the living is not yet dead." Bukowski was not especially sociable, anyway. He saw himself as withdrawn and introverted, often with nothing to say; a cross-country trip for a social visit was out of the question. Corrington perceived Bukowski's remarks as suggesting the invitation was made from a sense of obligation. He would have none of this: "You are a raft of mistakes: Neither Joyce nor I are hospitable from a sense of obligation. We want you to come here if you are within a crawl or a gallop of BR. It is not necessary to talk. I get a bellyful of that. You could sit and drink beer and watch my baby boy drooling on the floor and crawling through it, leaving a path like a demented and outsize snail."

In the fall of 1964, the Corringtons were newly back from England, where Bill had completed his Ph.D. Soon after their return to New Orleans, Bukowski sent a letter of congratulations with the salutation "Dear Dr. Corrington," and went on to praise Corrington's new poetry collection, *The Anatomy of Love*. He had written a good review of the book for *Chat Noir* and was convinced that the novel Corrington was finishing "sounds rife with fresh delights." The Webbs' party was a chance, finally, for the two men to go beyond the camaraderie of letters and see one another as men. One of the Corrington children was ill that evening, so Joyce didn't come for the visit. In her place, Corrington brought a teaching colleague and fellow poet, Miller Williams. Corrington was excited about finally meeting Bukowski and wore a jacket and tie as signs of respect. When Corrington and Williams arrived, they were met by Jon, Bukowski, Ed Blair, and Ben C. Toledano. Blair later recalled that Corrington talked a great deal, but Bukowski was quiet: "I was in awe of Bukowski. I talked a bit about the races at Fair Grounds with him. We both liked the chances of Dapper Delegate to move on to Derby. I know I was intimidated by the crowd. I recall no arguments or feuding while I was there. After an hour or so I left with Ben C. and I believe the others stayed. Bukowski's reaction to the meeting was lasting. With the academic talk I'm sure Hank [Bukowski's nickname] went into a shell and someone like Williams or Corrington would not have necessarily noticed his feelings."

In letters Bukowski and Corrington had been intellectually in sync. In the flesh, there was no connection. As Bukowski had told Corrington two years earlier, he was not comfortable with small talk, and conversation was sporadic and strained. To fill the awkward silence that began the evening, Corrington and Williams chatted about university life, and Toledano chipped in about his work as a lawyer. This line of conversation made Bukowski even more uncomfortable, and he and Corrington ended up bickering about the academy and politics, enduring the evening until it was time for Corrington

and Williams to leave. Williams later told Bukowski biographer Howard
Sounes that Corrington was deeply hurt by Bukowski's behavior. Still, Williams never believed the break between Corrington and Bukowski was cata-
clysmic: "Neither ever told me that he was turning his back on the other,
and I know that each of them admired the other's work. Both of them were
important to my life, but Hank was a dear friend while Bill was a brother.
I was not aware of any change in their relationship after the New Orleans
meeting, except perhaps for a slight stepping back. Neither said anything to
me about a cooling of the relationship, and I think they would have if they
had been seriously concerned."

This is not to say that each man was not stung by the meeting. Bukowski
gave his side of things in a letter to his friend Douglas Blazek, a poet and
editor of the little magazine *Ole*. He told Blazek that Corrington was "all
right, mostly more so once, but gone off on tangent of success and power,
and maybe he's right, shit, I don't know, I don't know." Bukowski complained
about the meeting being in a "room full of prefessers [*sic*] and laymen hy-
men lawyers and bigwigs." He claimed not to have said anything "which was
cowardly, but on the other hand, they didn't give me much chance to." This
was a completely foreign world for Bukowski. "All that exposition of bril-
liance and nobody really wanting to get drunnk" [*sic*].

If Corrington's time in England had not already brought distance between him and the Webbs, this meeting signaled the end of his close work
with Loujon. He kept up with Jon and Louise through the years, but it was
clear he would not be working on *Crucifix in a Deathhand*, and further opportunities for collaboration did not appear. Another of the Webbs' friends,
the painter Noel Rockmore, did help with the book, providing the artwork
for its cover. Rockmore created a nightmare cityscape peopled with hideous
characters. The scene was in keeping with some of Rockmore's recurring
themes, such as the downtrodden of New York's Bowery, where he had his
first studio, and the hidden world of circus performers.

Rockmore was a well-known artist who had been successful from an
early age, with shows at New York's Metropolitan Museum of Art in 1952
and the Whitney Museum of American Art in 1958. He had also presented
at Philadelphia's Pennsylvania Academy of the Fine Arts and the Cleveland
Institute of Art. He met the Webbs soon after their return from one of their
western trips. Jon and Louise were drinking in a bar; Rockmore came in-

side and soon noticed Louise. He approached her and asked if he could do her portrait.

"When? Now?" Louise asked. "Who are you?"

Rockmore introduced himself and, after some conversation, Louise agreed to sit for him. Over time, Rockmore painted dozens of pictures of Louise, including a large portrait of her in a blue dress, cigarette butts littering the floor at her feet. Louise liked the painting, and Rockmore gave it to her, after signing it, "For Gypsy, love you, Rockmore." Louise had the painting on her wall only a few days when Rockmore brought a woman to the Webbs' apartment to see it. The woman loved the painting and wanted to buy it. "No, you can't. That's mine!" Louise told the woman. She turned to Rockmore and said, "You gave it to me!" None of this mattered to Rockmore. He took the painting back and sold it to the woman for five thousand dollars. Rockmore promised Louise he would give her another painting, but he never did.

One of Rockmore's best-known works remains *Homage to the French Quarter*, a stew of images of actual Quarter residents. Jon and Louise are featured, Jon wearing a beret and Louise holding a fish. In a follow-up painting, *Homage to the French Quarter IV*, Rockmore painted himself full body into the foreground, but the dominant image, by far, was Louise Webb. Rockmore painted Louise twice the size of his figure and had her covering most of the left side of the painting. She stood forlorn in a festive dress, eyes averted down and to her right, this time holding a dead, plucked chicken by the neck.

Rockmore's help was a boost for *Crucifix*, and perhaps he functioned as surrogate for Corrington. Even without the unpleasantness with Bukowski, it would have been a strain for Corrington to continue devoting a great deal of time to Loujon. He was the father of two young children and, with his doctorate in hand, had recently been promoted from instructor to assistant professor of English at Louisiana State University. He had also taken on duties as a reader in fiction for the LSU Press. In short, he was a busy man. But the silence between Corrington and Webb came from both directions. In December 1964, Jon finally contacted Corrington after a long enough time for Corrington to suspect Jon had been sick. Jon told him of progress on *Crucifix in a Deathhand*. "The new Buk book sounds fine," a gracious Corrington told Jon. "I'll be the first to order one (or probably the last) & look forward to seeing it."

If Corrington was already willing to put the unpleasant meeting with Bukowski behind him, Bukowski was not. Bukowski savaged Corrington in the winter 1965–1966 issue of *Steppenwolf* under the guise of a review of Corrington's latest book, *Lines to the South and Other Poems*. Bukowski titled his review "Another Burial of a Once-Talent," and was vituperative in the extreme. He saved his only praise for "Surreal for Lorca," which had appeared in the second issue of the *Outsider*, the poem that had earlier led him to say that he and Corrington were developing similar styles. Dismayed, Corrington sent Webb a copy of Bukowski's review. Enclosed with the review was a letter which looked back on the early Loujon days when Webb and Corrington were thinking of the future: "Somewhere back there, you and I were writing back and forth, wondering how IT CATCHES would affect Chas, who had been a good man and a good poet, and who then was not known two blocks from his house. We decided something like, 'he's good, and he deserves a good book.' And yet I remember we both still wondered." To Corrington, Bukowski's attack was like having a friend die. He described Bukowski's review as a betrayal of "somebody who has done the best he could by you," an action which negated "that fine luxury you call loyalty."

Webb was not entirely sympathetic to Corrington's hurt feelings. He confided to Blair that Bukowski's review of Corrington's work was "damned brilliant." Acknowledging that Corrington was "quite hurt and upset," Webb reminded Blair of what he perceived as Corrington's bungling of his face-to-face meeting with Bukowski. Corrington, Webb wrote, "had to keep at the academic talk of university stuff, and of degrees he had and others had, which put Buk way down." Webb was less candid with Corrington. He had his own reasons for being angry with Bukowski and used them to help commiserate with Corrington's situation: "As for Buk attacking you, he's done things to us of late too. In *Literary Times* he gave best top 3 lit mags going, and put above us in #1 and #2 places first *Ole*, a crappy little mimeo high school kid editor sloppy little mag using just about nothing but poems full of four-letter words, by smart alecky kid writers (tho they can write better stuff at times) and second place to him, though we didn't too much mind that, *Wormwood Rev.*"

Despite any awkwardness the problems with Bukowski may have caused the Corrington-Webb relationship, Corrington remained a friend to Jon and Louise. Soon after he sent them Bukowski's review, Corrington wrote an undated letter to say that a care package was on its way: "Let me know when the stuff I'm mailing arrives. I sure hope it'll be of some use. Keep in touch, & if things get real bad, phone me collect." Corrington decided to put Bukowski's attack on his book behind him and was willing, still, to start anew with his old friend. He felt uneasy about writing Bukowski himself, but told Jon "when you see him, or write, tell him to drop me a line." Not much later, Bukowski and Corrington resumed their correspondence. Their letters still had the spark of friendship, though each wrote far less often than before.

Bukowski had his mind on other things. The upcoming book pleased him, but he had misgivings about Stuart's plans to charge seven and a half dollars per copy. The press run was to be over three thousand, and he feared that they would not sell at that price. "Most of the people, I think, who might buy my poems, most of them don't even have $7.50 and if they did they'd prob. buy something to drink," he wrote a friend. On the other hand, the Stuart deal called for royalties for Bukowski, which made this book a welcome milestone. As before, he worked to drum up support, writing friends and urging them to order copies at the prepublication price of three dollars per book. Bukowski told Sherri Martinelli that Jon needed the money, "and it's going to be another beauty-mad product of format inventiveness."

Jon worked on marketing *Crucifix* locally, and a community newspaper provided good, free advertising. Ormonde Plater, a columnist for the *Vieux Carré Courier*, interviewed the Webbs in their "cluttered dungeon they call the Loujon Press" at 1109 Royal Street. Louise worked with glue as Jon talked about Bukowski's recent visit. He told Plater that Bukowski was a tough writer, but a gentle human being who stood six foot six. "He drinks about a case of beer a day, and that doesn't stop him from writing 30 poems a week." The brief column was filled with similar hyperbole, and when Bukowski learned of this, he was not pleased. He was certain that his work was strong enough to stand alone without exaggeration about his life from the editor.

This was not the only time Bukowski took exception to Jon making exaggerated claims on his behalf. Bukowski was engaged in his own project to write his life large in poetry, and Jon's efforts, well intended as they were, sometimes got in the way. A case in point is Jon's claim that Jean-Paul Sartre and Jean Genet proclaimed Bukowski as the greatest living American poet. Jon promoted Bukowski's books with these claims, and one day, while the two of them were drinking together, Bukowski finally asked Jon to tell him the truth. "Somebody read Genet your poem, 'Old Man Dead in a Room' and Genet said it was a great poem," Jon said. "But that's not the same as the other," Bukowski replied. "He didn't say I was the best poet in America. I don't want you to use this blurb." Jon just stared at Bukowski, and that was the end of the discussion.

Marcus J. Grapes enjoyed a fairly close association with the Webbs during the making of *Crucifix in a Deathhand*. One of his visits came on a rainy night when the apartment was packed with unbound pages of the book. Jon sat at a makeshift desk, a piece of plywood laid over two orange crates, with a big can of glue and a large paintbrush, fixing pages into their bindings. Jon reminded Grapes of Tom Sawyer, working his paintbrush on the books. Even more striking to Grapes was the tool Webb used to cut pages. Rather than a professional-grade paper cutter, Webb relied on a machete for this delicate task. Years after that night, in a letter to Webb, Grapes reminisced about "you and Lou and the nights I came down desperate with despair into your tiny room, bed and books piled high for glue, sitting on the little crate next to your desk talking about 'it all.'"

Grapes became a regular at the Webbs' home, though he consciously kept an emotional wall between his hosts and himself. The usual routine was for Grapes to show Jon his poetry and Jon to critique it. Grapes didn't allow himself to appear emotional during these meetings, because he wanted Jon to see him as a tough poet, like Bukowski or some of the other hard-nosed writers who published in the *Outsider*. Grapes's first impression of Jon, taken from a photograph on the back cover of the debut issue of the *Outsider*, was of "a rather avuncular presence with receding hair line and lots of gray hair fanning out behind him." Jon had changed by the time the two met. Now, "there was no hair at all; he looked older, thinner, more fit, and his eyes were razor sharp, penetrating, tough."

Grapes was intimidated. "I'd read that he was an ex-con, and I knew he'd hung out with the poets shooting up on Rue git Le Cour in Paris, a street I was to later visit on his instructions." Jon's presence, more than his history, gave Grapes pause. "Jon looked at you and small though he was, you felt he was melting you down to see what you were really made of. He wore a cap, not a baseball cap, but something like that. It was a cross between a banker's visor and a tug-boat captain's hat. And it was the end of summer in New Orleans, maybe late September, when the heat and humidity are at their worst, and he was sitting on that orange crate, white tee-shirt and pants tightened with a thin belt." Grapes soon decided Jon was a con artist. "You could tell he was trying to figure what your angle was so he could wedge in his angle. My angle? I had no angle. Well, maybe I did. But I was so flummoxed by the notion of it that I could barely talk." Grapes's "angle," such as it was, was to convince Jon to read and critique his poetry. He handed Jon his pages, and Jon's response was a hard stare. "And Lou's sitting on another orange crate next to her drawings leaning up against the brick front of the building and she's jabbering with the people passing by, a little crazy, a little miraculous."

"You want me to publish them?" Jon asked. "You handing these in for publication?"

"No," Grapes said. "I was just hoping you'd look them over and tell me what you think. I've read the *Outsider* and . . ." Grapes became tongue-tied and decided that Jon was no longer listening to him. He thought the entire exchange was like something from a Raymond Chandler story, "because I swear, he had this sneer, and it was as if I'd handed him a packet filled with stolen jewels and I was asking him if he could fence them."

"Okay," Jon said. "Come back next week." Grapes felt as though he had stepped inside a new world, "and I felt this fear, this apprehension that whatever boulder I'd set rolling down the hill, it was too late to stop it."

Grapes became interested in helping Jon and Louise with their press, and when he could he gave Jon money. It was never a great deal, but enough to make some difference in their lives. Grapes was conflicted. He was pleased that he could come to the aid of two people he greatly admired, but he wanted to be published in the *Outsider*, too. If there were ever a hint that Jon would take his poetry because of the money, it would destroy any victory that the publication would otherwise give. This was a fantastic new world he had entered, and Grapes wanted it to remain pure.

The fantastic did not just come from Jon's poetry critiques or the literature he exposed Grapes to through the *Outsider*. Grapes saw what Jon accomplished with *It Catches My Heart in Its Hands* and *Crucifix in a Deathhand* as physical artifacts and became fascinated with the book arts. He decided to try his hand at this delicious work, though making books per se was not new for Grapes. He had experimented with chapbooks and other small projects for years, but the Loujon books showed him that there were dimensions to the craft that he had not dreamed of. Grapes began haunting local stationery stores, seeking the right combination of exotic papers. He ended up finding most of what he needed, "various sheets of tissue paper used for wrapping presents, all sorts of mixed colors, mottled and dripping with various colors," at a five-and-dime store down the street from his home. Grapes brought his books, done in editions of one hundred, to Jon, who seemed to approve.

No doubt it was flattering to have a talented young man become inspired by his work and create art in the same vein. But his own work was the thing, and Jon kept hard at his new book until it was finished. In April 1965, Loujon made delivery of 3,100 copies of *Crucifix in a Deathhand* to Lyle Stuart in New York. The book was "handset in Bulmer Roman, American Uncial & others," and printed "handfed in single-page impressions on Linweave Spectre paper in shades of ivory white peacock, gobelin, bayberry, bittersweeet & saffron, on an 8 by 12 C. & P. Letterpress." Jon was proud of the book and wasted no time in sending a copy to the Patchens. The "crazy but equally astonishing" book clearly impressed them. "Anyway, by now what you do only *continues* to amaze us," Miriam wrote. "By now we realize you can do anything so the shock element is gone . . . but, but it still is extraordinary."

Even with Miriam and Kenneth's praise of *Crucifix*, hope for the Patchen book was almost gone. Everyone concerned came to realize that, for the foreseeable future, the book had to be shelved. "As a consolation Jon got Patchen to send work that had been shown at City Lights to New Orleans where I was in charge of putting the show together," Ed Blair recalled. "The show took place at Glade Gallery. The poster was designed by Patchen as large mailer." A small controversy arose when the Patchens asked that the paintings be sold for three hundred dollars each. Blair was certain that this was too much and prevailed upon Jon to ask that the price be reduced. In the end, seven paintings sold, each priced at thirty-five dollars. Jon and Louise were back in New Orleans for the show, but left the day after it opened, on June 15, 1965, their twenty-sixth wedding anniversary.

That same month brought the unexpected news that *Crucifix* had been nominated for the Pulitzer Prize. Jon was pleased, but told Blair the nomination was "amusing, for it can't compete with the Establishment." A few days later, the Pulitzer nomination still on Webb's mind, he wrote Blair again: "On the Pulitzer, natch he can't win—but at least Mrs. Trinkhaus of the P. Prize Committee requested a photo and brief bio of Buk last week, which I sent to her at Columbia U." After Jon told Bukowski of the nomination, Bukowski passed the news on to others in his circle. Poet William Wantling and his wife made such a happy fuss about the nomination that Bukowski became embarrassed and wished he had not mentioned anything to them. Like Webb, he understood that he had no chance of winning. "Shouldn't have told you about the Pulitzer nomination," he wrote the Wantlings, "because it's useless and futile, no chance, but thought it might amuse you in a kind of obscene manner, you know, maybe here I am dying and I am nominated for a longshot shit medal." Webb and Bukowski were correct in their predictions that *Crucifix* would not win the Pulitzer Prize; Richard Eberhart won for his *Selected Poems.*

Pulitzer nomination or not, Jon wasn't completely happy with the Lyle Stuart partnership. Stuart was slow to pay royalties, and Bukowski had been forced to write the publisher to ask for money, an effort which brought him a check for two hundred dollars. As Bukowski had predicted, Stuart complained that sales were slow. Jon thought the problem was Stuart not being aggressive enough in marketing *Crucifix.* He complained to Blair that, were he in charge of distribution, he would have already sold most of the press run. But *Crucifix* had a clear target audience, and when these people heard it had been published, they wanted to own a copy. One of these was Kenneth Rexroth, then living in Germany with his wife, poet Carol Tinker. Beginning his letter "Dear People," Rexroth asked the Webbs to send along a copy of *Crucifix.* "How did I miss it?" he asked. "I am a very strong Bukfan." Apparently forgetting his *New York Times* review of the first Loujon book, Rexroth asked: "Did you send me *It Catches?* If not, send that to bill. If you want them reviewed on KPFA—and feel like throwing around a lot of postage money—send them by air to my present address . . . and I will do them when I get home in the spring. More power to you & to Bukowski." Rexroth was referring to his weekly book review show on KPFA in San Francisco, the first listener-supported radio station in the United States. The station had been founded in 1949 by poet Lewis Hill, and had long been a cultural beacon for the Bay Area. A positive review by Rexroth on KPFA could boost the status, and sales, of most any book.

With *Crucifix* launched, the Webbs decided to leave New Orleans once again. Bukowski observed that "they had to get away from New Orleans, couldn't stand it—tourists, the Ku Klux Klan, thugs, bad weather for Lou's lungs." They again wandered for a time, moving variously to Laredo, Santa Fe, Phoenix, Cleveland, and back to Phoenix, before buying a house in Tucson.

❖ 8 ❖

TUCSON AND HENRY MILLER

THE WEBBS ARRIVED IN Tucson during what Jon described as "the worst rainy December in history here" and made a down payment on a small former grocery store at 1009 E. Elm Street, where they set up housekeeping. Jon did not tolerate the warm, rainy weather well. He wrote Blair that he was "just up from bed briefly—recovering from what Dr. said was going into pneumonia." Jon complained of a backache, the result of overextending himself in fixing up their new home. One unlikely problem came when rain caused an old cesspool under the patio to cave in, producing a hole, ten feet deep and six feet wide, in their backyard. At a loss as to what to do about the hole, for a time they settled on "using it for a rubbish box." Jon, Jr., was still in the army, and he and his family visited Tucson after a tour of duty in Meunchweiler, Germany. The family was on its way to their new home in Hayward, California, and stopped long enough to film some home movies with Jon, Jr.'s new 8 mm camera, to generally catch up on things, and have a lunch of barbequed chicken and refried beans. Sometime during the visit, Louise fell into the sinkhole and was almost buried under the rain of dirt that followed her down. Jon and Jon, Jr., had to gingerly climb down and pull her to safety.

Marcus Grapes had married, and he and his wife also paid the Webbs a visit in Tucson. They were moving to Los Angeles, and Tucson was more or less on the way. Before he pulled his car into the Webbs' driveway, Grapes still was unsure of his standing with Jon and Louise. The relationship had never progressed past Jon critiquing Grapes's poetry and Grapes playing the occasional benefactor, but this time "there were hugs all around, and suddenly I realized that there was something deeper there, that there was affection, not that I was like a son or anything, but that there was some kind of teacher/mentor thing there, that he and Lou just liked me. I dropped my guard then and let be what was going to be."

It was good to have visitors, but as always, the Webbs soon turned their attention to work. With little money, certainly not enough to finance a new

issue of the *Outsider*, they hit upon a plan for a more modest business venture. "We are going to open a quality used paperback—some new later—
& little mag bookshop to get a bit of bread and butter money," Jon wrote
Blair. He was counting on the fact that the couple's new home was only a
few blocks from the University of Arizona campus to provide business for
the bookshop. To get things going, Jon asked Blair if he might send "any
old paperbacks you don't want," and asked about a New York City bookseller that might sell him stock at a reasonable price. Since helping finance
the first Bukowski book, Blair had been someone Jon could rely on, and Blair
often helped by sending small amounts of cash. When this happened, Jon
always sent something in return. "Jon always gave more than he got," Blair
said. "At least that was my experience. Lou did things like make pictures of
clowns for my kids."

Jon soon decided it had been an error to impose upon Blair for free stock,
and took back the request. He told Blair that some items had already been
donated "from here and there, not much, but maybe soon we can get a bookshop look." Blair later recalled that the "bookstore idea in Tucson never developed but Jon did put out a flier which he sent to friends. It was a deal
where he did not have any books himself, but as he got orders he'd pass the
orders on to a distributor and got a percentage of the sale. Most of the books
were sex oriented—how to manuals. The only book of literary substance was
Henry Miller's *Tropic of Cancer*. A really weird selection."

When the bookstore plan died, Jon realized it was time to get back to the
work of the Loujon Press. His greatest successes had come with the Bukowski
books, and he decided to try a third go with Bukowski. Jon planned to produce a phonograph record of Bukowski, a cheaper and easier endeavor than
publishing a new issue of the magazine. In an interesting twist, Bukowski
would be speaking off the cuff, not reading from his poetry. It would be
a chance for listeners to get a more intimate feel for the man behind the
poems. Bukowski agreed to the deal, and "Bukowski Talking" was in the
works. The idea for a record came after Jon managed to get free advertising
space in the Chicago-based *Literary Times* because of an apparent misstate-
ment the *Literary Times* made about his criminal record. "This is a secret,
but I got the ad free—I raised holy hell about their putting in that phony ex-
convict stuff, phony in that they didn't qualify the term in application to me,
and Nash got over-whelmed and donated this $500 page ad to us. And may
give us another one next issue, and another. If what he promised is done,"

Webb told Blair. Unfortunately, Loujon had no new material to promote with this free advertisement, and Jon, under a tight deadline to get the advertising copy to Chicago, "got some beers and sweated on what to promote and finally decided best to promote a record." He worried that the record might be a bust, but felt that he was committed to following through with it. Still, another issue of the *Outsider* was Jon's primary goal, and he believed Tucson was a good location from which to produce that issue. "This setup ideal for #4 and we're rolling the ball on paper work steadily toward it, and its coming out is a sure thing in time."

The record, it turned out, was less of a sure thing. Before the month was over, Jon was already having second thoughts. He believed that even though Bukowski planned to visit him and Louise in Tucson at his own expense, at which time several hours of material could be taped, the record would "be quite a gamble." Henry Miller further complicated things. Jon told Bukowski in February 1966 that the record might have to be postponed, because he was considering publishing a manuscript Miller had offered. He emphasized to Bukowski the money Loujon stood to make on the project. Bukowski understood the financial incentive and also Miller's desire for a Loujon-quality book. "He wants the wondrous Loujon format and you can't blame him," Bukowski told Jon. "You'd like it yourself, for yourself, wouldn't you?"

"Bukowski Talking" was supposed to come out in April, and Bukowski, in constant pain from recent hemorrhoid surgery, rushed to complete the recordings. Bukowski saw the record as a favor to Jon, and his willingness to work through the pain was admirable. On April 1, he wrote Martinelli that he had "finished cutting the tapes for the record Webb has advertised. So that's that. Now he can finance his Patchen issue and run his Henry Miller book. What a good boyscout I am, never asking royalties. Or maybe I am a fool. But I don't want to get tangled in all that." As Bukowski's letter to Martinelli suggests, for a while Jon hedged his bets, trying to find a way to produce the record and publish Miller. He told Bukowski that he didn't have the six hundred dollars it would take to press the record and bought time by suggesting October might be a better time for that project. With this, he turned his attention to Miller. In truth, the *Literary Times* ad had only generated twenty or so orders, not enough to inspire confidence that this would be a money-making proposition. It "would be a slow mover," Jon confided to Blair. Soon after, the record deal was off.

Bukowski was becoming disenchanted with the Webbs. He was unhappy with the way Jon handled the "Bukowski Talking" situation, and he disapproved of Jon and Louise's recent series of moves, which he thought foolish. He wrote Douglas Blazek that Jon had "blown thousands of dollars running around the country for a year looking for a new Taos, a new Carmel, a new something." While he understood this was not his business, Bukowski marveled that "he's running around in special trains with his wife, 2 dogs, the printing press, tons of cartons of paper, type, books, manuscripts." Every place the Webbs landed, Bukowski wrote, seemed perfect at first, but they quickly found something wrong. "I get postcards from this city, then that: 'I believe this is it. Everything fine.' Then a week later, another card: 'Oh, we can't stand it here!' and there goes the press and the dogs and works somewhere else."

Jon was not overly concerned with Bukowski's ire. After all, he had given the poet two first-rate books and brought him to national prominence. If he now had the chance to publish an established icon of the avant-garde, he saw no reason pass up the opportunity. Still, even with the Miller book, Jon had misgivings. He worried about money and, since he had yet to see Miller's manuscript, was concerned it might be unworthy of the "all-out treatment in format and over-all presentation" that distinguished Loujon books. Once he saw the manuscript, though, the misgivings faded. It was brief, which meant less production work, and it was unique. The manuscript was in the form of an extended letter to Miller's friend, painter Hans Reichel, a compatriot from 1920s Paris. Jon decided he could complete the book in four months and realize enough profit to underwrite the next issue of the *Outsider*. He believed most who had preordered the Bukowski record would take the Miller book instead or accept a refund. Now, Jon moved quickly to take advantage of the situation and get Miller on board for future projects. Miller was quicker to answer Louise's letters, so Jon had her write to suggest Miller write a children's book. Webb got the idea after reading *Art and Outrage*, a volume of correspondence between Miller's friends Lawrence Durrell and Alfred Perles, which indicated that Miller was like "a magnet to kids, likes them and gets along fine with them." Jon sensed an opportunity to publish a unique book and seemed to believe it might happen. "Wouldn't that be a switch?" he asked Blair. "Kids going around with a Henry Miller book under their arms. The author's name in big letters." Miller admitted he liked the idea of writing for children, but didn't see where he could find the time. Jon read some hope in this response and, for a while, continued planning the project. In the end, Miller did not write the book, but in an intriguing case of what-might-have-been, Jon confided to Blair that "Andy Warhol (of the Velvet Underground, N.Y.C.) would like to illustrate the Miller book."

Once again, Jon contacted Lyle Stuart to test the waters on collaboration. Stuart was interested and asked Jon to get back with him after reading the manuscript. By the end of March, Jon had a change of heart, telling Stuart he wanted to work alone. With Stuart out of the picture, Jon faced the problem of generating enough prepublication orders to get the book started. Even getting word out was expensive. This would take strategic advertising and quality brochures to send to people on Miller's mailing list. Jon believed that the only effective venues for advertising this book would be pricey, nationally circulated publications such as the *Village Voice*, which now seemed out of reach. Still, by late March, prepublication orders were already starting to arrive, mostly from word-of-mouth publicity.

Everything was expensive, and these orders helped keep the project on track. Jon contemplated setting the volume in Paganini typeface, which he would have to order from Milan. In addition to the cost of the typeface itself, Jon knew that the airmail expenses would be high. The extravagance was necessary, he reasoned, because he had to "make it worth the price I'm going to ask for it." Jon wrote Blair to ask for a new book by poet and master printer William Everson, who had joined a religious order and taken the name Brother Antoninus. He didn't want to copy the design, but to keep abreast of what was being done by other fine press publishers. "We're still in the throes of a definite format," Jon wrote. "No place here to examine fine late books in limited editions." Wanting to publish the best-designed book he could, Jon asked Blair to also send any new and exciting books he might have.

As Jon became more involved with Miller's book, titled *Order and Chaos chez Hans Reichel*, another small publisher, Black Sparrow Press, came into being with the express purpose of publishing Bukowski. John Martin, the Los Angeles office supply manager who had helped Jon and Bukowski with supplies, was a bibliophile with a valuable collection of modern first editions. When Martin realized that Bukowski lived in Los Angeles, he arranged a visit. After looking through a large pile of poems Bukowski had stuck away in his closet, Martin offered to publish several as broadsides, maybe even pay royalties. Martin sold his book collection to the University of California, Santa Barbara, Libraries to generate start-up money, and Black Sparrow was launched. The press's first publication, a broadside of Bukowski's "True Story," appeared in April.

Jon did not concern himself with Bukowski's deal with Black Sparrow. He was more interested in Miller now. By early June, his confidence in the Miller project was strong, even with the inevitable problems of fine press work. A ninety-six-thousand-page paper order had been improperly cut, necessitating that repairs be made and shipments routed through Phoenix and Los Angeles before Jon could finally get his hands on the paper, all of which resulted in a two-week production delay. Still, the delay allowed Jon to attend to a number of other preliminary details, and he believed that the "Miller book promises to be a big thing for us."

Jon even planned to make the publication announcement, a folded brochure printed with fine type on heavy, deckled paper, a collectors' item. He sent the brochure to the almost seven hundred names provided by the Henry Miller Literary Society, a group of collectors from around the world. Miller, too, sent a long list of names and addresses of a number of high-profile collectors. Miller's list included Charlie Chaplin, Henri Matisse, and Elizabeth Taylor, "and other queens of the screen, and actors, and most of the living world-known writers, and millionaires in chateaus in Europe, and so on." Jon planned on publishing both premium and economy editions and believed the premium editions would sell out quickly. Production costs were high, of course, and Jon estimated that, "counting brochures, mailing, packing, etc., and ads, so on," the project would cost about five thousand dollars to complete. This meant that any money that came into the household went to fund the book, but Jon saw the project as a windfall. He hoped to realize enough profit to buy a new, bigger press, along with "a cutter, binding equipment, a folder, and such," as well as paper and ink in quantities large enough to publish the fourth issue of the *Outsider*. The next *Outsider* would likely mark a return to Loujon's roots: "Will do #4 in New Orleans, we're pretty sure," Jon told Blair in early June.

By the middle of the month, Jon had already experimented with several formats and invested eight hundred dollars in design ideas he subsequently discarded. Another eight hundred dollars went to adding a small design flourish that came to him as he was well into production. Jon wanted this book to surpass his previous efforts, and compared it to the "bunch-of-Indians-whooping" style of *It Catches My Heart in Its Hands*, which he called a "merry-go-round" of ease, in comparison. The hard work paid off, resulting in a book arguably more complex and beautiful than either of the Bukowski volumes. But it also exacted a heavy price on Jon. Sometime around the beginning of July, he suffered a small stroke. His doctor prescribed vasodilation medication, which Jon was to take for the rest of his life. He also ordered Jon to swim a half hour each day. Swimming was out of the question, because Jon did not drive and there were no pools near home, "but," he wrote Blair, "I'll be damned if this exercise at the press many hours a day plus many other swimming movements I make daily, and the swimming I do in quandaries on where is the next dime coming from to pay the mounting Miller book bills, is not enough to keep me alive."

In mid-November, Corrington wrote to congratulate the Webbs on the Miller book, and to let them know he would be sending a check for a copy of one of the less-expensive editions. Corrington's career was going well. He was now teaching at Loyola University in New Orleans and had a novel in press with Putnam in both the United States and England. He was keen on the Webbs returning to New Orleans and offered his services as "a kind of address while you're in transit." "New Orleans isn't much," he wrote, "but you all will surely brighten it." Jon and Louise visited New Orleans sometime in 1966 or 1967 in hopes of settling there again. Ed Blair drove them around the city looking for places to rent outside the French Quarter. The search for a New Orleans home did not pan out, and soon Jon and Louise were back in Tucson.

Soon after they were again settled in Tucson, it was time to begin shipping the first copies of their new book. Copies of *Order and Chaos* went to preorder customers as early as February 1967, with most orders shipping in March and April. Bukowski received his copy by mail on April 6, one day after receiving two copies of *Crucifix in a Deathhand*. If he was still unhappy with the Webbs, he did not let that stand in the way of gushing over the book. One day earlier, he wrote a letter anticipating the new book: "I saw your press before it was dropped and smashed by the movers. Surely only the prayers of the immortal mad in love with quiet beauty could have held that, that ... marvelous God damned *washing machine* together thru this one! They will never know, those who see this Miller book will never know. Nor will they know the accomplishment gut-gamble of keeping yourself alive on nothing, grabbing at your own Thrifty Drugstore giveaway advance order sales in order to get type, ink, paper, food, rent, clothes, oil, light, heat, energy to start the thing from zero to miracle." Bukowski wrote again the next day, after the book arrived: "How does one talk about a Lou & Jon creation—*Order & Chaos*—? I could roll cigarettes and drink beer all night and write about it and end up with all the pages, and perhaps myself, on the floor and still not have said it."

Bukowski's response was far from unique. Jory Sherman was overwhelmed: "The Henry Miller book is the most beautiful book I've ever seen, a piece of art in its own right. It damn sure was worth your struggle and worth waiting for by all of us who are privileged to own it. Every detail adds up until the impact is almost overpowering!" For Marcus Grapes, the contents were solid, but the book as artifact was more compelling: "It could be the writings of Mrs. Barbara May Harris of the Women's Guild, a guidebook to better gardening, and I think I'll still go nuts just feeling it, touching the pages, looking at its strange beauty changing into something new each time I see it. I know you get hundreds of more important people telling you how great the book is, but you must feel some sense of . . . what's the word, pride? No . . . some strange sense of . . . majesty, of strong victory. You're doing something much more than genius."

Book lovers across the United States joined in the congratulations. Orders came from Nancy Sinatra, Ella Fitzgerald, Red Skelton, Louis Armstrong, and Jonathan Winters. One customer wrote that "It's awesome to hear of this kind of book being made in a country where 'existence for profit' squelches loving production." A college student in Bowling Green, Ohio, wrote that it was the book's craftsmanship that made it so appealing. "Most people," he wrote, "are especially amazed that in 1967 there are still good people like you & Lou who still care about the product of their work." John F. Font, of San Jose, California, with whom the Webbs had carried on some correspondence but had never met, wrote that he and his wife, Lolly, "feel we know you so well, and are in many ways close to you both." These warm feelings translated into action. "We talked about you to some friends last evening and showed them the Miller & Bukowski books. They became as enchanted with you both as we are. I told them about the press and the life subscriptions. The check books came out and they are enclosed, as is ours. Each would like the subscription and a Henry Miller book."

John Martin understood the effort Jon and Louise had put into the book, and felt compelled "to write and tell you that *Order and Chaos* is a most beautiful book. It is beautifully printed, and the bindery work on this limited edition is superb. I know it will be very successful and will sell out quickly, and I just hope when everything is done there is enough profit left to compensate you both (at least in part) for all the love and labor that certainly went into this great project." Martin was expecting a proof copy of the book, and reminded Webb that he had sent a check for "the regular issue" of the *Outsider*. He now sent another check for an additional copy of the magazine and offered his help as he could: "Do you need any tape or other supplies? If so, just ask."

At Eastern Michigan University, Mrs. Solveiga Rush, head of the humanities division, wrote of her copies of *Order and Chaos*, "They are so beautiful!" and placed an order for five more, also asking to reserve an additional copy for the EMU library, which, she promised, would soon send an invoice. Robert L. Volz, a librarian at Maine's Bowdoin College, ordered personal copies of both *Order and Chaos* and *Crucifix in a Deathhand*, telling Webb, "The library will get these books when I am done with them." Danish journalist Jorgen Aldrich wrote to let the Webbs know that he had published a small article on the Loujon Press in Denmark. Aldrich called Loujon books "magnificent" and assured the Webbs that *Order and Chaos* had a place of honor among his rare book collection. Al Woodbury, who orchestrated scores for Hollywood films such as *Porgy and Bess*, *Bye Bye Birdie*, and *My Fair Lady*, ordered multiple copies of several editions of *Order and Chaos*, some of which said he intended to give to friends as presents. "All who have seen my copy have drooled," Woodbury wrote.

Orin Borsten, who wrote the script for Burt Reynolds's screen debut, *Angel Baby* (1961), and for television shows like *The Outer Limits*, offered: "Nothing like it has ever graced my bookshelf." Borsten was eloquent in speculating how the book came to be: "It is the work of gifted creators who have for many years loved the feel, touch and weight of books, the texture of bindings, the fragrance of glue and printer's ink—and who, because of this great love for the book, have shown the world how beautiful a book can really be, how papers and binding can become an extension of the writer's raging talent, lyricism, joy in life."

Not surprisingly, people involved in the book trade appreciated Loujon's efforts. Melissa Maytag, owner of Los Angeles's Unicorn Bookshop, wrote: "I had been in awe of Bukowski's two beautiful books, but these are even more precious." Mary Jo Tasto worked as a clerk for Books Universal in Livermore, California, and had her own money problems. Even so, she sent checks totaling more than one hundred dollars for a personal subscription and copies of *Order and Chaos*. Soon after, Tasto wrote for additional copies of *Order and Chaos* and *Crucifix in a Deathhand*. She asked the Webbs to hold copies of the books for about a week, when she would send payment. Tasto understood that the Webbs might not be able to hold the copies back for her. "In any case—I shall send the money Jan. 2nd and if your supply is gone—keep the money. Use it as you see fit and have a wonderful new year."

In February 1967, Ed Blair suggested that he and William Wisdom, a well-connected New Orleans friend, might be able to negotiate a deal with either the William Faulkner or the Thomas Wolfe estate to publish a book with the Loujon Press. Jon was delighted with the idea and had "ideas exploding in me on format already." He would pull out the stops for such a book. If it were Faulkner, he might house the book in "a wood slipcase—with thin pine from Faulkner's country around Oxford." After publishing Miller, a book by either of these giants would surely cement Loujon's place as one of the premier small presses in America. Jon told Blair he was praying a deal could be made concerning either Faulkner or Wolfe, but nothing came through.

Better news came the following month when the Type Directors Club of New York honored the cork edition with an exhibition at the Mead Library of Ideas on Park Avenue as part of the club's thirteenth annual awards show. As part of the award, the book was also featured in the spring 1968 issue of *Art Direction* magazine. Delighted, Jon scribbled a note to Miller, telling him of the Type Directors Club Award and that Reichel's widow had sent a "long letter of delight & thanks for book's format."

Bukowski visited in June, just as the commotion about *Order and Chaos* began to quiet. There had been talk of reviving the record project, but the concept had changed. Now, the idea was to record Bukowski reading from his poetry. There was talk of recording the poems during his visit, so that Jon could pick through them later and choose what he liked. Louise's father was visiting from Cleveland, so Jon arranged for Bukowski to stay at a poet's cottage on the University of Arizona campus. Bukowski still had his luggage in tow when, in the late afternoon of the day of his arrival, Jon took him to a bar near the Webbs' home. They lived in what Bukowski considered a bad part of town. The bar was a Hispanic hangout, and when the two of them entered, the bartender twice rang a small bell. Bukowski took this as a signal to the regulars that two "gringos" had arrived, and it made him uneasy. He was tired from the trip and felt uncomfortable there with his ragged suitcase, but he sat at the bar with Jon and they talked for a while

and drank beer. Bukowski eventually excused himself to go to the bathroom. Two men followed him inside. While he was urinating, one of them
spoke up in a loud voice.

"Hello!" the man said. Bukowski, thinking the man was speaking to his
companion, didn't respond. "Hello!" the man said again, louder.

"You talking to me, man?" asked Bukowski. The man said he was, and
cursed Bukowski for not speaking back. Bukowski assumed the man wanted
to fight and resigned himself to this. They exchanged a few words, Bukowski
doing his best to keep the situation under control. The man was clearly hos-
tile, but nothing more happened, and Bukowski was able to leave the bathroom in peace. He returned to the bar and told Jon about the incident. Jon
chided Bukowski for being worried and said nothing bad ever happened in
this bar until nightfall. He admitted, though, that a man had been stabbed
on the steps outside the bar the night before. Bukowski reminded Jon that
it was getting on toward night and suggested they should leave. As they left
the bar, they passed two more men coming inside. Bukowski heard one of
them mutter, "There's that artist," meaning Jon, who, wearing a black beret,
looked the part. Bukowski got the idea that Jon was safe there, but wasn't so
sure about himself. He was happy when they were safely away.

The visit did not get much better for Bukowski. It was a hot summer,
and he was miserable. He didn't like the heat, and he disapproved of Jon
and Louise's frequent trips to Las Vegas to play the slot machines. Jon had
dyed his white hair red, which Bukowski found ridiculous. On top of all this,
after that first visit to a bar, the only person who would drink with him was
Louise's father. At one point Bukowsi and Louise talked about the problems
she and Jon faced in Tucson. They had pawned many of their belongings to
bring money into the house. This was not unusual, but Louise was worried
about her health and Jon's. She understood that the eleven years' difference in
their ages was becoming ever more significant and worried what would become of her if anything were to happen to Jon. Bukowski was sympathetic,
but this did nothing to make him more comfortable with his visit.

Jon was oblivious to Bukowski's misery. The day before Bukowski returned to California, Jon wrote Blair that "all's gone well so far, no arguments or fights. He's consuming his usual case of beer a day too." Their biggest problem, as far as Jon could tell, was Bukowski's irritation over Jon's
success in betting at the track. "He keeps bringing up tho how I ruined his

system in N.O. by winning all day, and how my horse in the last race which was the dumbest bet a man could ever make came up out of nowhere from the tailend and whipped his, the favorite." Bukowski blamed Jon for his lost money. "Seems if it hadn't been for my betting on the worst horse in the lot it wouldn't have won."

When he returned to Hollywood, Bukowski wrote about the trip in his column, Notes of a Dirty Old Man, which he had recently begun contributing to *Open City*, an alternative newspaper published in Los Angeles. Bukowski painted himself as a fool in the column, socially inept, drunken, and obnoxious. His portrait of the Webbs wasn't especially flattering, but neither was it particularly harsh. The worst things he said of them were that they were getting old and that "The Great Editor" had published him for ten years and still did not know who he was. The column made it clear, though, that Bukowski had hated the visit. The Webbs would likely have regarded Bukowski's visit in much the same affectionate, if bemused, way that they had previous meetings, had Bukowski not sent a copy of his column to a Tucson newspaper reporter. The reporter shared the column with Jon, who became hurt and angry. Bukowski wrote Jon soon after, but Jon did not write back. Bukowski later told Corrington that "Jon is a very sensitive cat, not a sloppy hardened beerhead like me, but I guess he figured it as a kind of disloyalty, just like people figured I was being disloyal to you when I attacked one of your books of poetry." Whether to justify himself or to make amends with Corrington, Bukowski argued that "it isn't disloyalty; I would be the first to come up with blackjack and snub-nosed automatic to blast a hole in some human wall or inhuman wall if you were in a jam and needed to get on through. There's still some German in me. Which means loyalty, honor, all those old-fashioned words, and I half expected both you and Jon to understand this."

The strained relationship with Bukowski was unpleasant, but Jon had little time to worry about this problem. He and Louise focused their attention on the new *Outsider*, which was in preproduction by the middle of 1967, complete with the long-anticipated Patchen tribute. But, as so often happened, there was a snag: the Patchens wanted some important materials back. Miriam understood that she was asking at a bad time, but they needed "all the photographs, couple paintings, etc. you have from us for the Patchen issue." She assured Jon that he could have them back later, if he wished, but they were needed now for a planned New Directions volume. Miriam's request terrified Jon. "Now on the material back, considering all the time and expense we've put out up to now on the Patchen issue I most certainly am reluctant to part with the material without absolute assurance I'll have the material back very soon," he wrote. "We've put hundreds and hundreds of hours into the planning of this issue, have notified thousands of people about its coming, have spent hundreds of dollars in stamps and paper and envelopes, and in general because of the wide publicity we've given the issue as the 'Patchen issue' are more or less committed to do the issue—the #4 issue of the *Outsider*."

It would be inconvenient to work around the material Miriam wanted back. Even worse, if New Directions published the work before the *Outsider*, it would diminish Loujon's prestige, perhaps make the new *Outsider* less marketable. With their household finances intimately bound to their publishing finances, this would be a disaster. With no real recourse, Jon returned three negatives to the Patchens in mid-April 1969, one of them for a dust jacket photograph on the New Directions book. In July, Miriam assured Jon that the material he had on hand was still his to use. This was a relief, but any talk of Loujon publishing a Patchen book was finished. Miller was now in the Loujon family, and there was talk of a new project, a portfolio of Miller's watercolors and accompanying book. Still, the Webb-Patchen relationship transcended their publishing deals, and the friendship remained. By the end of the year, Miriam was back to her regular correspondence with Jon and indulging in her usual practice of describing Kenneth's ongoing agonies. She also offered her congratulations on a press clipping Jon sent describing an astonishing and unexpected gift.

The gift was orchestrated by Donald Borzak, a commercial printer in Chicago. Borzak read an article about Loujon in the trade journal *Book Production Industry* describing Loujon's excellence and the hardships the Webbs faced getting their books and magazine into print. Borzak was fascinated and wanted to help. His solution was to organize a group of donors to buy the Webbs the press of their dreams. The only stipulation was that all donors would receive one copy of every Loujon Press book published from then on. "I admire what you and your wife are trying to do—our operation is much more commercial—and I would get a great thrill out of helping you if I could," Borzak told Jon. Noting that his wife was a college English teacher who admired both Miller and Lawrence Durrell, another author Loujon had considered publishing, Borzak included a twenty-five-dollar check with his letter, to cover the cost of a cork-edition copy of *Order and Chaos*. Webb replied at once. Borzak's letter, Webb wrote, made him pale as he read it. In contrast to Borzak's brief note, Webb typed a five-page, single-spaced letter, offering a detailed history of the Loujon Press. Webb told Borzak that "I've daydreamed of something of this sort coming to pass someday, but never really expected it to happen. So the fearsomeness is a trepidation warning me to be careful: don't say anything wrong, don't scare the man away!" Later, after declaring Borzak's letter to be "strong and sweetly beautiful like Purcell's music," Webb asked his unknown benefactor, "Are you real? Is it true? Are there such people left in the world? We can't grasp it as a reality." In his gratitude, Webb acknowledged Borzak's order of the cork edition of *Order and Chaos*, but told him the book would be sent gratis. Borzak's twenty-five dollars bought him an autographed copy of the book's more lavish Blue Oasis edition, an autographed copy of *Crucifix in a Death-hand*, and issue three of the *Outsider*.

Finally, Webb addressed the central question raised by Borzak's offer, that of the press. Webb's choice—though he admitted the choice was not necessarily well thought out, since he had never expected to be in such a position—was an automatic feed Heidelberg. Heidelberg was an expensive brand, however, and Webb understood that asking Borzak to consider it might sound presumptuous. "Do note please here I'm speaking of used presses when I mention the magic word Heidelberg. I know what they cost, and could be I'm saying the wrong thing already, bringing up a Heidelberg. A C & P rebuilt, or one plenty old but still in excellent working condition, would make us happy as hell, be sure."

Webb's uncertainty over his apparent good fortune was obvious as he wrote of the high-quality work he and Louise managed with both the *Outsider* and their books on their old Chandler and Price. "So surely 10 by 15 would suffice, except I've always wished for a press that would do two of the *Outsider* pages at one time, cutting the presstime in half. 12 by 18 would. Would 10 by 15? Not likely." Webb understood that this was "a tall order, I know—for a press I will be getting free. But you know it would do us no good to get a press merely because it is motorized and wasn't capable of satisfying our demands of it." After finishing the letter, Webb again considered his needs and added a short note, telling Borzak that perhaps Loujon's requirements would be better met with a press other than a Heidelberg, as he was unsure if the Heidelberg could adequately handle the deckle-edged pages that were a hallmark of Loujon books. He planned to check with printers he knew in the Tucson area and report back.

It took almost a year to gather the money and iron out the details, but Borzak was as good as his word. Jon apparently decided to trust his first instincts, and Borzak complied, as Type & Press of Illinois shipped the Webbs a Heidelberg press in early December 1967. With this press they could speed production from one page every few days to two pages a day. Borzak's group, which now numbered in the dozens, also offered to buy a paper cutter, but Jon requested they instead give him the money directly. The Webbs might be leaving Tucson soon, and the paper cutter would be expensive to move. The money, on the other hand, would help make issue four of the *Outsider* possible. More money arrived from a new push for lifetime subscribers. The subscriptions cost fifty dollars, and Jon solicited everyone on his mailing list, even those who already had lifetime subscriptions. A few subscribers grumbled, but a good portion of them took advantage of the offer just to support Loujon. A few people chided Jon for asking too little for the lifetime subscriptions, and some of these sent double the asking price and asked nothing extra in return.

Swamped with their usual barrage of correspondence, and with both Jon and Louise battling myriad health problems, Jon found the time to acquire the heavy sixty-pound book stock he wanted to use for the upcoming issue. The paper cost almost a thousand dollars, an expense on top of three thousand dollars in medical bills Jon and Louise had accrued in recent months. Louise had chronic respiratory issues, dating back at least to her first weeks in New Orleans at Marc Antony's interior design shop. Jon suffered problems with his prostate. Their health problems did not prevent them from working, however. "Since paper arrived we have been going day and night—have a lot of copy set up and ready to go." Jon assured the Patchens that he had enough tribute material to do the issue, but hoped for more. He was especially pleased with a Patchen interview done by Gene Detro, a tape of which Miriam had sent. Loujon still lacked cover stock, but Jon and Louise forged ahead.

EDITOR'S BIT AND OBIT

LOUJON'S FINANCES GOT A boost in August 1968, with a thousand-dollar grant from the New Orleans-based Fidelis Foundation, an organization chaired by Blair's friend William Wisdom. The foundation praised the press's innovations in all areas of the book arts, including typography, format, and design. Soon after, another thousand-dollar grant came through, this one from the National Endowment for the Arts and the Coordinating Council of Literary Magazines. The money surely came in handy as the Webbs continued with their brutal production schedule for the new *Outsider*.

Jon took the night shift and Louise took the day; they rarely saw one another awake. Jon often left Louise notes to remind her of chores that needed doing, like buying more stamps or ordering paper. One of her jobs was gluing in the magazine's endpapers. This was tedious binder's work, and Louise doing it freed Jon to concentrate on printing. "Thanks, honey," he told her, "for relieving me of a big part of the job on *Outsider 4/5*." Sometimes Jon commented on his health. "I sure have felt a lot better (almost no pain) since you know when. A thousand thanks, honey." In this same note, Jon joked to Louise that good work would be rewarded. "If you do this good—I'll think about giving you a raise. (That's the sense of humor the astrology said I'd have tonight, in paper)." Work went much faster than it had with *Order and Chaos chez Hans Reichel*. "Best day yet at the press—look at pile of stuff done today on shelves. Five runs through press. Used to take a week or more for that on Miller book." Jon pushed himself to keep on track. "Got to try to keep up this pace this month—Soon be back at the poems—about this time next week," he wrote. "Should have Patchen section about done." One of the things that kept Jon going was Louise's cooking. "Your meatloaf sure delicious at 4:30 a.m.," he told her.

In addition to the normal pressures of producing an issue of the *Outsider*, the Webbs were trying to sell their house and plan their next move. They were determined to leave Tucson and considered buying a motor home. And it was beginning to weigh on Jon's mind that time was catching up with them. He was eleven years older than Louise and worried he might die and leave her stranded in a strange city. Perhaps New Orleans would be best, if Louise could be happy there. "Maybe we should take a trip there and see. Years make a big change, & of course it is not the N. O. now we knew. Or you take a trip by yourself, tho I'd miss you." Still working one morning sometime after 4 a.m., he wrote, "Good to make progress each day. Got to do more than been doing—tho today did 3 pages. Before we know it we'll know if house is sold or not. I'd say we'll know by Dec. 3—or that week, for sure. Be a great thing to get off our minds." The note also suggested a normal domestic tension, no doubt made worse by the pressures of magazine production. "So got to keep busy till then—& forgive me when I don't watch TV with you. Love you & want to—but later, honey." He ended the note with a drawing of a valentine heart and his signature.

In early 1968, Jon asked Miller about another collaboration, this one an album of Miller's watercolors. Miller was intrigued, but he worried about financing and distribution. He had given Loujon *Order and Chaos* with no expectation of royalties, but wasn't willing to enter into a similar arrangement now. He wanted to make money and assumed that Jon did, too. Miller worried that Loujon tended to make small profits or lose money on most projects and wanted Jon to give him the particulars of the deal: number of watercolors per set, what the album would sell for, and how long it would take to do the job. Miller toyed with the idea of two separate projects. The first of these he called the "Insomnia Series," eleven watercolors with extensive annotation by Miller. He called these paintings "very special" and suggested that he might write a brief text to accompany them. His other idea was to gather a dozen or more of his paintings held by collectors and issue them with no accompanying text. These would be "pure water colors, including some of my very best."

Miller and Jon negotiated the details of the project over the first half of 1968. Miller worried that Jon was estimating costs too low and perhaps aiming at too grand a production. His fears were based in his experience with the Webbs on *Order and Chaos*. Miller had not been completely satisfied with his first Loujon book. He acknowledged that *Order and Chaos* was beautiful, but felt it was generally overdone, without enough distinction between the regular and deluxe editions to warrant their difference in price. On the new project, he thought Jon's proposed selling price of fifteen to twenty dollars per copy was too low, and suggested twenty-five to thirty-five dollars would be more reasonable for the regular edition, with a higher price for a deluxe edition. "That is, if you are thinking to make a profit for yourselves this time, which I hope to god you are. I see no good reason why a beautiful job should not earn money for the doer."

In June, Miller gave Loujon the go-ahead to publish the "Insomnia Series." Miller had earlier suggested that the watercolors be sold by subscription only, thus cutting out the large discounts demanded by bookstores. When Jon told him that this was not feasible—he still had many unsold copies of *Order and Chaos*, which had been sold both to subscribers and through bookstores—Miller agreed that Jon's original high-end price (twenty dollars) would probably produce more sales. Regardless, Miller didn't want the project at all if it couldn't be done right, and he knew this would take money. If Jon couldn't arrange the financing, Miller believed they should abandon their plans.

Webb found a backer in Ben Sackheim, a former New York advertising executive who had turned to bookselling. Sackheim operated his business from offices at 91 Central Park West in New York City, but had a residence in Tucson, which is probably where Jon met him. Sackheim told Webb he might be interested in backing *Insomnia* if Miller finished writing the manuscript which was now planned to accompany the paintings. Like Miller, Sackheim worried about price, quality, and profit. Sackheim suggested creating an exclusive book club, limited to two hundred fifty to three hundred members, who would pay an annual subscription of perhaps five hundred dollars for twelve to eighteen collector's editions per year. *Insomnia* would be one of the club's selections. This would be similar to the subscription plan Miller had suggested, but with *Insomnia* as part of a larger package, there was a much greater likelihood of strong sales and a reasonable profit. Loujon could make even more money publishing and selling additional copies. Better still, Sackheim might advance Jon production costs before the book went to press.

With negotiations on *Insomnia* ongoing, the Webbs immersed themselves in the next issue of the *Outsider*, pushing themselves almost to the breaking point. Jon collapsed from exhaustion and was hospitalized. At some point during production, he suffered another small stroke, which partially disabled the left side of his body for about two weeks. At another point, he required prostate surgery. The day he got home from that operation, Louise put a record on the stereo and danced in celebration, only to double over in pain and crumple to the floor. Her problem was a strangulated intestine, a potentially fatal condition that required immediate surgery. Fortunately, Jon was able to get Louise to the hospital quickly, and her operation was a success.

They had been making steady progress on the new *Outsider* before Louise's surgery, and freshly printed pages of the magazine lay stacked in the print shop, along with the Webbs' remaining copies of *Order and Chaos*. The day Louise returned home from the hospital was no doubt set aside for recuperation, but that was not to be. A flash flood, of all things, saw to that. The *Tucson Daily Citizen* reported: "Heavy rains sluiced beneath the print shop up front and sprung in geysers through joints in the floor in the rear of the house. Gypsy, home from the hospital less than 12 hours following major surgery, had to be restrained from fighting the rising waters. Jon, released from another hospital only days earlier . . . hefted 150-pound packages of paper around, and swept vainly at the water—then jumping a six-inch high door sill into the bedroom—like the sorcerer's apprentice." The floodwaters swept dozens of copies of *Order and Chaos* and many pages set for the new *Outsider* into the backyard sinkhole where they joined the trash Jon and Louise had dumped there and were covered with debris, ruined and lost.

The flood was devastating, but there was little choice but to resume working on the magazine. Somehow, Jon maintained his steady and voluminous correspondence, even as he and Louise continued work on the *Outsider* 4/5. Poet Robert Bly was among Jon's correspondents. Bly published an important literary journal named for the decades in which it was published: in the 1950s, the magazine was called *The Fifties*; in the 1960s, it was called *The Sixties*. Bly respected the *Outsider* and had hoped to visit the Webbs during a trip to Tucson, though other engagements got in the way. As was common with Jon's correspondents who commented upon the flood, Bly was stunned by the Webbs' troubles: "Sorry I'm late—I've been running around trying to get some money for my own press. But thank God we don't have floods here! Fantastic thing—I hope you're both well and working again now."

Jon set the last page on February 9, 1969, and printed it the next day. Then came the enormous task of collating and binding the fat, 211-page issue of what had now become a "book periodical." The issue featured a cover photo of a bedridden Patchen in full body cast, wearing dark glasses and holding a cigarette in his upraised right hand, his ashtray, lighter and cigarette pack within reach on his bed. The issue bore the dedication "For Kenneth Patchen." Against all odds, there was a new *Outsider*.

Elizabeth Bartlett (1920–1994), whose poem "the walnut tree," appeared in the issue, promoted the magazine to friends and worked hard to interest them in Loujon's newly reextended lifetime subscription offer, which Jon had limited to twenty subscribers. She also personally sold several copies. Soon after receiving her contributor's copy, Bartlett wrote to thank the Webbs for publishing her poem and to congratulate them on what she described as "a beautiful job—heartbreakingly so." She sold a copy to Kenneth and Melissa Maytag, who owned the well-known Unicorn Bookstore, and provided names of ten more friends she thought might be interested in purchasing copies. She told Webb to tell these people that Elizabeth Bartlett had suggested he contact them. Bartlett sold copies to faculty members at the University of California at Riverside and at UC Santa Barbara. She charged ten dollars for each copy of the magazine, "since *Outsider* 4/5 is a collector's item." She later wrote that she would be "getting a chance for more *Outsider* orders next week, when I go to UCLA."

Bartlett's commitment to helping the Webbs continued at least through the waning months of 1969, when she planned a "Loujon Party" fund-raiser in Santa Barbara. Bartlett asked the Webbs to send her fifty copies of his column, which he now called the Editor's Bit and Obit, to include with her invitations. The event was well organized and ambitious: "Finally, we have a date on Sunday, Dec. 14, P.M. for our Loujon Party. Mailing lists and invitations are in process—the goal, 50 people, $250. A church in Isla Vista, the UCSB student community, has extended its kitchen and lounge facilities, and if the weather permits, dining outdoors on the lawn. Menu: a Margarita cocktail, choice of turkey, ham, roast beef, tongue, with slaw, potato salad, relishes, cherry tomatoes, hard rolls, ice cream, cookies, coffee. Plus door prizes of your Miller, Bukowski, and *Outsider* 4/5. Here's to success!" Melissa Maytag helped with the event, as did Carol Tinker, who brought the cole slaw. In addition to whatever money she raised at Isla Vista, Bartlett planned to send the Webbs fifty dollars and hoped it would reach them by Christmas. "I know how much it takes for normal expenditures, not to mention your others."

Others tried to help in different ways. When William Cagle of Indiana University's Lilly Library received the *Outsider* 4/5, he sent congratulations and a bit of unsolicited advice on increasing Loujon's cash flow. Cagle feared appearing like a "self-appointed business manager, but asked: "Why not follow this up with two or three short, 20 or 30 page works before you tackle another big job?" Cagle realized that many of the contributors to the current *Outsider* were widely collected by both individuals and libraries. A brief, limited edition book from any of these writers would probably turn a nice profit for Loujon, Cagle believed. "Book shops like House of Books and Phoenix would place good orders, I am sure, and you might make a little profit before your next work of love."

Cagle was responsible for the Lilly Library's aggressive collection policies toward a number of American and British authors and in this capacity had been a real friend to Loujon. Soon after joining the staff as librarian for English in 1962, Cagle convinced library director David Randall to establish standing orders for several important authors, Henry Miller among them. Cagle's plan included works from commercial publishers, private presses, and limited editions, as well as any subsets of these publications. Because of this policy, Lilly wound up with copies of the entire run of *Order and Chaos chez Hans Reichel.* "I imagine the Webbs were pleased and thought me totally mad," Cagle later wrote. The Loujon books stood out in the Lilly collection because the library didn't make any particular efforts to collect material from private presses per se. But Cagle admired what the Webbs were doing, "and so we may have been a bit more inclusive in their case."

The little magazine world had not stood still while the *Outsider* was on hiatus. *Lines, Kayak,* and *My Own Mag* were just a few magazines which commenced publishing in 1964. A rich batch of new titles appeared over the next four years, including *Quixote* (1965), *Angel Hair* (1966), *The Ant's Forefoot* (1967), and *Adventures in Poetry* (1968). By 1967, d. a. levy had become a well-known poet and publisher of *The Buddhist 3rd Class Junkmail Oracle.* The authorities in his hometown considered him a rabble-rouser, and he was arrested in Cleveland with Asphodel Bookshop owner Jim Lowell on charges of distributing obscenity stemming from little magazine sales there. The arrest was probably the result of his outspoken support of legalized marijuana and denunciation of the war in Vietnam. Jon had accepted levy's poem "for the pigs, sheep & various adorable other mammals of cleveland, o.," a reprint from *Grist,* for the new *Outsider.* It was a powerful poem, containing the lines "I am moving / I am moving / & not only my body is in motion / for anyone foolish enough to look / I give warning / I am leaving behind tons of rubbish & dust / don't look at it—look at the love in you still buried / and my love for you."

The demons levy faced in himself and the harassment by the Cleveland police department had marked him and resonated through his poem. Levy sank into depression and told Jon that "it just goes round & round my head like a merry-go-round except it's not so much fun anymore—I put myself together 1,000 different ways but there is still no place for me on this planet— & I am very tired most of the time—things were easier when I just wanted to write—now I'm fighting all kinds of illusions that pretend to be living or life—there's very little life on this planet—& I'm bored with all the bad movies. What ever happened to d. a. levy who used to write poems & believed in them? I live too close to the riots." Levy shot and killed himself on November 4, 1968. Jon included a full-page memorial facing levy's poem.

The winter 1968–1969 *Outsider* was a bittersweet affair. This issue was a major departure from earlier numbers, moving from a soft-cover publication that was recognizably a magazine into the book format Jon had considered when in talks with Stuart. It was also considerably thicker than previous issues. This combined number 4–5 followed the previous issue by more than five years, plenty of time to collect a wealth of new material. Among the dozens of contributors were Clarence Major, Diane di Prima, levy, Jean Cocteau, and Bukowski. Denise Levertov finally placed work there, saying now that her original distaste for the magazine came from its inclusion of Bukowski and Peter Orlovsky, "both of whose work I think is awful, though I have seen (since) one poem by each I thought was good."

In the Editor's Bit and Obit Jon wrote of the horrors of the flood. He told readers that "The Outsider is/was published by Loujon Press. Address until June 15, 1969, is 1009 East Elm, Tucson, Arizona 85719. Sold home & workshop to help put this issue out—must move." Jon asked readers to buy extra issues, or just send money. "Otherwise, it's done for, for good. We love it, and we don't want that to happen, praying it won't."

The issue's centerpiece, planned, aborted, and planned again since 1963, was the forty-six-page "Homage to Kenneth Patchen." The Patchen tribute relied heavily upon Miriam's lists of potential contributors. Webb pulled together tributes and commentary on Patchen from a broad range of writers, producing what could be described as a biography in pastiche. Novelist, Guggenheim recipient (1935), and editor of leftist political journals such as *The Anvil* and *The New Anvil*, Jack Conroy, in his short essay, noted that "Since my friend Webb has enjoined me from any critical evaluation I'll have to rely on tangential and peripheral items," but went on to observe that Patchen was a link between 1920s-era Dadaism and the Beat culture of the 1950s and beyond. Frederick Eckman reaffirmed a suggestion he had made a decade earlier that Patchen compared favorably with William Blake. *Trace's* James Boyer May submitted a piece written for a long-planned but finally shelved tribute in *Views*. May wrote that "The central key to his character lies in his love for all that lives: plants, animals, man . . . and stars."

Of course, the magazine was more than just the Patchen tribute. This issue was "Handset, Mostly & Hand Bound At Loujon's Desert Workshop Printery, Arizona U.S.A. by Lou & Jon Webb, and the Ghost of an Indian," according to an inscription appearing just after the table of contents. A series of cartoons from Kelsie Harder added an overtly political cast to the issue. One cartoon played off Archibald McNeal Willard's painting, *Spirit of '76*. Instead of their musical instruments, the patriots now carried rifles with long scopes, which they gleefully aimed at an unseen target. Later in the issue, Harder's cartoons engaged religion, cultural imperialism, war and peace, gender wars, marijuana, and other social concerns prominent in the late 1960s. *Camels Coming* editor Richard Morris, who introduced Harder's work, said Harder "courts ridiculousness with his political statements," but "Kelsie tells it like it is."

Webb had sent Marcus Grapes repeated requests for a submission for the *Outsider* 4/5, but since Grapes had given Jon money over the years, these requests made Grapes uneasy. He finally gave in and submitted work, telling Jon to "do what you want with the poetry." After sending his love to Louise and asking Jon to take care of himself, Grapes closed the letter: "Maybe someday, we'll get a chance to really know each other. The hard way." Webb accepted the poems and showcased them in "A Marcus J. Grapes Album of Untitled Poems." Grapes's fifteen poems ran for eight pages. The album was sandwiched around a design element characteristic of Webb's attention to artistic detail, a tissue-thin page which held a caricature-portrait of Grapes, "a pen and ink portrait by N. O. French Quarter artist F. McBride." The poet was shown in the incongruous mixture of ruffled, dainty collar and Captain Marvel T-shirt, a book grasped in his hand and an ear horn hanging in the air beside his head.

The *Outsider* 4/5 was well received. Conroy proclaimed the new issue was "a humming bird and a lulu," and assured Webb that he was "spreading the word" to potential customers. Conroy added that he might get to review the magazine for the *Kansas City Star* newspaper. Dustbooks editor and publisher Len Fulton, who also served as chairman of the Committee of Small

Magazines Editors and Publishers, wrote the Webbs that "OUTSIDER 4/5 is FANTASTIC! But I imagine you've heard that already, eh? Your dedication and labours are UNMATCHED in this world, believe." Fulton, unable to send money, offered to give Loujon a free full-page ad in the upcoming fifth number of *Small Press Review*. Allen Ginsberg sent a check for fifty dollars, describing the gift as "small balm for some troubles."

And so it went. The *Los Angeles Free Press* gushed that Loujon was "the Rolls Royce of publishers!" Issue 4/5 "is jacketed with some elegant oriental rice paper, engraved of course. The paper is rich and varied, different colors, different textures, different as hell. If you've never seen a Rolls Royce, how could I really describe it to you?" William Cagle called the issue "most impressive," and predicted "the publicity from this—both in the press and from the attention it will attract itself—will put you back in the spotlight." *Library Journal*'s Magazines columnist William Katz called the new issue "the bargain of the year."

The issue amazed even Bukowski, who wrote a congratulatory letter filled with praise for Jon and Louise's efforts over the lifetime of their press. He understood that their own story transcended the value of the books and *Outsiders* they published and urged them to write a memoir, even supplying a potential title: *The Adventures of Loujon in a Low-Down Clime*. Bukowski reveled at the stories such a book might tell: "All the times the press went in and out the window, sometimes the same window, out, in, out again. The time of the attempted robbery. The time Bukowski tried to gas you. The bed up in the air. The bathtub filled with pages. That ugly and cold Santa Fe scene. The crazy and dull visitors. The madmen. The gangsters who push their bad work almost with threat. The pests. The sickness again and again. Flood, fire. Old papa with his beer. Bukowski vomiting in the University trashcan. The old handpress. The madness and agony of everything. All the things I do not know. Lou on the corner trying to sell paintings. The deaf and dumb guy in the bar. City after city. All the odd benefactors with strings attached. The whole crazy wild story." Bukowski knew a great story when he saw one, and to him, Loujon's seemed practically unmatched: "I'm sure that there has never been a press and a time like yours, and I think that it would be a shame and an error if it were not recorded, because someday somebody is going to do it and they'll get it all WRONG."

It seemed that everything, for once, was going well. In December, the National Council on the Arts awarded the *Outsider* a $250 grant on the strength of Elizabeth Bartlett's contribution to the issue, "the walnut tree," being selected for a Viking Press anthology. This grant, along with money they made selling production materials and other items associated with the new issue, financed the Webbs' next move. They had trouble deciding on where to go next. Louise wanted to return to New Orleans or maybe Cleveland, where she still had family; Jon preferred a new city altogether and had his eye on Nashville, Tennessee. Jon considered Nashville to be a publishing hub, which would make getting press supplies easier, and eventually convinced Louise that this was the right move for them. Jon wrote Ed Blair that Nashville was "a big gamble—& crazy, considering we're about broke, but that's our life, sink or swim."

Jon was much more positive about the move in his notes to Louise. Nashville, he told her, would be ideal, because the city was situated at the midpoint between New Orleans and Cleveland, making it a happy compromise: "And it's perfect—our both agreeing on Nashville. It's exactly midway between Cleveland & N. O. too.—532 to Cleveland—& 530 to N. O. What could be better? So we have got to like the place." He told Louise that he could not find a single thing wrong with the move, but added that it would be best for him to fly to Nashville first and find them a place to live, rather than the couple simply packing their belongings and finding lodging when they arrived in the new town.

Such a trip would come at the expense of a trip they had been planning to Las Vegas. Jon pointed out that the Las Vegas trip would cost at least five hundred dollars and that it would be wiser to invest that money into finding a good home in Nashville: "It's the smart thing to do. We'll study the paper ads, & soon as we get a good picture of costs of places there—& the rentals—& have several good prospects to look at, I'll fly to Nashville & it would be perfect if we had our place with address all settled before we leave Tucson."

For Jon, the difference between Nashville and the other places he and Louise had discussed was a comfort with the city itself. He wrote: "It'll be a trip this time without the misgivings I had with Vegas, or even Kingman— because with them I just was not sold on those places as being right for us. I am 100% sure with Nashville. I would have had the same misgivings with Cleveland or N. O.—if I'd gone to those places. But I'm sold beforehand on Nashville, so I wouldn't be going there to find a place there, feeling it's not the town for me, or us. It's the one town in the U.S. I want to go to—so I've got to find a place, & will." Jon became more enthusiastic about the proposed move as he continued writing. He realized that he had "always had a feeling for Nashville." The location was good for Loujon's future prospects, "And you know basically I've always liked country music—or 'hillbilly records' as I used to call them."

That Jon's enthusiasm for this move was greater than was Louise's is reflected in his admonition that "Whether we like it or not AT FIRST, we've got to face it—Nashville is right for us, and we're going to make it work." He saw a future not only for himself and Louise in Nashville, but also for the *Outsider*, suggesting that the city could provide material for their magazine which might mirror their earlier success in New Orleans: "So here we come, NASHVILLE! Same as I did a section in the *Outsider* on traditional jazz— why not a section in *Outsider* #6 on the famous old timers of the Nashville sound? With photos, etc. Get to meet a few—& maybe even interest one or two in trying out a song by you. Not impossible. You know how important a connection is in show biz." Settling on Nashville seemed right professionally and was also good for Jon's health. He told Louise that the decision took a big load from his mind and that "My head has been aching for days, down to back of my neck, and of a sudden the ache is gone."

They moved to Nashville in May 1969 and in researching Jon's proposed country music feature for the *Outsider* met singers Mel Tillis, Johnny Cash, and June Carter Cash, becoming friendly enough with the Cashes that Louise got into the habit of sending birthday cards to their son, John Carter Cash, who was born in March 1970. But, as had happened so often in the past, Nashville wasn't the fit Jon believed it would be. Other than meeting a few country stars, they made no real progress in getting the next *Outsider* under way. In February 1970, they left Nashville for New Orleans and an apartment at 607 Dumaine Street. They moved again a month later, landing this time in Albuquerque, near the campus of the University of New Mexico. Jon was writing again. He had picked up "Go Lieth Down South, Oh, Lover," and was intent on finishing it.

As always, Jon pushed himself hard. He was tired and still stressed from their ordeal in Tucson. One way he relieved the stress of work was through the gaming tables of Las Vegas, only fifty minutes away by air. Jon took a scientific approach to gambling, spending more than sixty dollars on how-to-win books, which he studied religiously. On one trip, he took fifty dollars, intending to play the dice tables. About ten o'clock the night he left,

Jon called home and told Louise, "Honey, I just wired you one thousand dollars." Louise was overjoyed. "Oh, my God, that's great!" she exclaimed and went back to bed. "And then the phone rang again. He did it four times. The second time he won another thousand, then I think he went across the street to the Fremont and he won two thousand there. And each time he wired it. He wired me six thousand dollars and he had gone with fifty bucks." Jon wired Louise his entire bankroll and had to get her to send cab fair for him to make it home from the airport. He later told Louise, "If I had known I could win that much money, to hell with the magazine and writing!" Jon brought his lucky dice home and gave them to Louise. For years after that, she and Jon, Jr., each wore one on a chain around their necks.

In early June, the Webbs received a final visit from Bukowski and another friend, poet Gregory Corso. A photograph taken during this visit showing Jon with Bukowski and Corso is remarkable for the relative vitality of everyone but Corso, who is slumped over, disheveled and thin, almost asleep. Webb sits perched above Corso staring down at him while Bukowski grins directly into the camera. Sometime during this visit, Bukowski gave a reading for which Jon printed a publicity flyer. After a quote from Miller, calling Bukowski the "poet satyr of today's underground," and another from Bukowski, "Sexual intercourse is kicking death in the ass while singing," Jon worked to lure an audience to see the "world famous poet, critic and storyteller whose *Notes of a Dirty Old Man* so far has sold 250,000 copies & whose *All the Assholes in the World & Mine* berserked the establishment to billyclub screams of outrage." The flyer sported a photograph of Bukowski which looked more like a particularly unsavory police mug shot than a portrait of a celebrated author, but the irony was almost certainly intended.

Of course, there was still the serious business of a new Miller book to publish, and word of a new Miller-Webb collaboration began to trickle out. Donald Borzak used news of this development to keep members of the Chicago investors group updated on Loujon activities. Borzak, first noting the problems the Webbs had experienced due to the Tucson flood, wrote to his coinvestors: "They also have been in contact with Henry Miller regarding an opportunity he has given them to do a book of his watercolors. I hope the Webbs will be able to start on it when this issue of the *Outsider* is finished. I've got copies of Jon's and Mr. Miller's correspondence with each other and it is very exciting to me—but just too lengthy to send you copies." If the Chicago investors felt they had any reason to worry about the Webbs continuing to produce quality work after their recent hardships, this news likely assuaged those worries. Borzak did his part to jumpstart the project, using his connections in the printing community to get Loujon a large discount on high-quality color separations for the watercolor prints.

For several months, Sackheim remained interested in financing the project. During this time he and Jon spoke often via long distance telephone calls. Sackheim made many of these calls, one of which lasted two hours, but Jon made his share of calls, too, running up sizeable phone bills. He didn't worry about the costs, though, because he was sure, if the work could be done for fifteen thousand dollars, Sackheim would put up the money. Sackheim had concerns, however. He worried that Miller might die before he could autograph the more than two thousand watercolor prints that comprised the bulk of the project. He worried that Miller's text, about twenty typed pages, was too brief. At the same time, Miller worried over trying to expand the text.

The negotiations became moot in early 1970 when Sackheim informed Jon he had lost a great deal of money in the stock market and withdrew from the deal. Jon wasn't convinced that Sackheim was entirely truthful. He told Miller that Sackheim had often mentioned his fear of investing so much money into the publication of a very brief manuscript and worried that it would likely take a long time to see a return on the investment. By this time, though, Miller was convinced that the project should go forward. In April, after Jon told him he could begin production with five thousand dollars, Miller obliged. He loaned Jon three thousand dollars with which to begin production. A month later, he sent another loan of two thousand dollars.

Jon had not finalized his plans for *Insomnia*, and Miller kept in close touch with his own suggestions and reactions to Jon's. Jon still hoped that Miller might expand the text. For a while, Miller was adamant that he had said what he wanted to say, and any additions would be anticlimactic. He later relented and added a postscript, which he styled a "cadenza," about the watercolors themselves. Jon didn't get his way in all things, though. He wanted Miller to make a recording of himself either talking about *Insomnia* or reading from the text, but Miller thought this was a bad idea. He didn't like the idea of doing the recording and worried that some who bought *Insomnia* wouldn't have the equipment to play it. Miller ultimately left pricing decisions up to Jon, though he worried that Jon was asking more than most people on Miller's mailing list could afford. Webb now proposed thirty-six dollars for the economy edition, all the way to one thousand dollars for the deluxe edition, which would be limited to twelve copies. For their thousand dollars, buyers would also receive an original Miller watercolor.

Jon and Miller eventually settled on the title *Insomnia, or the Devil at Large*. This mixed-media production included a fine-press book, a portfolio of Miller's watercolors, and a hand-crafted wooden case to house the material. Jon saw this as a potential economic bonanza and spared nothing in making *Insomnia* a fully realized masterpiece. Jon was more convinced of *Insomnia*'s financial potential than was Louise, who apparently did not hesitate to make her objections clear. After all, Jon had said the same of *Order and Chaos*, and sales had been disappointing. Jon insisted that things were different this time. *Insomnia*, he was sure, would allow the two of them to become financially independent: "So, honey, don't gripe at this Miller job— it's really our jackpot for the future."

❖ 10 ❖

DEATH IN NASHVILLE

If *Insomnia* was going to make the kind of money Jon hoped it would, he knew it would have to be well promoted. Loujon announced this latest publication with a lavish, detailed broadside, which described "this most monumental production yet to be designed, handcrafted and published by Loujon Press." *Insomnia* would consist of a total of 999 copies divided into seven "deluxe editions." The main attraction was a portfolio of Miller's watercolors. Along with the paintings came an introductory book "candidly detailing the courting by 'this reputedly famous old man' (his words) of Hoki Hioko Tokuda, the young Japanese singer Miller undodderingly escorted not long ago to the altar, & to whom the book & portfolio are dedicated." Among the recipients of this advertising matter was Gerald Locklin, a member of the English faculty at California State College at Long Beach. Locklin, whose unadorned poetry had much the same power as Bukowski's, was becoming an established poet, with "stuff all over the magazines and a couple of small books." Jon had accepted his poem "cunt" for an upcoming issue of the *Outsider* in the days before the Tucson flood, and Locklin was curious about whether Jon was again reading manuscripts. Locklin was twenty-nine years old, twice married, and the father of three; money was tight. He wrote that, if he couldn't afford to buy *Insomnia*, he would still recommend it to the college library, which he believed would make the purchase.

The advertisement noted, not unexpectedly, that "a private press is always in need of cash," and offered a prepublication purchase of *Insomnia* at a 40 percent discount. Miller liked the broadside, though he thought Jon lifted too much text from the book. He was also leery of the large prepublication discounts Jon offered. Still, he asked for 150 copies to send to potential buyers. Even better, Miller sent Jon another thousand dollars. Miller was almost apologetic about the amount, but he assured Jon this was the best he could do. His own finances were suddenly shaky, and he worried about money.

Even with Miller's help, the Webbs were obliged to continue their practice of finding whatever outside assistance they could to make the new book a reality. Webb, for example, requested and received free production materials from a major paper manufacturer, Brown-Bridge Mills, Inc., of Troy, Ohio. A company official empathized with Loujon's predicament: "We, too, are finding it equally as hard to produce a quality product in a society where price, and not quality, dictate who gets the order." Webb also sought in-kind assistance for the new project. Literary agent and photographer William Webb enthusiastically agreed to allow the use of one of his pictures in exchange for a copy of *Insomnia*: "What fool wouldn't accept your generous offer of a Miller portfolio in exchange for a mere photograph!"

In June, Jon entered into discussions with Durrett Wagner of Swallow Press about making *Insomnia* a joint venture. Wagner, an old friend of Donald and Lenore Borzak, had once been a dean at Kendall College, where he hired Lenore to be on the English faculty. He and a partner had acquired Swallow Press in 1967 after the death of founder Alan Swallow. Wagner saw the Miller publication as natural for Swallow, as the press was a longtime publisher of Miller's Paris muse and protégé, Anaïs Nin. He also knew, from Borzak, that Loujon needed money. There was talk of Miller receiving ten thousand dollars from this collaboration. Miller was intrigued, but still worried that the money would cut into Jon's potential profits. It soon became clear, though, that Wagner wanted Miller to spice up *Insomnia* in ways that he was not willing to do, and the deal ultimately fell through. "I don't like the attitude of Swallow's editor at all," he told Webb. "I never had any intention of going into sex life biz in this text. And, as you know, I never try to oblige editors as to what or how long contents should be." Talk of the joint venture ceased in February 1970 when Wagner bowed out, pleading overcommitment to other projects.

As time passed and *Insomnia* seemed no closer to production, Miller became increasingly concerned with his investment. He was hoping for royalties from a film based on his *Quiet Days in Clichy*, which had done well in Europe, but so far he had not seen a penny. Miller had made loans on several ventures in recent months and from these, too, he had not seen a return. It did not go over well when Jon floated the idea of not treating the money Miller had sent as a traditional loan. In October, Miller, obviously concerned about the money, asked, "I take it you didn't want to repay as one would a loan. How was it to be, if you can tell me briefly?" Jon apparently wanted to mix his repayment of the loans with Miller's profits from *Insomnia*, but Miller rejected this idea, telling Webb that he should repay the loans before sending profits from sales. Miller softened his request by saying, "This doesn't mean I am prodding you to pay something *now*, only that the money, when it comes, comes as 'return of loan.'" Still, it was clear he expected his money back and his share of the profits from *Insomnia*.

Jon, meanwhile, was telling potential buyers that the best Loujon could hope for on *Insomnia* was to clear enough money to publish two more issues of the *Outsider*. As the project neared completion, Jon sent letters headlined "Forgive the Delay" to preorder customers. The letters outlined the ordeal he and Louise had endured to publish the book and portfolio, and thanked their customers for being patient. Webb described the effort required simply to construct the wooden cases that housed the book and prints: "From the stack of original 4-by-8-foot wood sheets to the finished handmade portfolios, more than 30 separate hand operations were labored through. And only the two of us on this job—seven morning-to-midnight days a week for almost a year." Privately, Jon was convinced *Insomnia* was their ticket to financial freedom. In a handwritten note to Louise, much of which was concerned with a recent discussion of which of them might die first and what financial security the other might have, Jon assured Louise that *Insomnia* would be a windfall which would provide them "more money in a few months than any of your family or mine can make & see in the bank in 5 or 10 years. That's why on this Miller book I want to add at least $20,000—or more—to our (or your) never needing to beg for support as you grow older, either with me or alone without me."

Finally, all that remained to finish *Insomnia* was filling the boxes with books and Miller's watercolors and shipping them to buyers. In November 1970, in the midst of this phase of the project, Jon suffered another small stroke, similar to the one he had suffered in Tucson during production of the *Outsider* 4/5. As before, his left side was affected; he couldn't exert pressure with the fingers of his left hand. He told Donald Borzak that he had suffered a number of small strokes in recent years and had problems with his blood pressure. "A few weeks ago, pressure jumped from 140 to 198, and have been on pressure medication for about 3 years." Louise had her health problems, too. "Now, too, the altitude is beginning to hit Lou (perhaps me too)—a mile up and we're used to low altitude—New Orleans for our 20 years there was sea level. Lou's emphysema is starting to show signs of acting up again, now that cold weather is setting in—so means we will have to get out."

Jon's point in telling Borzak all of this was that he wanted to sell the

Heidelberg press. The press did great work, but in many ways it was a burden. The Webbs moved frequently, and each move meant packing and shipping the three-thousand-pound press and setting it up anew in their new home. Each move was expensive, and every time it was in transit, the press had been damaged. The Heidelberg was operating at diminished capacity now, adding to Jon's tension at work. He feared that all of this might lead to a fatal attack. His proposed solution was to sell the press in Albuquerque and buy a smaller replacement with the profits after they relocated, perhaps to Boulder City, Nevada, where they were considering spending the winter. Borzak's motive had always been to help the Webbs as best he could, and he gave Jon his blessing to sell the press. A week later, Jon told Miller that he had commissioned the Heinsohn company of Albuquerque, a subsidiary of the Heidelberg company in Germany, to sell the press.

Insomnia, published in nine separate editions in 1970 and 1971, received attention on a par with previous Loujon publications. As sometimes happened when admirers received Loujon publications, *Insomnia* became cause for a fund-raising event. Bernadine Szold-Fritz, a well-connected Beverly Hills matron who years later would appear as herself in the motion picture *Reds*, one of the witnesses to the literary idylls of socialist author Jack Reed's circle of friends, was "enthralled with the *Insomnia*! And at the same time, a little unhappy because I find my belly shriveling up to think of how much labor it took—loving labor of course, but oh dear, you have put all of yourselves into it—and HOPE you get it all back, with bonuses." Szold-Fritz told Louise that she intended to host a party "and invite special friends—and potential buyers—in for a 'viewing.'" Szold-Fritz, claiming shame because the book "ought to cost a dozen times what you stipulate," ordered a second copy to give as a birthday present to actress Jennifer Jones. She was in a rush to get the gift copy before Jones's birthday party. "However, if it does not come in time I'll give her this one, and wait for the other, for myself. It's just about the most superb production I can remember ever having seen."

It was good to be finished with *Insomnia* and undoubtedly gratifying to receive the lavish praise the portfolio drew from collectors. But, the project being finished, there was nothing holding the Webbs to Albuquerque, and it was again time to move. Their wanderlust was part of the reason for this move, but it was also for health reasons. The "frosty weather setting in this mile-high Albuquerque climate" aggravated Louise's chronic lung problems, which had earlier been bothered by the "copper-smelter-air-polluted"

Tucson air. They were soon back on the road, relocating to 1131 South 10th Street, Las Vegas. Jon, Jr., retired from the army in 1967 and was now back in school, working toward a degree in chiropractic medicine. On one occasion, Jon, Jr., and two of his children, Cynthia and Larry, climbed into the family's VW bus and made the more-than-five-hundred-mile journey to visit Jon and Louise. As he had done on a previous visit, Jon, Jr., brought a home movie camera along and filmed Jon and Louise clowning around their home.

Jon didn't have a great deal of faith in his son's chosen field, but at one point during the visit he complained that his neck had been hurting and agreed to let the young man work on him. Jon lay down on a small couch, and his son gave him an adjustment. Immediately, Jon rolled to the floor, seemingly in convulsions. Jon, Jr., was terrified until his father stood and said, "See? See? You could have done that, couldn't you?" Jon, Jr., was too relieved to remain angry with his father. The two of them later went gambling at the Circus Circus casino and got separated at the slot machines. When he needed to locate his son, Jon had him paged as "Ernest Hemingway." "He was always playing jokes like this," Jon, Jr., recalled years later.

Jon and Louise lived only briefly in Las Vegas before returning to Nashville. This time, the move was probably Louise's idea. Jon loved Las Vegas, and it was hard for him to leave. Louise watched him as their train pulled away from the city and never forgot how he kept his eyes on the skyline until it was out of sight. The plan for Nashville was to establish Louise as a songwriter, though Jon, too, was writing songs.

They had only been in town a few months when Max York, a reporter for the *Nashville Tennessean*, interviewed them for a story to appear in the paper's Sunday magazine. York planned to write about the Webbs' successes with their press and their plans for another issue of the *Outsider*. For an angle of local interest, York would mention their coming to Nashville in order to give the country music industry a try. Jon admitted that the move was a gamble. "But we felt we were ready," he told York. "Lou's been writing songs for 20 years. I'm a good editor. I'll help her." They had a "pretty good" portfolio of material on hand and planned to start making the rounds to music publishers when they had compiled one hundred good songs.

The Webbs were not entirely honest with York, because they had already decided that this second move to Nashville was a mistake. While living in Las Vegas, they had made friends with a young blackjack dealer named Mike Newman. Jon wrote Newman that they could not get used to the humidity and, worse, were having second thoughts about their ability to make it in country music: "Can't get in register here. I've been turning out song-poems, for the wastebasket, feeling my way, trying to find out whether I have any pro in me, which if I have could only mean years of bucking the usual hard row to hoe ferreting out recognition—and then what, acclaim on the brink of six feet under?" Jon felt like he was in prison again. Success offered the possibility of parole, but he was "too lazy or something beyond words to get up and hit the bricks." Even if they were set on being songwriters, Jon had decided they could write songs anywhere. He wished for a motor home, or even an old school bus converted so they could live in it and wander the country, but even if they could afford one, this was a pipe dream. Neither of them could drive. There was also the question of publishing the next *Outsider*. Jon wanted to get started, but not until they were settled somewhere they could stay and be happy until the job was finished. He just kept asking himself, "What the hell are we doing here?"

The Webbs had lived in Nashville about four months when Jon began complaining of vertigo. When he and Louise made their decision to move to Nashville the first time, he had found relief from nagging headaches. Whether or not the earlier pain was related to his dizziness, it soon became clear that Jon had a serious health problem. A rash of dizzy spells became acute, and Webb went to the emergency room at the Vanderbilt University hospital. The vertigo, tests revealed, resulted from problems with his carotid artery, and Jon was admitted to the hospital where he had to endure a series of painful tests. Doctors quickly determined that Jon suffered from high blood pressure and detected bruit sounds, anomalous noises emanating from both of his carotid arteries. He underwent an arteriogram, which produced intense burning sensations in his leg and jaw and the sense of a phantom hemorrhage in his mouth. His physicians told him there appeared to be a lesion on his carotid artery. The next step was surgery. Though the procedure was considered relatively safe, doctors told Jon there was a one-in-five-hundred chance of death. Jon, Jr., telephoned in an attempt to reassure his father, but Jon was worried. He pointedly told his son that if there were a one-in-five-hundred chance of dying when he got onto an airplane, he would never fly.

Jon, his "nerves shot," was also going through nicotine withdrawal after not smoking a cigarette in ten days. Father and son spoke in some depth of

Webb's symptoms. Jon, frightened, asked about the nature of neurosurgery and the definition of lesions—wondering if lesions could mean "an abscess in the brain." Jon, Jr., calmly explained the medical definitions of each symptom and condition his father brought up. After speaking with his son for about ten minutes, Jon spoke to his daughter-in-law, Lore, and each of his grandchildren. While he was honest about his fear with his son and daughter-in-law, with the grandchildren, each of whom addressed him as "Jon," he was just an affectionate grandfather, asking about school and their other activities.

In a telephone conversation of June 1, 1971, the day before he was scheduled for surgery, Jon told his son the doctors had found "something unusual" in their tests. Seeking to cheer his father, Jon, Jr., quipped, "That you've got brains?" followed by nervous laughter. The problem, Jon said, was that "for at least several years there's been a complete occlusion in my right carotid artery." The condition of Webb's right carotid artery was so poor, he said, that the doctors were unwilling to disturb it for fear of making matters worse. His left carotid artery also showed signs of occlusion, and it was here the doctors would operate. Jon, Jr., reassured his father that his condition did not appear grave and that the procedure on his neck would amount to no more than a "plumbing job." He told his father that he should be out of the hospital in three days, and then spend two weeks recovering. Jon was to be prepped for surgery at 6:30 the following morning, with the procedure to commence at 8:00 a.m.

About forty-five minutes after this conversation, Jon, Jr., again telephoned his father. The son asked if Bukowski had been in touch, and Webb said he had not. He then asked if his father had heard from Miller. He had, and Miller had told him of a circulatory problem in his leg. Jon, Jr., suggested he might be able to help Miller with chiropractic treatments. They discussed Jon's desire to move west after his surgery, perhaps back to Las Vegas. Jon wanted to resurrect the *Outsider*, though he believed his health would force him to hire a printer for future issues. During all of this, Louise only reluctantly left Jon's side. She had been with him constantly until he sent her home for rest, with the understanding that she would return at 6:30 the following morning so they could have time together before his operation.

The doctors had asked Jon if, knowing the risks, he still wanted to go through with the surgery. "What am I going to do," he asked his son, "chicken out with them all looking down at me?" Before hanging up the telephone, Jon, Jr., asked his father if he should care for Louise, should the worst happen. Jon answered yes, followed by "she'll be a wreck, though," before his voice drifted away. Jon, Jr., told his father, "Well, the *Outsider* will live on" and promised to call Bukowski with an update on Jon's condition. They discussed, vaguely, plans for a forthcoming issue of the *Outsider*, which, Jon now said, would be the final issue of the magazine, but would be a triple issue, numbers six, seven, and eight. Though Jon, Jr., and Lore, also a health care professional, repeatedly reassured Jon that his surgery was to be relatively minor, they were terribly worried. Jon, Jr., was sure that his father was anxious. Since they were halfway across the country, there was little Jon, Jr., and Lore could do to help, but they contacted a friend on the hospital staff and asked her to check on Jon after the procedure and report back to them. Probably reflecting how serious they actually felt the surgery to be, they cautioned the friend not to contact Louise.

Sometime before his 8:00 a.m. surgery, Webb found himself alone and spent some of the time writing a poem. These lines reveal more regret than fear. Jon was uncertain if he had been a success in life:

Going on down,
Changing with the weather.
Doing our best at staying together.
Raining in our hearts,
Snowing in our brains . . .
Adrift in lonely depots,
Missing all the trains.

He was wheeled into the recovery room at 9:25 with a clear artery and a good prognosis. For a day, all seemed well. Louise worried over Jon's condition, but believed that he would recover and they would get on with their lives. There were still so many places to see, so much to do. Another issue of the *Outsider* might be on the horizon, maybe a return to Las Vegas, perhaps New Orleans. There was still a future to discover. But that future went dark the morning of June 2 when, unexpectedly, Jon suffered a massive stroke and sank into a coma. Within hours his kidneys failed; soon after that he was placed on a respirator. Doctors told Louise there was little hope. If Jon were to survive, he would likely be an invalid or worse. Louise told the doctors that all she cared about was Jon's life. If he were impaired, so be it, so long as he lived. She hoped Jon, Jr., could come to Nashville, but neither had money to pay for the trip. A round-trip train fare between Los Angeles and Nashville was $325.70, and the family was not able to gather the money. Louise suggested that Jon, Jr., borrow from Bukowski, but quickly realized that this would not work, because he, too, was poor. Doctors allowed Louise five-minute visits with Jon every other hour. Otherwise alone, she faced the prospect of Jon's death in the company of her sister and brother-in-law. Louise remarked to Jon, Jr., that there were still a number of unfinished volumes of Miller's *Insomnia* at the Webbs' home that could be completed and sold, her only hope for immediate income.

Jon, Jr., made a point to keep Bukowski and Miller up to date on his father's condition. On June 5, he visited Bukowski and reminisced about Jon's work with the *Outsider* and Bukowski's visits with Jon and Louise. Probably trying to preserve Bukowski's impressions of Jon for posterity, Jon, Jr., asked, "What the hell was he working for, Hank? All those years, what do you think?" But Bukowski was not interested in this line of conversation. "I don't know, man," he said. "I think you spoil things by coming right out and saying, oh, 'He was going to do a great thing,' and 'I'm a great poet'; you know, that sours everything. . . . You just go ahead and make your moves until the game quits on you." This did not mean Bukowski failed to appreciate what Jon had done for him. "Old Jon picked me up out of nowhere," Bukowski said. "[He] just planned the beautiful pages." Two days later, the younger Webb called Miller. Hearing that Jon had been in a coma for five days, Miller exclaimed: "Five days? My God. I'm sorry to hear. He's had one thing after the other. I don't know what to say." Miller asked how long Jon might last and, when Jon, Jr., responded that he had seen people survive for three weeks in such a state, Miller said, "He's survived most everything, hasn't he?" Repeating that he didn't know what to say, Miller told Jon, Jr., that "If you talk to Gypsy, give her my best and my hopes."

Jon, Jr., also kept in close contact with Louise, speaking with her by telephone several times each day. Louise told Jon, Jr., that her sister was waiting with her at the hospital for Jon to die so that they could return together to the sister's home in Cleveland. Louise did not want to go to Cleveland, and Jon, Jr., repeated to her a promise he had made to his father: if Jon were to die, Louise would have a home with him. By this time, though, it was clear to everyone that "if" was no longer part of the equation; death was near. Jon's fight ended on June 9, 1971. He was sixty-eight years old. Jon's wish in his twenty-first anniversary note to Louise had come true. He had asked for half as much more time as they had spent together, and that's almost exactly what he got.

Jon's wish was to be cremated, but through a quirk in Tennessee law, Louise could not arrange for cremation herself. If she donated his body to Vanderbilt, there would be no problem. Louise agreed to do this. Before Jon died, Louise asked a nurse for his dentures, which she wanted as a keepsake, but was told she could not have them because they were university property. Louise was determined to have the dentures and asked repeatedly that they be returned. She was rebuffed each time. After Jon's death, she gathered up her dog, Tina, and made a night visit to the morgue. She wandered from door to door, each time saying, "Hi, Jon," until she finally found the correct room; Jon lay on slab C 3006. Louise took Jon's dentures and, satisfied, said to her dog, "Come on, Tina. We've got to go home, babe." After the cremation, she made repeated requests for Jon's ashes, but ran into the same problems she had encountered in trying to get his dentures: everyone she asked told her the ashes were university property. Finally, a pathologist relented and gave Louise the ashes in a paper carton. She was angry about what she considered shabby treatment, but relieved to have some part of Jon returned to her. Jon had always been partial to the color yellow, so Louise bought a yellow planter and placed the ashes within. She kept them close by until her family prevailed upon her to bury them in a family plot in Cleveland. Louise agreed, but secretly kept out a handful of ashes with bits of bone that had not been consumed by the fire.

Louise made the necessary calls to tell friends of Jon's death. One of the first of these calls went to Ed Blair, who was in Washington, D.C., on business. Blair had not known the seriousness of Jon's condition, and the unexpected news hit him hard. "Next to my own father's death I had never been so moved," he remembered decades later. "I can still remember crying in the hotel shower after hanging up the phone." The night of Jon's death or the next, Louise called Bukowski to tell him the news. When the telephone rang, Bukowski was at work on a eulogy for d. a. levy for *The Serif*, a magazine of the Kent State University Libraries. Bukowski turned the eulogy into a tribute to both men. "The music plays," he wrote. "I smoke half a cigar stub, there's a beer . . . levy, levy, levy, you're gone. jon, jon, jon, you're gone too. my heart heaves out the belly of itself." Soon after Jon's death, Louise used a nail to scratch a memoriam in a backyard tree, after the age-old fashion of young lovers. Someone took her picture holding Tina in her arms and leaning, eyes closed, against the tree. Dug deeply into the bark is the legend "6/9/71. I love you Jon. Lou."

Max York's cover story for the *Sunday Tennessean*, July 18, 1971, under the headline "A Good Man Dies," was a farewell to Jon and the Loujon Press. "Death came the other day to a gentle man. He was a stranger in town, and few of us mourned his passing. But since his death, poems have been written in his honor. We had written a magazine story about his coming to Nashville and about his good works and his hopes for a good future here. He died before it could be printed. Now that story becomes this." Back in New Orleans, an obituary quoted Ben C. Toledano on Jon's importance to local culture. "This man is the closest thing we've had to a real literary figure in New Orleans within the avant-garde framework within the past 20 years," Toledano said. "He is one of the few people we've had who has been in the mainstream of things."

With Jon's death, Lou was left near destitute, pending the settlement of her husband's life insurance policy. Just as Jon had worried, she found herself alone in an unfamiliar city where she knew few people. She had no money to pay Jon's three-thousand-dollar hospital bill, nor did she have money for rent. Her assets included a few pieces of furniture and some leftover Miller prints, which she hoped to sell to a local bookstore. Louise told York: "Jon never cared for money. It was just something he could use to buy paper and ink. He didn't care for money just to have money."

When Jon's insurance money became available, she traveled briefly, going to Las Vegas and then to California to see Jon, Jr., and his family. This was just a visit, though, not a permanent arrangement. She suggested to Jon, Jr., that they publish another issue of the *Outsider*, though both knew this was all but impossible. There was no money with which to do it, and no Jon to see it through. After the California visit, Louise drifted back to Ohio, where she stayed briefly with relatives. Finally, she moved back to New Orleans and lived for a time in an apartment above a Bourbon Street bar in a building owned by Larry Borenstein and supported herself working in a T-shirt shop. She eventually developed a treatable lung cancer and moved in with her sister, who now lived near New Orleans.

For a time, Louise considered publishing a tribute to Jon in the form of a "photobiog." She alerted potential customers to the project through little magazines such as *Literary Times* and *Wormwood Review*. Following the Loujon standard, she hoped to finance the project through advance orders, which she offered for twenty-five dollars. But the same problems held up the book that prevented Louise from publishing another *Outsider*. She lacked Jon's skills, and she lacked money. Still, his death did not go unnoticed in the little magazine community, nor did his memory quickly fade. In 1974, *Wormwood Review* editor Marvin Malone arranged publication of Jon's short story "The Crowded Tomb" in Curt Johnson's little magazine, *December*. In a letter to Louise, Malone wrote that the story "will have a good audience there," and indicated that the only changes Johnson had made were for punctuation, typographical errors, and repeated words. For his part, Johnson wrote of the piece, "Good story. Got style."

This was not the first time Marvin Malone had attempted to sustain Jon's memory. Malone devoted the entirety of issue 45 of his magazine to a Webb memorial and a reprint of Webb's story "All Prickles, No Petals." In a brief prefatory note, Malone praised the *Outsider* as "the best little magazine of the 1960s." He described his memorial issue as an attempt to bring together three generations of writers who were affected by Jon Webb: Henry Miller, Charles Bukowski, and Marcus J. Grapes. Two out of the three came through. Miller sent a brief note to decline the invitation: "I'm afraid I'm of no use to you. I never met Jon Webb and our correspondence was limited to discussion of the 2 books he printed. Besides, I'm over my head in work—and am sick of work. Want only to write what I want to write for my own pleasure." Malone printed Miller's response without comment.

Grapes's contribution was a letter speaking directly to Jon: "What did they want from you? It wasn't the poems in THE OUTSIDER, or the poets. Some you liked and some you didn't like. Some you heard of, some you hadn't heard of and never did again. Some were Bukowski. But that wasn't it. And the books, the beautiful books, sure there was no arguing with the format, or the design, the sheer poetry not in them but of them. It was something else. Something they couldn't define. THE OUTSIDER was so totally outside of anything else, so totally itself, so much you and Lou." Grapes finished his tribute with the suggestion that the *Outsider* offered poets a journal that was fundamentally different from other, more staid "footnotes and tea parties" publishing venues. "It stood there, what it was, and it pointed in directions even further away."

Bukowski's contribution was similar in tone. He listed many of the "names" who had published in the magazine, but he argued that the names were not what made the *Outsider* great. "It was simply that the *flame* bent toward the *Outsider*. It was the gathering place, the tavern, the cave of the gods and the cave of the devils . . . it was the place, it was in . . . it was literature jumping and screaming, it was a record of voices and it was a record of the time, it was the *Outsider*, it was Jon and Louise Webb, and now Jon Webb . . . has vanished." As was sometimes his custom in the 1960s and early 1970s, Malone made a punning play on the magazine's title, using the pun as a substitute title for that issue. On the cover of this particular issue, beneath a stock photo of a full-blown, traditional New Orleans jazz funeral, complete with a horse-drawn hearse and scores of people lining the streets, the title read, "Jon Could See True."

POSTSCRIPT: WHAT BECAME OF THEM

IN 1994, LOUISE participated in another tribute to the Loujon Press, helping with the production of two fine art prints designed from original printing blocks from the *Outsider*. Commissioned by Ed Blair, they were printed by New Orleans printmaker Francis Swaggart from blocks Blair "retrieved from a damp French Quarter attic." Blair did not see Louise for four or five years after Jon's death, but his friendship with her never wavered, and he never lost his admiration for the romance of Jon and Louise's life together.

Through the years Blair was always a rock for Louise to rely on. He had long wanted to publish a tribute to Jon, and in 1983 he toyed with the idea of a memorial book which would follow the line of Jon's creative life. The book would begin with excerpts from *The New Day* and *Four Steps to the Wall*, and include a long section on the *Outsider* and the Loujon Press, correspondence between Jon and Bukowski or Jon and Henry Miller, a section on Jon and Louise's travels, and a Bukowski short story about the Webbs. While the memorial book did not materialize, the fine prints were published and well received. Louise not only inspected the work as it was being done, but added contextual annotations. The prints were designated *Skyscraper* and *Ursulines*, after the two New Orleans addresses where the *Outsider* was published. This was fine work, done on "heavy cotton, acid-free paper, with black and terra cotta ink on cream, and fine additional Japanese colored papers." William S. Burroughs was among the first to order a set of prints. A review noted that "the significance of the *Outsider*, and its regeneration through *Skyscraper* and *Ursulines*, is both historical and contemporary, a timely reminder of what was and what is."

Jon, Jr., idolized his father and considered him a genius. There was a wall between them that was never quite breeched: "He had quite a temper and I couldn't work too close to him sometimes because he couldn't stand some of my mistakes." Even so, "at a distance we were great." Jon, Jr., did not see his father again after the visit in Las Vegas. He was devastated by Jon's death and, about a year later, began writing him a series of letters. It was almost like they were there together, drinking a beer, with easy talk between them. He recalled his long-ago hitchhike to New Orleans and the good times there with Jon and Louise. It was a grueling trip, but "I wanted to come to you. I have always felt that way ... always wanting to come to you ... I guess that

New Orleans thing in the forties is the only time we ever were together, that I can really say was together. It didn't last long." Jon, Jr., mused over the film he shot of Jon and Louise in Tucson. The movie showed the pair "prancing around looking cheerful. Yet, since then, as I replay those movies, Lou and you sure looked other than cheerful in some of the runs. Though you clowned a lot, as I do, when being photographed, you had a very serious and tragic hint in some of the shots, quickly corrected in the camera's sweep on you. Prophetic? Lou had the same thing."

Jon Edgar Webb, Jr., remained in California and had a successful career as a doctor of chiropractic medicine. In 2003, Beat Scene Press published his brief memoir, *Jon, Lou, Bukowski and Me,* and he has other Loujon- and Bukowski-related projects in various stages of development. Jon became a widower in 2005 with the death of his beloved Lore.

Other players in this story went their own ways.

David Goodis left Hollywood soon after his involvement with *Four Steps to the Wall* ended. He returned to his hometown of Philadelphia, where he lived with his parents and wrote more than a dozen successful novels describing the tawdry lives of down-and-out men and the women they desire. Books like *The Blonde on the Street Corner, The Moon in the Gutter,* and *Of Tender Sin* sold well but failed to establish their author beyond the pulp fiction market. His biggest seller was probably 1951's *Cassidy's Girl,* which reportedly sold more than one million copies in paperback. Eleven of Goodis's books or stories have thus far been adapted to film, including François Truffaut's acclaimed 1960 version of *Shoot the Piano Player* (1956). The film was a *New York Times* Critic's Pick. Goodis died of a stroke on January 7, 1967, in Philadelphia's Albert Einstein Medical Center, leaving an estate of more than two hundred thousand dollars. He has remained a popular writer in France. Since 1987, many of his books have been reissued in the United States and his work has attracted an increasing amount of scholarly attention.

Marcus J. Grapes took Loujon's example to heart and made it financially viable. In 1989, as Jack Grapes, he founded Bombshelter Press, which has since published scores of books from Los Angeles poets. Bombshelter also sporadically publishes a fat, beautifully made literary magazine, *onthebus,* a clear descendant of the *Outsider.* Grapes has distinguished himself as a playwright, an actor, and a teacher. He wrote and starred in a critically praised comic play, *Circle of Will.* Four times a year, he conducts private, nine week writing workshops in Los Angeles.

Marvin Bell graduated from the University of Iowa's Writers' Workshop and went on to a distinguished career. The most recent of his nineteen books are *Iris of Creation, The Book of the Dead Man, Ardor, Nightworks: Poems 1962-2000, Rampant,* and *Mars Being Red.* He was for many years the Flannery O'Connor Professor of Letters at the University of Iowa and has served as the state of Iowa's Poet Laureate. His former students include Rita Dove, James Tate, Denis Johnson, and John Irving. He now teaches for Pacific University and divides his time between Iowa and Washington State.

Not long before Jon's death, Walter Lowenfels published a critical work, *The Tenderest Lover: The Erotic Poetry of Walt Whitman.* In 1973, he compiled the writings of Chicanos, Eskimos, Hawaiians, Indians, and Puerto Ricans in *From the Belly of the Shark: A New Anthology of Native Americans.* He edited another volume two years later, *For Neruda, For Chile: An International Anthology. Library Journal* published a scathing review of this book, condemning both the quality of the poetry and its unashamed leftist leanings. Lowenfels died of cancer in Tarrytown, New York, in 1976. Talisman Press published his *Reality Prime: Selected Poems* twenty-two years later.

On February 2, 1962, Bill Corrington wrote Bukowski to make what he considered a terrible confession: "My demon has been since 15 the desire to become a legend. Not just fame, surely not money, but to become a mythical creature like Achilles or Stonewall Jackson or Shakespeare or James Joyce. Shameful. A man should care only for the work and for doing the work honestly and well. I am a pretender, a cuckoo amidst you nightingales. Ah woe!" Perhaps it was this that pushed Corrington to reinvent himself more than once. The rough-and-tumble young man became the English professor Jon knew, but Corrington's complaints about academic life were real, and finally he left it behind. He published a steady stream of books, beginning in 1962 with Charioteer Press's *Where We Are.* These books included poetry collections, like 1964's *The Anatomy of Love and Other Poems* and *Mr. Clean and Other Poems*; a short story collection, *The Lonesome Traveler and Other Stories* in 1968; and novels, such as *And Wait for the Night* in 1964 and *The Upper Hand* in 1967. Corrington's first big shift, in 1969, was to the movies. With Joyce, he wrote the screenplay for *Von Richthofen and Brown* (also known as *The Red Baron*), a low-budget film directed by Roger Corman and released through United Artists. The next year, the Corringtons wrote the script for *The Omega Man,* a major motion picture starring Charlton Heston and Anthony Zerbe. In rapid succession, they wrote Martin Scorsese's first feature film, *Boxcar Bertha*, followed by *The Arena* (also known as *Naked Warriors*), *The Battle for the Planet of the Apes*, and a television movie, *The Killer Bees*. Corrington took a law degree at Tulane University in 1975 and practiced in New Orleans until 1978, but he and Joyce were already hooked on the entertainment industry; and besides, Bill was a writer to the bone. In 1978, they formed Corrington Productions, Ltd., and made the switch to television. From 1975 through 1985, the couple worked off and on as script writers for network soap operas. Bill was head writer for *Search for Tomorrow* (CBS, 1978–1980), *General Hospital* (ABC, 1982) and *One Life to Live* (ABC, 1984–85). He created and wrote for the short-lived *Texas* (NBC 1980–81). He produced and served as head writer for the syndicated *Superior Court* (1986–88). Corrington continued to publish serious fiction during these years, including both novels and short story collections. With Joyce, he wrote a series of detective novels featuring New Orleans police detective Ralph "Rat" Trapp. Bill Corrington died of a heart attack in 1988, leaving behind Joyce and their four children. Joyce continued working in television. Probably as a result of her time with *Superior Court*, she became a producer of reality shows, notably MTV's *The Real World*. In 1991, Bill's undergraduate alma mater, Centenary College of Louisiana, founded the Corrington Award for Literary Excellence. The first recipient was Eudora Welty; she was followed by James Dickey, Miller Williams, and other prominent southern writers.

Jory Sherman also changed directions. He achieved some success as a poet, publishing a total of four collections of his work, but his triumph came in writing about the West. Since 1965, Sherman has published a staggering three hundred books. He writes western novels, short stories, and articles for western-themed magazines. His publishers include Doubleday, Avon, Bantam, and many others. His 1994 novel, *Grass Kingdom*, was nominated for the Pulitzer Prize in literature. One critic has suggested that "Among today's novelists of the Old American West, Jory Sherman has no peer for poetic, powerful storytelling."

Henry Miller remained a prolific author, publishing dozens of books after *Insomnia, or the Devil at Large*. Among his credits after Jon's death was a 1974 Doubleday reissue of *Insomnia*. Miller's marriage to Hoki was a disaster, though it lasted from 1967 to 1976. Hoki refused to have sex with the much older Miller, a humiliating situation for the famously sensuous author. After their divorce, Hoki ran a Tokyo nightclub called Tropic of Cancer. Miller died on June 7, 1980, in Pacific Palisades, California. He continues to have a worldwide readership.

Between the time of Jon's death and his own, Kenneth Patchen added two books to his large body of work, *Wonderings* and *Tell You That I Love You*, both published in 1971. Patchen never found relief from the agony of his back problems and succumbed finally to a heart attack on January 8, 1972. The City Lights Poets Theater in San Francisco hosted a tribute in Patchen's honor a few weeks after his death. *In Quest of Candlelighters* was published in May 1972, and a handful of other posthumous works, including *Patchen's Lost Plays* (1977), appeared in the ensuing years. The Experimental Theatre, a small New York venue, produced one of these plays, *The City Wears a Slouch Hat*, in August 2000. An authorized biography, Larry Smith's *Kenneth Patchen: Rebel Poet in America*, appeared in 2000.

After Kenneth's death, Miriam Patchen moved to San Jose, California, and turned her energy to protests against American military adventures. She found a companion, Laurent Frantz, a constitutional scholar with two law degrees. For fifteen years, she spent two hours each day on the corner of El Camino Real and Embarcadero Road holding signs protesting against the Cuban embargo, or incursions into El Salvador or Iraq, sometimes leaning against a shady sycamore tree for support. Frantz was there with her for many of those years, until his death, at age eighty-four, in 1998. Though the geographical hot spots they protested changed regularly, they kept another sign with the unchanging message: "Honk for Peace."

Miriam's activism was much broader than this daily ritual. Among the many causes she took up was the Cuba Friendship movement, in which she tried to get computers into Cuba by way of Mexico. She engaged in a number of candlelight vigils against the death penalty at San Quentin State Prison. Documentary filmmaker Kim Roberts released a study of Mrs. Patchen, *Miriam Is Not Amused*, in 1996. Among the accolades it received were the Isabella Liddell Art Award for Best Film about Women's Issues at the 1996 Ann Arbor Film Festival and Best Documentary at the 24th annual Student Academy Awards. Miriam died in 2000. She was eighty-five.

Charles Bukowski's long, prolific career is widely documented. He published dozens of books, mostly under the imprint of John Martin's Black Sparrow Press. In the early 1970s, Bukowski came to know Gerald Locklin, the young poet from Long Beach whose chance at publication in the *Outsider* ended with the Tucson flood. Locklin taught for many years at what is now California State University, Long Beach, and became one of Bukowski's most eloquent supporters within the academy. His 1995 volume, *Charles Bukowski: A Sure Bet*, remains a valuable resource. Locklin, with thousands of poems and dozens of books published over the years, is one of the few contemporary poets to rival Bukowski for output.

Bukowski married for the second time in 1985. His new wife, the former Linda Lee Beighle, helped him to eat sensibly and cut back some on his drinking. He often credited her with adding years to his life. Bukowski bought a house in San Pedro, California, not long before their marriage, and his years with Linda Lee were spent, more or less, in suburban happiness. Bukowski's work has been adapted for several movies, most famously *Barfly*, the only one for which Bukowski supplied the script. In 2003, a critically praised documentary, *Bukowski: Born into This*, appeared from novice filmmaker John Dullaghan. Bukowski's work is widely translated and, since the late 1970s, he has been popular in Europe. While he remains best known as a poet, he also published several short story collections and six novels. Bukowski died on March 9, 1994, after a lengthy battle with leukemia.

Sherri Martinelli probably achieved her greatest fame as the pseudonymous "Sheri Donatti" in Anatole Broyard's memoir of postwar Greenwich Village, *Kafka Was the Rage*. Broyard's depiction of "Donatti" was memorable, if unflattering. Martinelli died on November 3, 1996, in Falls Church, Virginia. Another bit player in the Loujon saga, Wally Shore, the erstwhile typesetter for the first issue of the *Outsider*, never forgot the Webbs. Shore lived in San Francisco in the mid-1990s and, mindful of the *Outsider* alumni there, sought Louise's permission to publish a sixth issue of the magazine as a tribute to Jon. Shore hoped to meet with Ferlinghetti and convince him to spread the word among his friends. The issue would be a mix of new poems and reprints from the *Outsider*. If any money came from this, it would go to Louise. Shore's tribute, unfortunately, did not happen.

Louise Webb sometimes shocked visitors through the years by eating bits of bone from Jon's and Tommy's ashes she kept in a locket worn around her neck. When the mood struck her, she took out a piece of bone and ate it. Noel Rockmore witnessed this act, as did Liza Williams, a one-time girlfriend of Bukowski's. "When I die," she told Williams, "we will be together, forever." At the time of this writing, Louise Webb still lives near New Orleans. Looking back on the sacrifices she made to help her husband pursue his dreams, she is unwavering: "I'm glad I did it. That's at least something good I did in this world."

APPENDIX:
CONTRIBUTORS TO *THE OUTSIDER*

Volume 1, Number 1, Fall 1961

Russell Edson	Untitled Fable
Jon Edgar Webb	The Editor's Bit: Public Square
Sinclair Beiles &	Metabolic C Movies
Stuart Gordon	
Gregory Corso	The American Way
Jon Edgar Webb, Jr.	A Peek over the Wall
Ann Giudici	Three Poems
Diane di Prima	Lord Jim
John Grant	On the Dot
Paul Haines	. . . had spent laughing
Gary Snyder	Xrist
Gael Turnbull	A Hill
Charles Olson	Untitled, "Borne down by the inability . . ."
Edward Dorn	Like a Message on Sunday
Allen Ginsberg	The End (to Kaddish)
Peter Orlovsky	Snail Poem
Langston Hughes	Doorknobs
Juan Martinez	Work Song
Gilbert Sorrentino	Ave Atque Vale
Walter Lowenfels	Good-bye Jargon
	Welcome Home to Cubby
Cid Corman	Post Mortem
	Sempre D'Amore
Lawrence Ferlinghetti	Underwear
Ray Bremser	On Prevalence
Margaret Randall	Series of Seven
Millen Brand	Swinging off Swamp Creek
Robert Creeley	The End of the Day
	"Mind's Heart"
	The Bird
Mike McClure	Spontaneous Hymn to Kundalini
Charles Bukowski	Hooray Say the Roses
	Pay Your Rent or Get Out
	Shoes

	I am with the Roots of Flowers
	Go with the Rockets and the Blondes
	A Real Thing, a Good Woman
	To a High Class Whore I Refused
	Old Man, Dead in a Room
	Love in a Back Room on the Row
	Nothing Subtle
	And then: Age
Robert Sward	Momma—, Mountain
Harland Ristau	M'sippi Town
Colin Wilson	Some Comments on The Beats and Angries
Jory Sherman	Dear Liz
Leslie Woolf Hedley	Naked in My Century
Henry Miller	Letters to Lowenfels
LeRoi Jones	The Southpaw
	Bo Peep
	"X"
	Boswell
	Dr. Jive
Marvin Bell	Portrait of a Skeleton
	Winter Poem
Lester Epstein	Demonstrate Your Culture by not Maltreating Flowers
	Moment
	Cold Coffee
Curtis Zahn	Reprimand for a Compromised Love-Object
William S. Burroughs	*Soft Machine* (Excerpt)
Kaja	From: The Emerald City . . . for Gregory Corso
Judson Crews	Rel Bore Speng Lule
	Pastoral
Tracy Thompson	Stranger
Paul Thompson	What did Your Face Look Like Before You Were Conceived by Your Father & Your Mother?
G. C. Oden	Lay Your Head Here
James Boyer May	The Salutary Snare . . . for Colin Wilson
Marc D. Schliefer	Here & There . . . for Marian's Show
Frederick Pfisterer III	Dolorous Somewhere Behind
Gene Frumkin	The Fat Pigeon
Jonathan Williams	The Big House . . . for Sherwood Anderson
William Corrington	Hard Man
Kay Boyle	Print from a Lucite Block
Paul Blackburn	Death Watch: Veille d'Hiver
Clayton Eshleman	Red Shoes . . . from *Songs for Exile*
Tuli Kupferberg	Great

Barbara Moraff   A Little Spur
Sam Abrams   Bodies Only
                   Formal Re:
Terence McGuire   Mid-Morning

Volume 1, Number 2, Summer 1962

William S. Burroughs Wilt Caught in Time
R. E. L. Masters   Untitled, "Before going to bed . . ."
Jon Edgar Webb   The Editor's Bit
Charles Bukowski   Sick Leave
                     To a Lady Who Believes Me Dead
Kay Johnson   From: The Fourth Hour
                     Poems from Paris
                     . . . Experience of 7 Consecutive Hours
                     . . . In Heaven at 9 Git-Le-Coeur
                     Quick, Someone's Coming
Joel Oppenheimer   A Long Way
                     The Present
Howard Nemerov   The Iron Characters
Russell Edson   There Was
Larry Eigner   Five Poems
                     "the sky cross the desert the dry . . ."
                     "visiting yesterday . . ."
                     "An easy death . . ."
                     "all these cripples . . ."
                     "that's odd . . ."
Edward Dorn   The Argument Is
                     Poems from Berlin
                     . . . First Week's Impression
                     . . . If I were a Young Berliner
                     . . . Suburban Night in Berlin
                     . . . ?
                     . . . City Night in Berlin
Ray Bremser   On the Nature
Richard Mayes   Lament
Gene Frumkin   The Poet on His Lunch Hour
Edward Morgan   Jean Genet: "A Legend, to be Legible"
Anselm Hollo   They Fatted the Calf
Carolyn Stoloff   Something Diseased
David B. Jacobson   Lecture
Jon Edgar Webb   Suddenly Over
Clarence Major   Dream in Ruins

Edward Field	Ah, Linger Awhile, Thou Art So Fair
Mason Jordan Mason	Mysterious as any Woman Be
Geoffrey Hazard	The Dubliner
Barbara Moraff	Dear Solomon
Frank Musial	Room
Ann Giudici	Hello
	Didn't He Ramble
G. C. Oden	Low Calvary
Marvin Bell	Pipecleaner . . . for Thin Dorothy
Kaja	From: Emerald City . . . for Gregory Corso
Jean Genet	From: Le Pecheur du Suquet (translated by Edwin Morgan)
A. W. Purdy	Love Poem
Louise Madaio	The Wine is Red . . . from Black Olives, a work in progress
Thomas McGrath	From: Letter to an Imaginary Friend
William Corrington	Surreal for Lorca
Jonathan Williams	The Anchorite
	Letter to the editor
Walter Lowenfels	Letter to the Editor Editorial
Lamantia	Last Days of San Francisco
Jack Kerouac	Sept. 16, 1961, Poem
Dave Margoshes	Denise Levertov
William J. Margolis	From: The Mendicant Notebook, VI (for Maxine)
Henry Miller	The Henry Miller to Lowenfels Letters
Ian Hamilton Finlay	Art Student
John Tagliabue	Five Poems
	Now and then in the Fluorescence a Slight Jerking Motion
	"I Got Important Contacts" Willy Loman Says
	Those Mysterious Events that Stir Us
	Tall Blonde Girl and Ballet Dancer
Kenneth Patchen	Letter and four drawings
Jack Micheline	Streetcall New Orleans

Oldest of the Living Old: A Documentary in Pictures of the Last of the Old-Time Musicians Playing Traditional New Orleans Jazz Live at Preservation Hall

Richard B. Allen, the Consultant	Preservation Hall, N'Orleans
Larry Borenstein, the Landlord	Untitled
Allan & Sandra Jaffe, the Mgrs.	Untitled
"Bill" Russell, the Historian	Untitled
Nat Hentoff	From *Hi-Fi Stereo Review*

John S. Wilson	From *The New York Times*
Godfrey Sperling, Jr.	From *The Christian Science Monitor*
From *Time*	Of Percy Humphrey's Crescent City Joymakers
From *Newsweek*	Of Billie & Dee Dee Pierce
Wilder Hobson	From *Saturday Review*
Hi-Fidelity	Of Kid Thomas & His Algiers Stompers
Riverside's Living Legends Series	"The New Orleans we had seen and heard (during the recording) can only last for a very little while longer."
Unsigned	A Typical Two-Week (different band each night) Preservation Hall Menu
The Editors	"We're not unaware that this first part of 'Oldest of the Living Old' leans a bit toward being more of a commentary than a documentary. . . ."
Unsigned	"Au Revoir" to Steve Angrum
Mezz Mezzrow	From: Really the Blues

Volume 1, Number 3, Spring 1963

Jon Edgar Webb	The Editor's Bit
Miriam Patchen	To the Editors (Six Letters)
Kenneth Patchen	Picture Poem (No. 3 Editorial)
Kay Johnson	The White Room
Gary Snyder	Some Square Comes
	Madly Whirling Downhill
Lionel Kearns	Stress-Axis Poems
	Vision
	Precipitation
	Letter to Webb on "stacked verse"
Robert Creeley	More on Kearns
Announcement	It Catches My Heart in Its Hands
Douglas Woolf	Visitation
Illustration	"What's this business everybody saying what a monument for our Fidel?"
Michael McClure	Three Mad Sonnets
Robert S. Sward	Donna is Her Name
	Museum
	Mr. Attis & Lady C.
William S. Burroughs	Take it to Cut City—U.S.A.
Sue Abbott Boyd	Journey
	The Following Morning
Robert Lewis Weeks	Grand Opening

Irving Layton	On Re-Reading the Beats
Jean Genet	A Colloquy . . . from Le Pecheur du Suquet (Translated by
	Edwin Morgan)
Roy Fisher	Chirico
	Something Unmade
Jon Edgar Webb	The Girl There
Diane Wakowski	The First Day
Harold Norse	The Pine Cone
Carl Solomon	The Madman in the Looking Glass

This section dedicated to poet Charles Bukowski selected by
the editors as deservedly the most inevitable recipient of
The Outsider's first annual "Outsider-of-the-Year" award (1962)

Editors Congratulate	Roy Miller, *The San Francisco Review*
	Gene Frumkin, *Coastlines*
	R. R. Cuscaden, *Midwest*
	Carl Larsen, 7 Poets Press
	John Bryan, *Renaissance*
	E. V. Griffith, *Hearse* and Hearse Press
	Margaret Randall, *The Plumed Horn*
	Norman Winski, *Breakthru Magazine*
	Evelyn Thorn & Will Tullos, *Epos*
	M. Malone & A. Taylor, *Wormwood Review*
	Edward Van Aelstyn, *Northwest Review*
	Helen Fowler, *Approach*
	Joseph Friedman, *Venture*
	E. R. Cole, *Experiment: An International Review*
	James Boyer May, *Trace*
	Anthony Linick, *Nomad*
	Sue Abbott Boyd, *South and West*
	W. L. Garner & Lloyd Alpaugh, *Target*
	Matthew Meade, *Satis*
	Felix Stefanile, *The Sparrow Magazine*
	Bukowski responds to the editors
R. R. Cuscaden	"Charles Bukowski: Poet in a Ruined Landscape"
William Corrington	"Charles Bukowski: Three Poems"
Charles Bukowski	The House
	Event
	Dinner, Rain & Transport
	Letters to the Editor
Henry Miller	The Henry Miller to Lowenfels Letters (Last of a Three-
	part Series)

Larry Eigner	Then:
William Corrington	Communion . . . from *Prayers for Mass in the Vernacular*
Alain Jouffroy	Fatherland
Anselm Hollo	Thalidomide . . . from a longer poem of this title
Barbara Moraff	Two for Syd
Willard Motley	The Burial
Reaburn Miller	The Drowned Boy
Larry Rubin	Etiquette for Americans

Oldest of the Living Old: a Documentary in Pictures of the Last of the Old-Time Musicians Playing Traditional New Orleans Jazz Live

Sam B. Charters	Jazz in New Orleans 1899 to 1957
	—words for Blues
E. L. Borenstein	1957 to 1963

Volume 2, Number 4/5, Winter 1968–69

Kenneth Patchen	Picture Poem ("My God the Sorrow of It")
Kelsie	Illustration (After "The Spirit of '76" by Archibald Willard)
Allan Kaprow	Moving: A Happening
Trevor Goodger-Hill	Editorial poem: "O shit that I could carve"
Charles Plymell	In Kansas
David Taylor	Panda
Russell Edson	The Toy Maker
	The Cult
Simon Perchik	Two Poems
Clarence Major	Weak Dynamite
William Wantling	That Night
Louise Webb	Illustration ("Safe to light up, Allen?")
Elizabeth Bartlett	The Walnut Tree
Alvin Greenberg	Taking a Stand
Bruce Severy	How We Do Things
	Mud
	From 400 Yards
Trevor Goodger-Hill	A Personal History
John Creighton	Green Hides (Lines to a Pale Lady)
Larry Eigner	Two Poems
	"March the route/highway is fields"
	"The great American ballot-box/leaflets"
Charles Bukowski	Kaakaa & Other Immolations

	Beef tongue . . . for J. T.
	Like a Flyswatter
	The Last Round
Diane di Prima	From her book: *Spring and Autumn Annals: A Celebration of the Seasons for Freddie*
Denise Levertov	Late June 1968
	Not to Have
Lawrence Durrell	?
Howard McCord	Descent into Birth
David Meltzer	This is a Nation of Keepers Who had No Time to Become Gods
Stanley Cooperman	New York: February, 1968
	Cappelbaum's Halloween
	One Kind of Tune
	& A More Similar Tune
Margaret Randall	Erongaricuaro—for my friends at the Molino
Jay Wright	Pastel
Kelsie	Political cartoons
Richard Morris	Introduction to Kelsie cartoons
Michael Hamburger	Travelling
Carolyn Stoloff	Wind and the Earth
Marcus J. Grapes	Album of Untitled Poems
	"I started dying again"
	"an old house"
	"oh, it wasn't so much"
	"too many years pass"
	"leaving this clumsy town"
	"could I believe"
	"if they send another bill"
	"the madness is power and what"
	"I spoke to Jenny/the other day"
	"legendary men in the forest"
	"and when they killed him"
	"finding new bones"
	"some jerk with Baltic-brained"
	"this tender minute"
	"some of us"
John Haines	Under the barracks
	In the Styrofoam Mountains
	From the Rooftops
Robert Kelly	Landing Cod (from *The Common Shore*)
David K. Gast	Teresa
Miriam Patchen	Dear Louise and Jon (Letter, June 27, 1968)

The Outsider's Book Issue 4/5 Homage to Kenneth Patchen, Peace 1968

David Sandberg   Untitled Poem "Please do not ring or knock"
Norman Thomas   Untitled Prose
Brother Antoninus   Untitled Prose
Allen Ginsberg   Untitled Prose
James Boyer May   Untitled Prose
Harold Norse   Untitled Prose
Millen Brand   Untitled Prose
Hugh Macdiarmid   Untitled Prose
David "Tony" Glover   Untitled Prose
Kenneth Rexroth   Untitled Prose
John William Corrington Untitled Prose
Bern Porter   Untitled Prose
Gene Detro   Patchen Interviewed by Gene Detro
Lawrence Ferlinghetti   Untitled Prose
Peter Yates   Untitled Poem ("Know him, this man Poetry does not
                          own")
David Meltzer   Untitled Prose
Lafe Young   Untitled Prose
Jack Conroy   Untitled Prose
Frederick Eckman   Untitled Prose
Henry Miller   From "Patchen: Man of Anger & Light," *Stand Still Like
                          the Hummingbird.* New Directions, 1962.

Douglas Blazek   A Few Small Things
Ted Enslin   Untitled poem, "As if it were my eye"
Al Purdy   The Jackhammer Syndrome
Richard Shelton   The Crossing
                        & The Scars will be Covered
Peter Wild   Engine
                        Snake Skin
                        Saturday Afternoon on Sugar Loaf Mtn
Brown Miller   The Dark Oval
Helen Duberstein   Joke
Douglas Flaherty   Mrs. Godkin's Son
Keith Wilson   All the Vanished Faces
                        The Wind Dragon in Spring
Barbara A. Holland   Dust-Devil Man
Gene Fowler   The Natural History of Woman
Gene Frumkin   Poem for Childhood
d. a. levy   for the pigs, sheep & adorable other mammals of
                          virtuous cleveland, o.

In Memoriam	Daryl Allen Levy 1942–1968
	Suicide, Nov. 24
Thomas Merton	Tibud Maclay
Robert Bly	Blown-up German Fortifications Near Collioure
Harold Norse	Return to Pompeii
Kent Gardien	Poem Based on a List by Luis Bunel
Dick Higgins	Four Degrees
David Antin	Sociology
Anselm Hollo	Bouzouki Music
Ruth Kraus	Drunk Boat
T. L. Kryss	Circus
	The Withered Lemming of the River
George Dowden	Morning Song for My Girl by the Sea
Michael Brown	The Seventh Month
Lenore Kandel	Muir Beach Mythology/September
Simon Perchik (Poet)	Four Photo-Poems
& Larence Shustak	Untitled "His death never reached . . ."
(Photographer)	Untitled "In the hieroglyphic a brick . . ."
	Untitled "While you wait keeps me alive"
	Untitled "Still growing a moon . . ."
Alison Knowles	Journal of the Identical Lunch
Emmett Williams	Untitled Poem "north is this way"
	Untitled Poem "i"
Jackson Mac Low	"Portable Ecstacies Might be Corked Up In a Pint
	Bottle" —De Quincy
Kay Johnson	The Emerald City (for Gregory Corso)
Jean Cocteau	Creation Before Life (Trans. From the French for *The*
	Outsider by Will Slotnikoff)
Ray Johnson	Face Collage (illustration)
Al Hansen	"gat" (illustration)
Florence Mars	Back cover
(photographer)	

SOURCE NOTES

Loujon Press publications quoted include four issues of *The Outsider* (no. 1, New Orleans, 1961; no. 2, New Orleans, 1962; no. 3, New Orleans, 1963; no. 4/5, Tucson, 1968-69) Charles Bukowski's books *It Catches My Heart in Its Hands* (New Orleans, 1963) and *Crucifix in a Deathhand* (New Orleans, 1965), and Henry Miller's books *Order and Chaos chez Hans Raichel* (Tucson, 1966) and *Insomnia, or The Devil at Large* (Las Vegas, 1970).

Public archives and private collections are cited by the following abbreviations:

Corrington Collection: Private collection of Joyce Corrington.
Lilly: Lilly Library, Indiana University, Bloomington, Indiana.
McCormick: Charles Deering McCormick Library of Special Collections at Northwestern University, Evanston, Illinois, Loujon Press and *The Outsider* Collections, Series XV.
Newberry: Newberry Library, Chicago, Illinois, Sherwood Anderson Papers, 1872-1992.
Webb Collection: Private collection of Dr. Jon Edgar Webb, Jr., ephemera related to the Webbs and Loujon Press, including unpublished interviews, correspondence, poems, clippings, and advertising material.

Introduction

As veteran Malcolm Cowley: Cowley, 5.
New Poets of England and America: Among the poets appearing in *New Poets of England and America* are Anthony Hecht, John Hollander, Donald Justice, Robert Lowell, William Meredith, Howard Nemerov, Adrienne Rich, James Wright, Richard Wilbur, James Wright, and Robert Pack.
"They are our avant-garde": quoted in Clay and Phillips, 13.
"In his young days": Rexroth, *Assays*, 167.
Zahn once said: Siegel.
While introducing Brautigan: Barber.
Corrington was born: Elkins.
Corrington argued that little magazines: Lowenfels, "Little Magazines (Part 3)," 38-40.
Philip Kaplan was a Russian-born artist: Simpson.
Charles Bukowski was a Los Angeles postal worker: Lowenfels, "Little Magazines (Part 3)," 43-45.
"little magazines fill a need": Lowenfels, "Little Magazines (Part 1)," 34.
"Generally, the littles are 'protesting'": ibid., 32-33.

"when most writers and editors": ibid., 26–27.

Beatitude editor William Margolis: Lowenfels, "Little Magazines (Part 2)," 52.

Brand chose to discuss Webb and *The Outsider*: Lowenfels, "Little Magazines(Part 1)," 33.

"were started in prison cells, speak-easy joints": ibid., 31.

"a desperate need" of new, young poets: ibid., 31–32.

"Little mag editors afraid to 'let go' ": ibid., 35–36.

Chapter 1. From Cleveland to New Orleans

Jon, Jr., recalled: Jon Edgar Webb, Jr., interview with author, 14 April 2002.

As he told it to his son: ibid.

"was shot in the calf": ibid.

The prison was designed: *Ohio Biographies.*

Mansfield was a dangerous place: Brummett.

"Years ago, so long ago": Lowenfels, "Little Magazines (Part 1)," 33.

"Mr. Webb's story in this issue": biographical note to JW, "All Prickles."

Like *Manuscript, Story* claimed: JW's biographical note in the August 1935 issue of *Story* mentions his jail time and praises his work with *The New Day*: "For thirty months was editor of the extremely well-edited prison weekly called '*The New Day*,' put out at the State Reformatory at Mansfield, Ohio. He is now living with his family in Ohio, on parole."

Indeed, Edward O'Brien: JW letter to Sherwood Anderson, 29 June 1940, Newberry.

"Before leaving the reformatory": JW, "Letters to the Editor," 8.

"They are both right and wrong": ibid., 105.

According to his son, Jon: Jon Edgar Webb, Jr., interview with author, 20 June 2006.

"a simply written episode": "Up and Down the Street," 1.

a then-unknown Harriette Simpson Arnow: Ballard.

"The man is the most": Miller, "First Impressions of Paris."

"the joy of our lives": Jon Edgar Webb, Jr., e-mail to author, 19 June 2006.

"It was easy for us": Herman Drezenski, "People, Etc.: Plot for Story—Dog 'Introduced' Writer and Wife," 1961; newspaper clipping, Webb Collection. The clipping contains no bibliographic information, but it is likely from the *Vieux Carré Courier*, a French Quarter newspaper sympathetic to the Webbs.

Jon, Jr., was curious: Jon Edgar Webb, Jr., interview with author, 14 April 2002.

To find privacy, Jon and Louise sometimes went walking: LW interview with author, 20 February 2005. Filmed by Wayne Ewing for *The Outsiders of New Orleans: Loujon Press.*

Louise loved Jon and liked Opal: ibid.

"a gigantic piece of work": JW letter to Anderson, 31 October 1936, Newberry.

Anderson liked the manuscript: JW letter to Mr. Wenning, 31 January 1962, Webb Collection.

"Anyway, I'm sure": JW letter to Anderson, 31 October 1936, Newberry.
The children were parceled: Jon Edgar Webb, Jr., e-mail to author, 26 June 2006.
"I can't work without a woman": JW letter to Anderson, 29 June 1940, Newberry.
About a month after their wedding: LW interview with author, 21 February 2005.
"Sweetheart, I gazed": JW poem, Webb Collection.
"What happened was, we went": Formento and Ferron, 9.
Jon's account to Anderson: JW letter to Anderson, 29 June 1940, Newberry.
"and before her a lot of other whores": JW letter to Anderson, 2 July 1940, Newberry.
"realizing the paint wasn't improving the room's looks": ibid.
"I know I have no right": JW letter to Anderson, 29 June 1940, Newberry.
Meeting with *Times-Picayune* reporter: JW letter to Anderson, 2 July 1949, Newberry.

Chapter 2. *Four Steps to the Wall* and Hollywood Dreams

As luck would have it: Louise's account of meeting O'Donnell differs from Jon's. In her memory, their first meeting was this encounter on the streets of the French Quarter. Since it is likely there is truth in both accounts, they are combined here. LW interview with author, 8 March 2002. JW letter to Anderson, 2 July 1949, Newberry.
O'Donnell decided to become a writer: "Delta Doings."
the year that Anderson had backed: Anderson letter to Houghton-Mifflin Company, 18 May 1936, Webb Collection. In a letter dated 3 August 1961, Webb claimed that he had been a protégé of Anderson's. Unfortunately, the name of Webb's correspondent, who was apparently considering the purchase of the original manuscripts published in *The Outsider*, is illegible. Webb Collection.
After O'Donnell won: "Delta Doings."
"except for a beggar woman": Mary King O'Donnell, *Those Other People*, 18.
"glamour and spectacular wickedness," Asbury.
"Everyone living there then": Formento and Ferron, 10.
L'Album littéraire: Journal des jeunes gens, amateurs de littérature: Dodson and Diouf.
Les Cenelles: ibid.
The city's first great literary light: Brown, 9–10.
In 1884, he published . . . *Dr. Sevier:* Long, 45.
Hearn is better known: ibid., 89.
"the best news and war correspondents": Whitman.
"One of my choice amusements": ibid.
In the late 1890s, William Sydney Porter: Long, 59.
Mark Twain visited his friend: Brown, 33.
In 1943, the neighborhood hosted: ibid, 35.
Two other transplanted Quarterites: Jolas, 82–84.

"Virginia is the best": Mencken.

The Jolases admired *The Double Dealer*: Jolas, 85–86.

He enjoyed the nightlife: Long, 154.

"Everybody congregated there": LW interview with author, 21 February 2005.

sometime in the 1940s that Jon met Ernest Hemingway: LW interview with author, 21 February 2005.

"I shined shoes": Weddle, "An Interview with Jon Edgar Webb, Jr.," 28.

The Webbs socialized with Pat O'Donnell: Jon Edgar Webb, Jr., letter to JW, 5 January 1972, Webb Collection.

"giant smile with the deep grooves lining his face": ibid.

"Go ahead, have a drink. Go ahead, have a puff": Jon Edgar Webb, Jr., letter to JW, 19 May 1972.

"I was awed, not only with New Orleans": Jon Edgar Webb, Jr., letter to JW, 19 May 1972, Webb Collection.

Louise's pregnancy and illness: LW interview with author, 20 February 2005.

Louise managed surreptitiously: According to Liza Williams, a one-time girlfriend of Charles Bukowski, many years later, after Jon's death, Louise kept a mixture of Tommy's and Jon's ashes in a locket she wore around her neck and sometimes ate bits of this ash. When Williams questioned her about this, Louise was said to have replied, "Sure, kiddo, everyday I eat a bit of him. I've got a whole box of the stuff with me, plenty. . . . When I die we will be together, forever." The story appears in the second issue of *Sure, the Charles Bukowski Newsletter*.

Louise was horrified: LW interview with author, 21 February 2005.

"what petty jewelry we had, my best suits, phonograph, radio, etc.": JW letter to Walter Winchel. Letter courtesy of John Martin.

"a sensational, typically corny prison novel": ibid.

"dizzy and weak from not eating, a thousand miles from home": ibid.

"THIS LETTER IS NOT A PLEA FOR PUBLICITY": ibid.

"It is a grim tale, and the author": Eugene A. Plumb, "Clevelander Depicts Life in Columbus Pen," newspaper clipping with no bibliographic information, Webb Collection.

"In Jon Edgar Webb's first novel, *Four Steps to the Wall*": Davidson. The Webb Collection contains a photocopy of the review and title page of *Four Steps to the Wall*, with the legend "Property of Mrs. Jon Edgar Webb 216 North Blvd. Slidell, La 70458" in LW's hand above the title. The review is apparently affixed to the inside front cover.

"To my darling husband—more like this to follow": Webb Collection.

"It was making nervous wrecks": JW letter to Jim Roman, 2 August 1963, McCormick, Box 15, Folder 2.

"Goodis' career by this time": Sallis.

"From the beginning, in the story he's writing": JW letter to Weintraub, 27 October 1949, Webb Collection.

"The screenplay has just been completed by David Goodis": JW letter to Joel, 17 November 1949, Webb Collection.

"So what I definitely would prefer to do": JW letter to Weintraub, 27 October 1949, Webb Collection.

"If only we could get a real prison for location": ibid.

"$5000 when shooting starts": JW letter to Joel, 17 November 1949, Webb Collection.

At Dial, George Joel wondered: JW letter to Joel, 29 November 1949, Webb Collection.

"from the beginning I could see no other guy": JW letter to Duryea, 12 February 1950, Webb Collection.

General Service was by no means: Wayne. Now known as Hollywood Center Studios, the lot Jon and Louise Webb knew as General Service Studios remains at this address and is still used in film and television production. A few years after the Webbs' experiences there, the television series *I Love Lucy* filmed its first two seasons at General Service Studios (Cobblestone Entertainment).

Jon was getting little writing done: JW letter to Israel Katz, 17 June 1950, Webb Collection.

Louise began visiting the studio: LW interview with author, 8 March 2002.

The guild found in Jon's favor: Edmund L. Hartman memo to members of the Screenwriters Guild, 6 April 1950, Webb Collection.

He tried unsuccessfully to make an end run: JW letter to Duryea, 12 February 1950, Webb Collection.

"And I'm getting more and more fascinated": JW letter to Shaw, 4 December 1949, Webb Collection.

He told Charlie Weintraub that money troubles: JW letter to Weintraub, 12 January 1950, Webb Collection.

"filled with prostitutes": Cherkovski, *Hank*, 126.

"good people; they'd let you do anything": LW interview with author, 21 February 2005.

"I feel that I should get": JW letter to Weintraub, 12 January 1950, Webb Collection. Jon's claim regarding his earlier income is likely an exaggeration, though he almost certainly generated income during the years in question through his freelance work with the pulp magazines.

Joel cautioned Jon: Joel letter to JW, 23 March 1950, Webb Collection.

"Lou and I and cats": JW letter to Joel, 25 October 1951, Webb Collection. Aside from Dan Duryea, only one of Jon's Hollywood associates had any real success in the movie business. A few years after the Webbs gave up on filming *Four Steps to the Wall*, Sam Shaw snapped one of the iconic photographs of the twentieth century, catching Marilyn Monroe's skirts billowing above a sidewalk grate during the filming of Twentieth Century Fox's *The Seven Year Itch*. He later published several highly regarded photographic collections of Ms. Monroe and became a sought-after member of the cinematic community.

Chapter 3. Outsiders in New Orleans

"I used to walk around": Formento and Ferron, 11.

Joe Hart story: ibid.

"I got better and better": Weddle, "Oh, We Were Soulmates," 10.

"She is perhaps the most startling": Lise LeLong, "Recycling Literary History," *Times Picayune*, n.d., Webb Collection. LW confirmed that this article was the origin of her famous nickname in a interview with author, 11 March 2002.

The striking image she cultivated: Aikman. Clipping in Webb Collection.

"Princess Bambi Loo Toy Webb": ibid. Princess Bambi Loo Toy was the runt of the litter, and the pet store owner who sold her to Jon was certain she would die young. The owner didn't want to sell Jon the cat, but Jon insisted, eventually paying twenty dollars for the sickly animal. He wanted the cat so badly because, like Louise, she was born on April 29, and Jon was sure Louise would love her. He was correct, and the princess remained a family pet until her death, eleven years later.

"For one thing, both of us used to drink": "Editor's Bit," *Outsider* 3: 131.

"I looked like a Coca-Cola truck": LW interview with author, 21 February 2005.

"I bet not many got in": Edwin Blair, e-mail to author, 27 February 2006.

"stalwart people that I hope": Formento, 20.

"It's true that we did not": Cassin, 78.

"Doesn't seem a whole 21 years ago": JW letter to LW, 15 June 1960, Webb Collection.

"Dear Webb" Mailer letter to JW, 12 April 1960, McCormick, Box 1.

In the teens, Ezra Pound advised: Hoffman, Allen, and Ulrich, 21.

When Harold Loeb decided: ibid., 102.

In situations more contemporaneous with the Webb-Lowenfels relationship: Kruchkow and Johnson, 107.

Bob Fey, editor-publisher of *eikon*: ibid. 234.

As a young expatriate in Paris: Hoffman, Allen, and Ulrich, 175.

In his 1936 novel, *Black Spring*: Lowenfels letter to JW, 23 August 1960, McCormick, Box 1.

"I am the only one": Lowenfels, "On Trial," 19, 22.

"we're writing for everybody": Lowenfels, "The Thirties and the Sixties," 44.

"voice of alienation": ibid, 46.

"It's the new audience": ibid, 44.

"a period of the greatest upsurge": ibid, 45.

As Lowenfels observed, this was a boom time: Clay and Phillips, 15–18.

"more poetry than prose": JW letter to Lowenfels, 13 July 1960, McCormick, Box 1.

"I promise a magazine": ibid.

"a sort of clearing house": Hoffman, Allen, and Ulrich, 104.

"Throughout, the unknown": ibid.

"passing-through 'beatnik' types": JW letter to Lowenfels, 13 July 1960, McCormick, Box 1.
to read aloud a recent letter: Lowenfels letter to JW, 18 June 1960, McCormick, Box 1.
"The way you and your friends": ibid.
"the best beat writer": Lowenfels letter to JW, 31 August 1960, McCormick, Box 1.
"Be choosy with everyone": Lowenfels letter to JW, 6 August 1960, McCormick, Box 1.
"Between us, you are probably": Lowenfels letter to JW, 23 August 1960, McCormick, Box 1.
"Is it because you tickle": Lowenfels letter to JW, 31 August 1960, McCormick, Box 1.
"primarily to avoid hurting anyone": Miller letter to JW, 8 August 1960, McCormick, Box 1.
"this letter stuff": JW letter to Lowenfels, 19 August 1960, McCormick, Box 1.
"hit the jackpot": Lowenfels letter to JW, 23 August 1960, McCormick, Box 1.
"Collectors, libraries": ibid.
"Everything I've written": Miller letter to JW, 23 August 1960, McCormick, Box 1.
"unfortunately, without guidance": Blair, "How to Start an Outsider," 80.

Chapter 4. Creating a Literary Network

"the only human": JW, birthday card to LW, 29 April 1961, McCormick, Box 1.
"Your post card": McDarrah letter to JW, 4 August 1960, McCormick, Box 1.
"Jon Edgar Man, the next time": McDarrah letter to JW, 9 August 1961, McCormick, Box 1.
Jon received a letter from Jack Fine: Fine letter to JW, 6 September 1960, McCormick, Box 1A. Fine established himself as one of the most accomplished proponents of New Orleans–style jazz, recording on dozens of albums. A longtime resident of the city, Fine was unable to evacuate as Hurricane Katrina bore down on the Gulf Coast in August 2005. He weathered the storm and, by chance, was among those interviewed by CNN in its aftermath. He eloquently described the devastation and lamented the cultural loss to the world that New Orleans's destruction represented. He maintained a sense of humor, though, answering a reporter's question on how he planned to survive in the days immediately following the storm with the quip "Well, I have a bottle of gin here" and suggesting that now he could practice his horn at will, since he no longer had neighbors who might object to the music.
"a good second-hand": JW letter to Lowenfels, 19 August 1960, McCormick, Box 1.
"From the size of it," Sherman wrote: Jory Sherman letter to JW, 3 September 1960, McCormick, Box 1A.
"he was drinking a lot": Weddle, "Oh, We Were Soulmates," 12.
Ferlinghetti gave a poetry reading: Wally Shore letter to LW, 16 August 1995, Webb Collection.

"To Honey Lou": JW note on "Prospectus," 8 October 1960, Webb Collection.

"It was a bitch": Weddle, "An Interview with Jon Edgar Webb, Jr.," 28.

"I would have thought": Weddle, "Oh, We Were Soulmates," 12.

Corrington was a poet: Halliburton, 172–75.

As he recalled years later: Corrington, "Homage to Kenneth Patchen," *The Outsider* 4/5 (1968–69).

"If nobody else wants to be": Mills, 2.

"New Orleans is coming to life": Corrington letter to JW, n.d., McCormick, Box 1.

Jon told Lowenfels that Denise Levertov: JW letter to Lowenfels, 21 September 1960, McCormick, Box 1.

"no taboo quarterly": JW letter to Carmine Austin, 22 June 1961, McCormick, Box 1.

As things turned out: Austin letter to JW, 27 June 1961, McCormick, Box 1A.

Jon and Wally Shore scavenged: Blair, 81.

Things were beginning to happen for Bukowski: Gregor, 30.

"thanks for word on *Outsider*": Bukowski letter to Sherman, 17 August 1960, in Bukowski, *Screams*.

"I believe right now": Bukowski letter to JW, November 1960, McCormick, Box 1.

"Chapbook for Buk sounds good": Sherman letter to JW, 8 August 1960, McCormick, Box 1A.

"anti-christ poets": Kerouac letter to JW, n.d., McCormick, Box 2.

"full of wild jazz": Corrington letter to Bukowski, 14 July 1961, Corrington Collection.

"a blah little mag": Corrington letter to Bukowski, 14 July 1961, Corrington Collection.

"because, without trying: Corrington letter to Bukowski, 21 July 1961, Corrington Collection.

"I got to thinking about you": Corrington letter to Bukowski, August 1961, Corrington Collection.

"You make all kinds of mistakes when you write": ibid.

"statement of Our Position": Burroughs letter to JW, 21 August 1960, McCormick, Box 1.

A week later, Burroughs wrote Jon again: Burroughs letter to JW, 30 August 1960, McCormick, Box 1.

Burroughs tried to help: Burroughs letter to JW, 12 September 1960, McCormick, Box 1.

"kif smoking abroad . . . effects of it on intellectuals": Bowles letter to JW, 20 November 1960, McCormick, Box 1.

"Morocco, the Sahara": ibid.

"I don't intend handing": Beiles letter to JW, 1 February 1960, McCormick, Box 1.

In July 1960, Beiles wrote Jon: 20 July 1960, McCormick, Box 1.

"I have the feeling": Beiles letter to JW, 13 September 1960, McCormick, Box 1.

"will let you have it": Hardiment letter to JW, 20 November 1960, McCormick, Box 1.

"work accepted/published": Bell letter to J W, 4 September 1960, McCormick, Box 1. Bell regularly published his poetry in the little magazines of the 1950s and 1960s. In a 2004 e-mail to the author, Bell described the place of little magazines during that era as a worthy publishing venue for serious poets and poetry: "The fifties and sixties were a rich time for individualistic editors and unusual magazines. The 'littles' were where the action was. Well-known poets such as William Carlos Williams and E. E. Cummings published regularly in the littles. They weren't so much looked upon as a stepping stone to more prestigious magazines but as a world unto themselves. It had a wonderful, and irreplaceable, mix of eccentricity and integrity, perhaps because the editors were amateurs, paying out of their own pockets, enthusiastic and alert. And after all, there were many fewer writers then. One could read it all."

"the most significant and worthwhile": Bell letter to J W, "Saturday" n.d., McCormick, Box 1.

"Now, *The Outsider*, with a concern": ibid.

Bell backed up his praise: Bell letter to J W, "Thursday" n.d., McCormick, Box 1.

"It's going to be a terrific magazine": Bell letter to J W, 6 June 1961, McCormick, Box 1.

"thrown three benefits here": Sherman to J W, 20 August 1960, McCormick, Box 1A.

"was written in a shithouse": Sherman to J W, 14 September 1960, McCormick, Box 1A.

New Directions publisher James Laughlin: Laughlin letter to J W, 6 March 1961, McCormick, Box 1.

"fascinating little circular": Laughlin letter to J W, 15 March 1961, McCormick, Box 1.

"Congratulations on No. 1": Ferlinghetti postcard to J W, n.d., McCormick, Box 1.

"Think Ginsberg pulling out": Sherman letter to J W, 20 August 1960, McCormick, Box 1A.

The younger Webb liked Sherman: Jon Edgar Webb, Jr., letter to J W, 5 December 1960, McCormick, Box 1A.

"a daisy chain affair": Sherman letter to J W, n.d., McCormick, Box 1A.

"These columnists having ball": Sherman letter to J W, 14 September 1960, McCormick, Box 1A.

"Of course, the arrangement": Thorn letter to J W, 26 October 1960, McCormick, Box 1A.

In a splendid show of solidarity: Turnbull letter to J W, 31 October [1960?], McCormick, Box 1A.

"still cranking away": Bukowski letter to Corrington, late June 1961, Corrington Collection.

"the best conversation the world": Anderson.

"for some years she pretty well succeeded": "Defining Uncle Alfred."

"thoroughly, totally, completely dead": Williams, 30.

"I got it and it's too much": Corrington letter to J W, 7 February 1961, McCormick, Box 1.

"Man, with a product like this": Corrington letter to JW, 25 July 1960, McCormick, Box 1.

"There were a whole bunch": Bukowski letter to JW, September 1961, McCormick, Box 2.

Chapter 5. The *Outsider* Flourishes

"explodes like fragrant": Johnson letter to JW, 9 May 1962, McCormick, Box 2.

She told Webb of a young Greek poet: ibid.

"downstairs having coffee": Johnson letter to JW, n.d., McCormick, Box 2.

"Yes, Jon, Burroughs is here...oh what a change": Johnson letter to JW, 4 July 1962, McCormick, Box 2.

"everyone loves what I write": Johnson letter to JW, n.d., McCormick, Box 2.

"read avidly standing": Johnson letter to JW, 9 May 1962, McCormick, Box 2.

"It freaked him out": Edwin Blair e-mail to author, 27 February 2006.

a photograph of Punch Miller: Louise wrote lyrics to Miller's "Long Distance Blues," which appeared on his album *The River's in Mourning* and as a single, backed with "St. Louis Blues," on the Icon label. The album, released on 1 February 1961, was pressed on red vinyl and sold for five dollars. Preservation Hall sold both the album and the single to customers, and Louise sold the single at her art stand.

"The outside cover was made with 110-screen plates": "Editor's Bit," *Outsider* 2: 91.

Dissension in the university's drama: Eness.

"we'd go over to the paper companies to scavenge": ibid., 6.

"a provocatively divergent assemblage of fifty-some 'voices' ": "Editor's Bit," *Outsider* 2: 91.

Like the Webbs, Patchen: Morgan, xi–xvi.

"You don't sell mags": Corrington letter to JW, 21 September 1961, Corrington Collection.

"O Lord, a bunch": ibid.

"Letter from Chaz": Corrington letter to JW, 24 September 1961, McCormick, Box 2.

"As each day passes": Corrington letter to JW, 2 February 1962, McCormick, Box 2.

"The difference between us parallels the difference": Corrington letter to Bukowski, [August 1961?], Corrington Collection. Lloyd Halliburton identifies only one instance approaching autobiography in Corrington's work, a 1972 short story entitled "Old Men Dream Dreams, Young Men See Visions." For a discussion of this, see Halliburton.

"When the letters catch": Bukowski letter to JW, 17 October 1962, in Bukowski, *Screams.*

"Nothing clearer": Corrington letter to Bukowski, [September 1961?], Corrington Collection.

"a thing of astute beauty": Bukowski letter to Corrington, [September 1961?], Corrington Collection.

"Now look, this is no idea": Corrington letter to Bukowski, 28 August 1961, Corrington Collection.

Bukowski agreed to do the chapbook: Bukowski letter to Corrington, [?] August 1961, Corrington Collection.

"not for vanity or the Big Time": Corrington letter to Bukowski, [?] September 1961, Corrington Collection.

"He has this frame": Corrington letter to Bukowski, [?] October 1961, Corrington Collection.

his editing of a submission from William Burroughs: manuscript of "Cuts from 'Word Line' William Burroughs for Hassan i Sabbah," n.d., McCormick, Box 2.

Johnson caught Bukowski's eye: Bukowski letter to JW, [5?] June 1961, McCormick, Box 2.

"[B]ut then it is always": Bukowski letter to JW, late July 1961, McCormick, Box 2.

"ah, well, I have gazed": Bukowski letter to JW, 15 October 1961, McCormick, Box 2.

"Kaja is real abstruse": Corrington letter to Bukowski, [?] October 1961, Corrington Collection. Unlike Bukowski and Corrington, Lowenfels remained enthusiastic about Johnson and hoped to forward her career. Publisher Carl Larson had visited him and seen Johnson's poem, "Eat Me Drink Me," and planned to include it in a "tape anthology" he was then putting together (Lowenfels letter to JW, 16 August 1961, McCormick, Box 2). By early 1962, Lowenfels asked Jon for Johnson's address, so that he could arrange a meeting between Johnson and his "friend and translator—who follows modern US poetry and wants to meet up with her" (Lowenfels letter to JW, 18 January 1962, McCormick, Box 2). Johnson later told Webb that Lowenfels's friend had indeed paid her a visit in Paris.

"[b]ut Smith will materialize": Corrington letter to Bukowski, 13 November 1961, Corrington Collection.

"Jon has taken one": Corrington letter to Bukowski, 8 January 1962, Corrington Collection.

"For all we know": Bukowski letter to Corrington, 12 January 1962, Corrington Collection.

"I reckon Jon has a right": Corrington letter to Bukowski, 8 January 1962, Corrington Collection.

"I will need it": Corrington letter to Bukowski, 13 February 1962.

"they will let me have a Ph.D.": Corrington letter to Bukowski, 18 June 1962, Corrington Collection.

"your roving European correspondent": Corrington letter to JW, 5 May 1962, McCormick, Box 2.

"maybe we both write like Synge": Bukowski letter to Corrington, 1 May 1962, Corrington Collection.

"A Letter to the Editor Editorial": From Lowenfels letter to JW, 7 April 1961, McCormick, Box 2. This essay was also published, in slightly different form, as "Literature and Society," in *Mainstream* 15, no. 6 (1962): 56–60.

"but the psychological thing": Lowenfels letter to JW, 9 February 1962, McCormick, Box 2.

"tell yourself every day": Lowenfels letter to JW, 24 February 1962, McCormick, Box 2.

"I can see generations": Lowenfels letter to JW, 14 February 1962, McCormick, Box 2.

"The third issue of *The Outsider*": "The Outsider 2, Poetry Magazine Published in Quarter, Now Available," n.d., *Vieux Carré Courier*, clipping in Webb Collection.

Burroughs sent congratulations: Burroughs letter to JW, 22 December 1961, McCormick, Box 2A.

"another terrific issue": Bell letter to JW, 25 June 1962, McCormick, Box 2.

"There are many men": Robert E. O'Brien letter to JW, 20 September 1962, McCormick, Box 3.

Chapter 6. A Focus on Bukowski

"would be pretty stupid": JW letter to Bukowski, 13 September 1962, McCormick, Box 3.

"But this is a quick letter": ibid.

"Mr. Webb, to close this thing": Bukowski letter to JW, n.d., McCormick, Box 3.

"I don't worry about legends": Bukowski letter to JW, n.d., McCormick, Box 3.

"Some will say": Bukowski letter to JW, 19 November 1962, McCormick, Box 3.

"damned good,": Corrington letter to JW, 8 November 1962, McCormick, Box 3.

Less than a week later, Corrington: Corrington letter to JW, 13 November 1962. McCormick, Box 3. "Charles Bukowski: Poet in a Ruined Landscape" appeared in *Satis*, a British journal, in 1963. It was reprinted in the third issue of *The Outsider*.

"'Old Man, Dead in a Room'": Corrington letter to JW, 3 December 1962, McCormick, Box 3.

"I may lean on that": Corrington letter to JW, 3 January 1962, McCormick, Box 3.

"The final cheap room": Corrington letter to JW, 9 January 1962, McCormick, Box A–D.

"That Willie would bother": Bukowski letter to JW, 19 November 1962. McCormick, Box 3.

Loujon wished to publish a substantial book: Webb's initial plan was to finance the book through collaboration with his friend Jim Roman, a Florida-based bookseller. They discussed making it a joint publication, with each getting roughly half of the 777-copy press run, each set carrying the imprint of its owner. When Roman ultimately declined to follow through on the deal, Jon used prepublication sales for the bulk of his operating capital. Roman remained a valuable friend to the Webbs, though, often sending gifts of cash to help them through difficult times.

"I will strictly be dreaming": Bukowski letter to JW, 28 December 1962, in Bukowski, *Screams*, 51–52.

"Another letter, but, I think": Bukowski letter to JW, 29 December 1962, McCormick, Box 3.

a paraphrase from "Hellenistics": For a succinct examination of Bukowski's debt to Jeffers, see Olson.

"50 bucks Thursday": Bukowski letter to JW, 28 December 1962, in Bukowski, *Screams*, 51–52.

"Several letters from Chas": Corrington letter to JW, 11 January 1963, McCormick, Box A–D.

"I'm sure they're off the cuff": Corrington Letter to JW, 3 January 1963, McCormick, Box A–D.

"I had to grit teeth to junk many": Corrington letter to JW, 11 January 1963, McCormick, Box A–D.

Corrington soon wrote again: Corrington letter to JW, 17 December 1962, McCormick, Box A–D.

"good about both #3": Corrington letter to JW, 22 January 1963, McCormick, Box A–D.

"when he gets butcher knife moods": Corrington letter to JW, 23 February 1963, McCormick, Box A–D.

"could be so neurotically pissed": Corrington letter to JW, 4 April 1963, McCormick, Box A–D.

"[E]ven without the poems": Bukowski letter to Martinelli, [5?] July 1963, in Bukowski, *Beerspit*, 297.

"Gotcher book": Martinelli letter to Bukowski, 10 February 1964, in Bukowski, *Beerspit*, 299. Martinelli was one of the first editors to publish Bukowski, and her early recognition of his talent created a bond between them. The two maintained a spirited, voluminous, and sometimes contentious correspondence between 1960 and 1967. Martinelli was an intense woman, beautiful and talented, who moved easily among the literati. In 1950s San Francisco, where she was friends with Ginsberg and his crowd, Martinelli was known as the "Queen of the Beats." She was, by turn, a *Vogue* model, an actress, a protégé of Anaïs Nin, a muse for Ezra Pound, and perhaps his lover (Steven Moore). Jon had asked Martinelli to contribute an essay on Pound to the first *Outsider*. She considered doing so, but the essay either went unwritten or Jon chose not to use it.

"talking it up": Gladys R. Scheffrin letter to JW, 3 February 1963, McCormick, Box 3.

"Still sweating OUTSIDER #3": Corrington letter to Bukowski, 2 March 1963, Corrington Collection.

Bryan wrote Jon in mid-October 1962: Bryan letter to JW, 12 October 1962, McCormick, Box 3.

"beautiful, fat magazine": Wakoski letter to JW, 20 March 1963, McCormick, Box 3.

"The real kick of the issue": Norse letter to JW, 11 April 1963, McCormick, Box 3.

"a sweetening of the pot": Miriam Patchen letter to JW, 23 July 1963, McCormick, Box 10.

"angel co-editor & backbone": JW note to LW, 14 April 1963, Webb Collection.

"You are free to misunderstand": Creeley letter to JW, 1 April 1963, McCormick, Box A–D.

"Well, if we are going": Corrington letter to JW, 20 April 1963, McCormick, Box A–D.

"The worst they can do": ibid.

"Jon is ready": Corrington letter to Bukowski, 4 April 1963, Corrington Collection.

"Editors, etc.": Snyder letter to JW, 15 March [1963?], McCormick, Box 3.

"cause of the pogrom": Miriam Patchen letter to LW and JW, 23 July 1963, McCormick, Box 10.

a young oil executive named Edwin Blair: quotes and information from Edwin Blair relayed in a series of e-mails from Blair to author, 23 January 2006, 18 February 2006, 27 February 2006, and 20 July 2006.

"Jon treated me": Years later, Blair was doing archival research in a Chicago library and found a letter Jon had written to another party. In this letter, he referred to Blair as his best friend in New Orleans.

"saddened and keep saddening us": JW letter to Miriam Patchen, 16 August 1963, McCormick, Box 10.

"You two are appalling!": Miriam Patchen letter to JW, 27 August 1963, McCormick, Box 10.

"We want to be printing": JW letter to Miriam Patchen, 24 August 1963, McCormick, Box 10.

"Knew each other": Miriam Patchen letter to JW, n.d., McCormick, Box 10.

Poet James Broughton sent his regrets: Broughton letter to JW, 14 April 1968, McCormick, Box A–D.

Miller, through his secretary, Gerald Robitaille, wrote: Gerald Robitaille to JW, 14 March 1968, McCormick, Box M–T.

A few, such as Laughlin: Broughton letter to JW, 18 March 1968, McCormick, Box 6.

"I've had a chance": Martin letter to JW, 11 February 1963, McCormick, Box 8.

"Charles Bukowski suffers": Rexroth, "There's Poetry."

"I couldn't believe it": Blair, e-mail to author, 2006.

"written in blood . . . and printed in blood": JW, from the colophon to Bukowski, *It Catches*.

"Never such a book": Bukowski letter to JW, 26 November 1963, McCormick.

"To Jon Webb, who makes Mencken": This copy of *It Catches My Heart in Its Hands* is in the private collection of Edwin Blair. The early date on the inscription is probably due to Bukowski signing pages before they were bound into the book.

Chapter 7. Meeting Bukowski

"It'll be great fun working on Patchen book": JW letter to Miriam Patchen, 24 August 1963, McCormick, Box 10.

"Kenneth doesn't want": Miriam Patchen letter to JW, 5 November 1963, McCormick, Box 10.

"Full steam ahead": Kenneth Patchen telegram to JW, 15 November 1963, McCormick, Box 10.

"I'm so glad": Miriam Patchen letter to JW, n.d., McCormick, Box 10.

"The few close friends": Miriam Patchen letter to JW, 26 April 1964, McCormick, Box 10.

"I have just heard from Jon": Bukowski letter to Corrington, 1 June 1964, Corrington Collection.

"We packed our stuff": LW, "Gypsy Lou Lands," *Vieux Carré Courier* 11, no. 2 (4 December 1964): 1, clipping in McCormick, Box 15A.

"I thank God": JW card to LW, 15 June 1964, Webb Collection.

"I wish you'd quickly": JW letter to Roman, 14 August 1965, McCormick, Box 10.

"an annual—a documentary annual of contemporary poetry & prose": JW letter to Roman, 14 August 1965, McCormick, Box 15.

The reason for the Webbs' Los Angeles visit: Cherkovski, *Bukowski: A Life*, 139.

Bukowski decided to pay Jon and Louise: quotes and details from Bukowski's visit to New Orleans, ibid. 145–47.

"I don't know when Grapes": Blair e-mail to author, 27 February 2006.

One evening, Jon asked Lou to buy some beer: Blair e-mail to author, 20 July 2006.

"You needn't worry": Bukowski letter to Corrington, September 1962, Corrington Collection.

"You are a raft of mistakes": Corrington letter to Bukowski, September 1962, Corrington Collection.

Bukowski sent a letter of congratulations: Bukowski letter to Corrington, 18 July 1964, Corrington Collection.

"I was in awe": Blair e-mail to author, 23 January 2006.

Corrington was deeply hurt: Sounes, *Charles Bukowski: Locked*, 71–72.

"Neither ever told me": Williams e-mail to author, 10 January 2006. Miller Williams has enjoyed a long and distinguished career as author or editor of more than twenty-five books. Williams also served for several years as director of the University of Arkansas Press. He read his poem "Of History and Hope" to a worldwide audience as part of President Bill Clinton's 1997 inaugural ceremonies. His daughter, Lucinda Williams, is a celebrated country music artist.

"all right, mostly more": Bukowski letter to Blazek, 14 July 1965, in Bukowski, *Screams*, 183.

"When? Now?" Louise asked. "Who are you?": LW interview with author, 21 February 2005.

"No, you can't. That's mine!": ibid.

"The new Buk book": Corrington letter to JW, 2 December 1964, McCormick, Box A–D.

"Somewhere back there": Corrington letter to JW, 1 January 1966, McCormick, Box A–D.

"damned brilliant": JW letter to Blair, 3 February 1966, Webb Collection.

"As for Buk attacking you": JW letter to Corrington, 15 March 1966, personal collection of the author.

"Let me know when": Corrington letter to JW, n.d., McCormick, Box A–D.

"Most of the people": Bukowski letter to Tom McNamara, 6 May 1965, in Bukowski, *Screams*, 151–53.

"and it's going to be": Bukowski letter to Martinelli, 24 July 1964, in Bukowski, *Beerspit*, 304.

"Somebody read Genet": Bukowski, *Reach for the Sun*, 99.

One of his visits came on a rainy night: Cherkovski, *Bukowski: A Life*, 149.

"you and Lou and the nights": Grapes letter to JW, 15 August 1968, McCormick, Box E–L.

"a rather avuncular presence": Grapes quotes and details from e-mail to author, 22 November 2005.

"crazy but equally astonishing": Miriam Patchen letter to JW, n.d., McCormick, Box 10. Still more extraordinary, the book was done on Loujon's creaky old Chandler and Price press. In August 1965, Jon had considered purchasing a press from St. Louis–based Mailing Machines, Inc., though this transaction did not occur because Jon decided he could not afford to make the purchase. Confusion resulting from the halting of this transaction cost Webb a $150 deposit he made on the machine (Beldner letter to Ben C. Toledano, 11 January 1966, Webb Collection).

"As a consolation": Blair e-mail to author, 27 February 2006.

"amusing, for it can't compete": JW letter to Blair, 2 June 1966, Webb Collection.

"On the Pulitzer": JW letter to Blair, 13 June 1966, Webb Collection.

"Shouldn't have told you": Bukowski letter to William and Ruth Wantling, 20 June 1966, in Bukowski, *Screams*, 263.

He complained to Blair: JW letter to Blair, 30 June 1966, Webb Collection.

Beginning his letter "Dear People": Rexroth letter to JW and LW, 1 December 1966, McCormick, Box M–T.

"they had to get away from New Orleans": Bukowski letter to Blazek, 6 April 1966, in Bukowski, *Screams*, 253.

They again wandered for a time: JW letter to Blair, 13 March 1966, Webb Collection. After Jon and Louise left New Orleans, another publication started up there that quickly gained a dedicated following. *NOLA Express* (1968–1974) was a biweekly publication that existed in a middle ground between the worlds of underground newspapers and literary magazines. Editor Darlene Fife later wrote that this was the only publication which belonged to both the Underground Press Syndicate (UPS) news organization and the Committee of Small Magazine Editors and Publishers (COSMEP) literary magazine organization. *NOLA Express* was a true example of the mimeograph revolution, and its concerns ranged from protest against the war in Vietnam to the publishing of fiction, poetry and art. Bukowski became a regular contributor. His provocative contributions—stories with titles, for example, like "The Fuck Machine"—brought more letters to the editor, both pro and con, than did the work of any other *NOLA Express* contributor. *NOLA Express* had its offices at 710 Ursulines St., not far from *The Outsider*'s first home, but Fife moved in different social and cultural circles than did the Webbs. She did not know Jon and Louise, but knew their work, later referring to Loujon's Bukowski volumes as "lovely hand-set editions." She also recalled that folklorist Gershon Legman described the Webbs as "super-annuated hippies." During the time Fife and the Webbs shared the Quarter, Fife held the Webbs in mild disdain. "In my view at the time, they were part of an art-literary crowd, people with mild eccentricities, which in the Vietnam war years held no interest for me. The Webbs, as I perceived them, lived in a literary timeless realm, the realm I had previously lived in." She later recalled her single encounter with Jon: "I only remember seeing Jon Webb once. I was walking by a Quarter restaurant where he sat at a window table and I recall his look of friendly curiosity. I did frequently see their friend, the artist, Noel Rockmore, whose art was on the cover of Bukowski's *Crucifix in a Deathhand*. Rockmore would be walking fast around the Quarter, leading by the hand some young woman of changing identity. I gave up nodding to him after the first few times since he never acknowledged my existence. I found it hard to believe he didn't know who I was, but this is certainly possible" (Fife, *Portraits*, 4; and Fife interview with author, 15 November 2005).

Chapter 8. Tucson and Henry Miller

"the worst rainy December": JW letter to Blair, 22 February 1966, Webb Collection.

Jon, Jr., was still in the army: Jon Edgar Webb, Jr., to JW, 5 January 1972, Webb Collection.

"there were hugs": Grapes e-mail to author, 10 November 2005.

"We are going to open": JW letter to Blair, 22 February 1966, Webb Collection.

"Jon always gave more": Blair e-mail to author, 19 July 2006.

"from here and there": JW letter to Blair, 3 February 1966, Webb Collection.

"bookstore idea in Tucson": Blair e-mail to author, 27 February 2006.

"This is a secret": JW letter to Blair, 3 February 1966, Webb Collection.

Jon told Bukowski in February 1966: JW letter to Blair, February 1966, Webb Collection.

"He wants the wondrous Loujon format": Bukowski letter to JW, 28 February 1966, in Bukowski, *Screams*, 240.

Bukowski, in constant pain: Bukowski had suffered from hemorrhoids for years prior to this surgery and frequently complained of the problem in letters to the Webbs and others.

"finished cutting the tapes": Bukowski letter to Martinelli, 1 April 1966, in Bukowski, *Beerspit*, 328–33.

"would be a slow mover": JW letter to Blair, 13 March 1966, Webb Collection.

"blown thousands of dollars": Bukowski letter to Blazek, 1 April 1966, in Bukowski, *Screams*, 253.

"all-out treatment in format": Bukowski letter to JW, 28 February 1966, in Bukowski, *Screams*, 240.

"a magnet to kids": JW letter to Blair, 13 March 1966, Webb Collection.

Jon believed that the only effective venues: ibid.

"make it worth the price": JW letter to Blair, 30 March 1966, Webb Collection.

"Miller book promises": ibid.

"and other queens of the screen": JW letter to Blair, 2 June 1966, Webb Collection.

"bunch-of-Indians-whooping": JW letter to Blair, 13 June 1966, Webb Collection.

"I'll be damned if this exercise": JW letter to Blair, 8 July 1966, Webb Collection.

"a kind of address": Corrington letter to JW and LW, 11 November, 1966, McCormick, Box A–D.

Ed Blair drove them: Blair e-mail to author, 27 February 2006. According to Blair, the Webbs had acquired some young traveling companions on the way to New Orleans. "During this period a very young couple was staying with them. The gal was asleep and Lou left the room. Jon said to me, 'I want to show you something.' Coyly, he went over and gently lifted the girl's skirt. 'See,' he said devilishly, 'see how these hippy kids dress, no underwear.' He got a kick out of that."

"I saw your press": Bukowski letter to JW, 5 April 1967, McCormick, Box 3.

"How does one talk": Bukowski letter to JW, 6 April 1967, McCormick, Box A–D.

"The Henry Miller book": Sherman letter to JW and LW, 13 April 1967, McCormick, Box 8.

"It could be the writings": Grapes letter to JW, 3 April 1967, McCormick, Box E–L.

"It's awesome to hear": Aaron Schneider letter to JW and LW, no date but annotated in JW's hand, "4/5," McCormick, Box 8.

"Most people," he wrote: John Petrie letter to JW, 1967 (no other date listed), McCormick, Box 8.

"feel we know you so well": Font letter to JW and LW, 7 December [1966?], McCormick, Box 8.

"to write and tell you": Martin letter to JW, 11 February [1968?], McCormick, Box 8.

"They are so beautiful!": Rush letter to JW, 1 December 1967, McCormick, Box 8.

"The library will get these": Volz letter to JW, 8 May 1968, McCormick, Box 8.

Aldrich called Loujon books "magnificent": Aldrich letter to JW and LW, 16 May 1967, McCormick, Box 8.

"All who have seen": Woodbury letter to JW and LW, 26 June 1967, McCormick, Box 8.

"Nothing like it": Borsten letter to JW, n.d., McCormick, Box 8.

"I had been in awe": Maytag letter to JW and LW, 1 March 1967, McCormick, Box 8.

Even so, she sent checks: Tasto letter to JW and LW, 6 December 1967, McCormick, Box 8.

"In any case—I shall send": Tasto letter to JW and LW, 28 December 1967, McCormick, Box 8.

"ideas exploding in me": JW letter to Blair, 25 February 1967, Webb Collection.

"long letter of delight": JW letter to Miller, 9 March 1967, McCormick, Box M–T.

he was miserable: Bukowski letter to Corrington, 15 November 1967, in Bukowski, *Living*, 77.

"all's gone well so far": JW letter to Blair, 4 June 1967, Webb Collection.

"Jon is a very sensitive cat": Bukowski letter to Corrington, 15 November 1967, in Bukowski, *Living*, 77.

"all the photographs": Miriam Patchen letter to JW, 11 May 1967, McCormick, Box 10.

"Now on the material back": JW letter to Kenneth and Miriam Patchen, 15 June 1967, McCormick, Box 10.

Jon returned three negatives: Miriam Patchen letter to JW, 14 April 1969, McCormick, Box 10.

In July, Miriam assured Jon: Miriam Patchen letter to JW, 22 July 1969, McCormick, Box 10.

a portfolio of Miller's watercolors: JW letter to Miller, 24 April 1968, McCormick, Box 10.

"I admire what you and your wife": Borzak letter to JW, 16 February 1967, McCormick, Box 15.

"I've daydreamed of something": JW letter to Borzak, February 1967, McCormick, Box 15.

Type & Press of Illinois shipped: William B. Gould letter to JW, 6 December 1967, Lilly.

Jon requested they instead give him the money: JW letter to Borzak, 25 December 1967, Lilly.

"Since paper arrived": JW letter to Kenneth and Miriam Patchen, 10 June 1968, McCormick, Box 10.

Chapter 9. Editor's Bit and Obit

"Thanks, honey": JW notes to LW, n.d., Webb Collection.

"Maybe we should take a trip": ibid.

"pure water colors": Miller letter to JW, 17 February 1968, McCormick, Box 1.

"That is, if you are thinking": Miller letter to JW, 28 April 1968, McCormick, Box 1.

In June, Miller gave Loujon: Miller letter to JW, 19 June 1968, Webb Collection.

he suffered another small stroke: JW letter to Donald Borzak, 9 November 1970, McCormick, Box 9.

strangulated intestine: Doctors later told Louise her condition had resulted from drinking too much tomato juice.

"Heavy rains sluiced": Pavillard. Clipping in Webb Collection.

Bly . . . had hoped to visit: Bly letter to JW, 8 August 1968, McCormick, Box A–D.

"Sorry I'm late": Bly letter to JW, 14 October 1968, Webb Collection; Bly's poem "blown-up german fortifications near collioure: in Disgust at Europe" appeared in *The Outsider* 4/5.

She also personally sold: Bartlett letter to JW and LW, 2 January 1968, McCormick, Box A–D.

"a beautiful job": Bartlett letter to JW and LW, 28 February 1969, McCormick, Box A–D.

"since *Outsider* 4/5": Bartlett letter to JW and LW, 20 March 1969, McCormick, Box A–D.

"getting a chance for more": Bartlett letter to JW, 19 July 1969, McCormick, Box A–D.

"Finally, we have a date": Bartlett letter to JW, 11 November 1969, McCormick, Box 8.

"self-appointed business manager": Cagle letter to JW, 13 March 1969, McCormick, Box A–D.

"I imagine the Webbs": Cagle e-mail to author, 18 December 2005.

"it just goes round": levy letter to JW, no date, McCormick, Box E–L.

"both of whose work": Levertov letter to JW, 12 May 1968, McCormick.

"do what you want": Grapes letter to JW, 10 September 1968, McCormick, Box E–L.

"a humming bird": Conroy letter to JW, 21 March 1969, McCormick, Box 8.

"OUTSIDER 4/5 is FANTASTIC!": Fulton letter to JW and LW, 28 March 1969, McCormick, Box E–L

"small balm for some troubles": Ginsberg letter to JW and LW, 18 March 1969, McCormick, Box E–L.

"the Rolls Royce": Gold, 42. Clipping in the Webb Collection.

"most impressive . . . the publicity": Cagle letter to JW, 13 March 1969, McCormick, Box A–D.

"All the times": Bukowski letter to JW, 5 February 1969, McCormick, Box 3.

National Council on the Arts awarded: Nancy Hanks letter to JW, 3 December 1969, McCormick, Box 9.

"a big gamble": JW letter to Blair, date partially obscured, 16 [?] 1969, Webb Collection.

"And it's perfect": JW notes to LW, n.d., Webb Collection.

"Honey, I just wired you": Formento and Ferron, 13.

"poet satyr of today's underground": Photocopy of original poster, Webb Collection; reprint of original poster in *Sure, the Charles Bukowski Newsletter*, no. 3 (3 December 1991), 10–11.

"They also have been in contact": Borzak letter addressed "Dear Group," 16 October 1968, McCormick, Box 8.

Borzak did his part: JW letter to Miller, 24 April 1968, McCormick, Box 9.

In April, after Jon told him: JW letter to Miller, 13 April 1970, McCormick, Box 10.

Miller thought this was a bad idea: Miller letter to JW, 26 May 1970, McCormick, Box 1.

"So, honey, don't gripe": JW note to LW, n.d., Webb Collection.

Chapter 10. Death in Nashville

"this most monumental production": *Insomnia* announcement, n.d., Webb Collection.

"stuff all over the magazines": Locklin letter to JW, 20 August 1970, McCormick, Box M–T.
Miller liked the broadside: Miller letter to JW, 27 July 1970, McCormick, Box 1.
"We, too, are finding": J. Adam Shartle, Jr., letter to JW, 21 June 1970, McCormick, Box 8.
"What fool wouldn't accept": William Webb letter to JW, 29 June 1970, McCormick, Box 8.4.
Wagner saw the Miller publication: Wagner letter to JW, 20 June 1969, Webb Collection.
"I don't like the attitude": Miller letter to JW, 18 November 1969, McCormick, Box 1.
Wagner bowed out: Wagner letter to JW, 2 February 1970, Webb Collection.
"I take it you didn't": Miller letter to JW, 11 October 1970, McCormick, Box 1.
"This doesn't mean": Miller letter to JW, 11 November 1970, McCormick, Box 1.
"Forgive the Delay": advertising matter for *Insomnia*, n.d., Webb Collection.
"more money in a few months": JW note to LW, 30 June 1970, Webb Collection.
"A few weeks ago": JW letter to Borzak, 10 September 1970, McCormick, Box 10.
Borzak's motive: Borzak letter to JW, 11 November 1970, McCormick, Box 8.
A week later, Jon told Miller: JW letter to Miller, 18 November 1970, McCormick, Box 10.
"enthralled with the *Insomnia*!": Szold-Fritz letter to LW, 3 December 1970, McCormick, Box 8.
"frosty weather setting in": "Forgive the Delay," advertising matter for *Insomnia*, n.d., Webb Collection.
On one occasion, Jon, Jr.: Jon Edgar Webb, Jr., letter to JW, 19 May 1972, Webb Collection. [Letter written to JW after JW's death as a form of therapy for Jon, Jr.
Louise watched him: LW interview with author, 21 February 2005.
"But we felt we were ready": York.
"Can't get in register": JW letter to Newman, 14 May 1971, Webb Collection.
Jon, Jr., telephoned: Audiotape recordings of telephone conversations between Jon Edgar Webb, Jr., JW, and LW, Webb Collection.
"Going on down": Weddle, "An Interview with Jon Edgar Webb, Jr.," *Chiron Review*, no. 70 (Autumn 2002), 22. This interview was reprinted in *Beat Scene*, no. 42 (Spring 2003).
Jon's wish was to be cremated: "LW interview with author, 21 February 2005.
"Next to my own father's": Blair e-mail to author, 19 July 2006.
"The music plays": Bukowski, *The Serif*.
Louise used a nail: Jon Edgar Webb, Jr., email to author, 4 December 2006.
"Death came the other day": York, 9.
"This man is the closest thing": "Literary Figure Jon E. Webb Dead at 66," n.d., newspaper clipping, Webb Collection. No date or other publication information appears on the clipping, though it likely was from the *Vieux Carré Courier*, a newspaper which had long been sympathetic to the Webbs and their work.

"Jon never cared for money": York, 11.

She suggested to Jon, Jr.: LW interview with author, 21 February 2005.

"will have a good audience there": Malone letter to LW, 17 June 1974, Webb Collection.

"Good story. Got style": Johnson letter to Malone, 7 June 1974, Webb Collection.

"the best little magazine": Malone.

"Jon Could See True": Yet another little magazine sprang up in New Orleans in 1988. *Mesechabe* began as an environmental advocacy publication in 1988, going through several editors and finally gaining the subtitle *A Journal of (Sur)regionalism* and shifting focus to art and literature. The last editor, Dennis Formento, saw Loujon as a watershed in New Orleans's cultural history and sought out Louise for an interview in 1997. "The first small press revolution was fought with typewriters and mimeograph machines in the back-a-towns and bohemias of America," Formento wrote in his introduction to that interview. "When it came to New Orleans, it was fought with a nine by twelve foot offset press operated by novelist Jon Webb and his wife, painter Louise Webb. . . ."

Postscript: What Became of Them

In 1994, Louise participated: McLellan.

he toyed with the idea: Blair letter to LW, 3 May 1983, Webb Collection.

"heavy cotton, acid-free": Susan Larson, "Recycling Literary History," New Orleans *Times-Picayune*, newspaper clipping, Webb Collection. No bibliographic information is available.

"the significance of *The Outsider*: McLellan.

"He had quite a temper": Weddle, "An Interview with Jon Edgar Webb, Jr.," 28.

"I wanted to come": Jon Edgar Webb, Jr., letter to JW, 19 May 1972, Webb Collection.

"The fifties and sixties": Bell e-mail to author, 21 June 2002.

"My demon has been": Corrington letter to Bukowski, 3 February 1962, Corrington Collection.

"Among today's novelists": Dale Walker, *Rocky Mountain News*, reprinted on http://www.jorysherman.com.

"When I die," she told Williams: Liza Williams, 19. A note accompanying the article from *Sure* editor Edward L. Smith reads: "I edited this piece from Liza's article that appeared in the *L.A. Free Press*, 1972."

"I'm glad I did it": LW interview with Wayne Ewing, 21 February 2005, for a still unfinished video documentary tentatively titled *Loujon Press: A Work in Progress*. The interview was conducted in New Orleans.

BIBLIOGRAPHY

Aikman, Leo. "A Gypsy Lady Known as Lou." *Atlanta Constitution.* 18 May 1955.

Anderson, Margaret. *My Thirty Years War: An Autobiography.* New York: Covici, Friede, 1930.

Asbury, Herbert. *The French Quarter: An Informal History of the New Orleans Underworld.* New York: Garden City, 1938.

Ballard, Sandra L. *The Collected Short Stories of Harriette Simpson Arnow.* Ann Arbor: Michigan State University Press, 2005.

Barber, John F. "Poetry: Uncollected Poems." Brautigan Bibliography plus+. http://www.nouspace.net/brautigan/uncollected-poems.

Bender, Sheila. "About the Author: Jack Grapes." Writing It Real. http://writingitreal.com/cgibin/get_bio.pl?name=Jack%20Grapes.

"Biography for Noel Rockmore." AskArt.com.

Blair, Edwin. "How to Start an Outsider." *Louisiana Literature* 13, no. 1 (Spring 1996).

Brown, Alan. *Literary Levees of New Orleans.* Montgomery, AL: Starhill, 1998.

Brummett, Phillip, Jr. KPI Investigations. 23 May 2006. http://www.kypinvestigations.tripod.com

Bukowski, Charles. *Beerspit Night and Cursing: The Correspondence of Charles Bukowski and Sheri Martinelli, 1960–1967.* Steven Moore, ed. Santa Rosa, CA: Black Sparrow Press, 2001.

———. "Death of a Once Talent." Review of *Lines to the South and Other Poems* by John William Corrington. *Steppenwolf* 1 (Winter 1965-1966).

———. *Living on Luck: Selected Letters, 1960s-1970s.* Seamus Cooney, ed. Santa Rosa, CA: Black Sparrow Press, 1995.

———. "The Outsider." *Wormwood Review* 12, no. 1, issue 45 (1972).

———. *Reach for the Sun: Selected Letters, 1978–94.* Seamus Cooney, ed. Santa Rosa: Black Sparrow, 1999.

———. *Screams from the Balcony: Selected Letters 1978–1994.* Seamus Cooney, ed. Santa Rosa, CA: Black Sparrow Press, 1993.

———. *The Serif* 8, no. 4 (December 1971).

———. *Sunlight Here I Am: Interviews and Encounters, 1963–1993.* David Stephen Calonne, ed. Northville, MI: Sundog Press, 2003.

Capra Press. "Collecting Capra Press Books: A Checklist." http://www.caprapress.com/checklist.php.

Cardon, Charlotte. "Relocated Publishers Demand Top Work for Hand-Printed Literary Magazine." *Arizona Daily,* 14 September 1966.

Cassin, Maxine. "Confessions of a Small Press Publisher." *Louisiana Literature* 13, no. 1 (1996).

Cherkovski, Neeli. *Bukowski: A Life.* South Royalton, VT: Steerforth, 1997.

204

❖ Bibliography ❖

——. *Hank: The Life of Charles Bukowski.* New York: Random House, 1991.
Chielens, Edward E. *American Literary Magazines: The Twentieth Century.* Westport, CT: Greenwood Press, 1992.
Clay, Steven, and Rodney Phillips. *A Secret Location on the Lower East Side: Adventures in Writing 1960–1980.* New York: New York Public Library, Granary Books, 1998.
Cobblestone Entertainment. Hollywood Renegades Archive. http://www.cobbles.com.
Coit, Cordley. "KaJa." Mesechabe: The Journal of (Sur)regionalism 19 (Summer 2000).
Cowley, Malcolm. "The Little Magazines Growing Up." *New York Times Book Review,* 14 September 1947.
Creekmore, Hubert. "Two Rewarding Volumes of Verse." *New York Times,* 30 January 1949. http://www.nytimes.com/books/01/04/22/specials/hughes-oneway.html
Davidson, David. "One Crucial Day Within Prison Walls." Review of *Four Steps to the Wall* by Jon Edgar Webb. *New York Herald Tribune,* 1946.
"Defining Uncle Alfred." Review of *The Little Magazine in America. Time,* 1 July 1946.
"Delta Doings." Review of *The Great Big Doorstep* by E. P. O'Donnell. *Time,* 5 October 1936.
Dial Books. Young Readers' Division. http://www.penguinputnam.com/static/html.
"Discovered by Manuscript." *Manuscript,* May-June 1935.
Dodson, Howard, and Sylviane A. Diouf, eds. "Haitian Immigration: Eighteenth and Nineteenth Centuries." *In Motion: The African-American Migration Experience.* Schomburg Center for Research in Black Culture. http://www.immotionaame.org/home.
Elkins, James R. "John William Corrington." Strangers to Us All: Lawyers and Poetry. http://www.wvu.edu/~lawfac/jelkins/lp-2001/corrington.html.
Eness, Jason. "Curtain Calls." *Look @ Tulane, the Online News Magazine.* http://www.2.tulane.edu/feature_curtain.cfm.
"Farley Story at Library." *Mansfield News-Journal,* 24 April 1948.
Fife, Darlene. *Portraits from Memory: New Orleans in the Sixties.* New Orleans: Surregional Press, 2000.
Formento, Dennis. "Welcome to the Society of the Marvelously Damned: An Interview with Robert Cass." *Mesechabe: The Journal of (Sur)regionalism,* 19 (Summer 2000).
Formento, Dennis, and Susan Ferron. "An Interview with the Outsider: Talking with Louise Webb." *Mesachabe: The Journal of (Sur)regionalism* 16 (Spring 1997).
"From Revolution to Romanticism." *In Motion The African-American Migration Experience.* Schomburg Center for Research in Black Culture. http://www.inmotionaame.org/home.cfm.
Gold, Robert. "The Outsider 4/5." *Los Angeles Free Press,* 9 May 1969: 42.
Grapes, Marcus. "Letter to Webb." *Wormwood Review* 12, no. 1, issue 45 (1972).
Gregor, David. "Collecting Charles Bukowski." *Firsts: Collecting Modern First Editions* 5, no. 1 (1995).
Halliburton, Lloyd. "Autobiography in Corrington's Fiction." In *John William Corring-*

ton: Southern Man of Letters, William Mills, ed. Conway: University of Central Arkansas Press, 1994.

Hoffman, Frederick, Charles Allen, and Carolyn F. Ulrich. *The Little Magazine: A History and a Bibliography*. Princeton: Princeton University Press, 1946.

Jolas, Eugene. *Man From Babel*. New Haven: Yale University Press, 1998.

Katz, William. "Magazines." *Library Journal* 94, no. 17 (1 October 1969).

"Kay Johnson—KaJa." Empty Mirror Books. http://www.emptymirrorbooks.com.

Kent State University Libraries. Special Collections. http://speccoll.library.kent.edu/ literature/misc/kaplan-laukhuff.html.

Kruchkow, Diane, and Curt Johnson, eds. *Green Isle in the Sea*. Highland Park, IL: December Press, 1985.

Locklin, Gerald. *Charles Bukowski: A Sure Bet*. Sudbury, MA: Water Row, 1995.

Long, Judy, ed. *Literary New Orleans*. Athens, GA: Hill Street Press LLC, 1999.

Lowenfels, Walter, ed. "Little Magazines in America: A Symposium (Part 1)." *Mainstream* 15, no. 11 (November 1962).

———, ed. "Little Magazines in America: A Symposium (Part Two)." *Mainstream* 15, no. 12 (December 1962).

———, ed. "Little Magazines in America: A Symposium (Part 3)." *Mainstream* 16, no. 6 (June 1963).

———. "On Trial." *Mainstream* 16, no. 3 (March 1963).

———. "The Thirties and the Sixties: An Interview with Walter Lowenfels." *Mainstream* 16, no. 5 (1963).

Malone, Marvin. *Wormwood Review* 12, no. 1, issue 45 (1972): 2.

May, James Boyer. "Towards Print." *Trace 1*, no. 1 (June 1952).

McDarrah, Fred W. *Beat Generation: Glory Days in Greenwich Village*. New York: Schirmer Books, 1996.

McLellan, Marian. "Francis Swaggart: Skyscraper and Ursulines." *Art Papers* (January/ February 1995).

Mencken, H. L., "The Sahara of the Bozart." *New York Evening Mail*, 13 November 1917.

Miles, Barry. *The Beat Hotel: Ginsberg, Burroughs, and Corso in Paris, 1958–1963*. New York: Grove, 2000.

Miller, Henry. "First Impressions of Paris." The Personal Archive of Henry Miller. Part I: Fine Modern Literature Including Selections from the Private Library of Seymour Lawrence, Publisher. http://www.pacificbook.com/catalogs/curcat137-2.html

———. *Wormwood Review* 12, no. 1, issue 45 (1972).

———. "Patchen: Man of Anger and Light." *Stand Still Like the Hummingbird*. Norfolk CT: New Directions, 1962.

Mills, William, ed. *John William Corrington: Southern Man of Letters*. Conway: University of Central Arkansas Press, 1994.

Moore, Dave. "Kerouac and *The Outsider*—A Puzzle." http://www.emptymirrorbooks. com/features/jack-kerouac-outsider.html

Moore, Steven. "Sherri Martinelli: A Modernist Muse." *Gargoyle* 41 (1998).

Morgan, Richard G., ed. *Kenneth Patchen: A Collection of Essays*. New York: AMS Press, 1977.

O'Donnell, E. P. *The Great Big Doorstep*. New York: Houghton-Mifflin, 1936.

———. *Green Margins*. New York: Houghton-Mifflin, 1937.

———. "Jesus Knew." *Harper's*, 1935.

———. "Manhood." *Collier's*, 1931.

———. "Transfusion." *Blues: A Magazine of New Rhythms*, 1929.

O'Donnell, Mary King. *Quincie Boliver*. Cambridge: Houghton Mifflin, 1941.

———. *Those Other People*. Cambridge: Houghton Mifflin, 1946.

Ohio Biographies. "Mrs. Elizabeth Clark Scofield." 13 February 2006. http://www. homepages.rootsweb.com/~rocky/oh_biographies/scofield.htm.

Olson, Ted. "Bukowski and Jeffers: Two Poets Listening to Life." *Sure, the Charles Bukowski Newsletter* 4 (1992).

Pavillard, Dan. "Downpour Swamps Webb Printery." *Tucson Daily Citizen*, 12 August 12, 1968: 2.

Rexroth, Kenneth. "There's Poetry in a Ragged Hitchhiker." *New York Times Book Review*, 5 July 1964.

———. *Assays*. Norfolk, CT: New Directions, 1951.

Rinck, Willima. "A Note on Kay Johnson." http://www.emptymirrorbooks.com/kaja. html.

Sallis, James. *Difficult Lives: Jim Thompson, David Goodis, Chester Himes*. Brooklyn: Gryphon, 1993.

Siegel, Sandy. "Screenwriters Need Not Apply." *Westside Weekly*, 19 January 1997.

Simpson, Craig. "Philip Kaplan and Hermine Laukhuff Papers, 1959–1985." Finding Aid. http://speccoll.library.kent.edu/literature/misc/kaplan-lauk haff.html.

Sounes, Howard. *Charles Bukowski: Locked in the Arms of a Crazy Life*. New York: Grove, 1999.

———. *Bukowski in Pictures*. Edinburgh: Canongate, 2000.

Southern Illinois University Carbondale Libraries. "Philip Kaplan Collection of Walter Lowenfels: Biography." http://www.lib.siu.edu/spcol/inventory/SC085.html.

Tailsiman House Catalog. http://www.talismanpublishers.com/catalog/realityprime. html.

University of Delaware Library Special Collections. "Howard McCord Papers." http://www.lib.udel.edu/ud/spec/findaids/mccordh.html.

"Up and Down the Street." *Mansfield News-Journal*, 19 February 1937.

Wayne, Gary. "Hollywood Center Studios." Seeing Stars in Hollywood. 2006. http:// www.seeing-stars.com/Studios/HollywoodCenterStudios.shtml.

Webb, Jon Edgar. "All Prickles, No Petals." *Manuscript* 11, no. 3 (May–June 1935): 3-10.

———. *Four Steps to the Wall*. New York: Dial, 1948.

———. "The Idiot in Cell 33." *Esquire* 19 (March 1937).

———. "The Key in the Lock." *Story* 43 (February 1936): 29-41.

———. "Letters to the Editor." *Story* 43 (February 1936).

———. "The Key in the Lock." *Story* No. 43. (February 1936).

———. "Night after Night." *Story* (August 1935).

Weddle, Jeff. "An Interview with Jon Edgar Webb, Jr." *Beat Scene* 42 (Spring 2003).

———. "Oh, We Were Soulmates." [Louise Webb interview]. *Chiron Review* 69 (Summer 2002).

Whitman, Walt. "New Orleans in 1848." *New Orleans Picayune*, 25 January 1887. http://www.bartleby.com/229/5017.html.

Williams, Liza. "True Love." *Sure, the Charles Bukowski Newsletter*, no. 2 (August 1991): 18–19.

Williams, William Carlos. "For a New Magazine." *Blues: The Magazine of New Rhythms* 1, no. 1 (February–July 1929): 30.

Wrong, Dennis H. "The American Left and Cuba." *Commentary* 33, no. 2 (February 1962).

Wyckoff, Geraldine. "Jazz All-Stars." *New Orleans Magazine* 37 (April 2004).

York, Max. "A Good Man Dies." *Nashville Sunday Tennessean*, 18 July 1971.

INDEX

Printed in the United States
By Bookmasters